My Layer Road

U's fans remember the Layer Road years

My Layer Road

U's fans remember the Layer Road years

Matt Hudson and Jim French

breedon **books**
PUBLISHING

Dedication

In loving memory of Margaret Hudson; a wonderful mother and friend

Matt Hudson

With Thanks

This book would not have been possible without the fantastic contributions, both written and photographic. Our written contributors are listed through the book, but we would also like to thank the following for their help with the book:

Rob Sambrook, Warren Page, Martin Bright, Chris Petty, Phil Unwin, David Amoss, Elaine Soame, Keith Beechener, Bob Riddle, Dick, Anne and Mark Graham, David May, Carl Marston, Lee Hyde, Kevin Barnes, Mike Middleton and everyone at Breedon Publishing

The majority of the photographs used in this book have come from club archives, supporters and families of current and ex-players, along with scrapbooks and albums. We have not intentionally infringed on any copyright and would be pleased to hear from anyone who feels this may be the case.

First published in Great Britain in 2009 by The Breedon Books Publishing Company Limited
Breedon House, 3 The Parker Centre, Derby, DE21 4SZ.

ISBN 978-1-85983-675-0   Printed and bound by MKT Print, Slovenia

Contents

Introduction .6

Remembering Emily 7

Chapter 1 – 1937 to 1945
The Birth of the U's 9

Chapter 2 – 1946 to 1948
Ted Fenton and his famous Southern League team
of Cup heroes 18

Chapter 3 – 1949 to 1955
Southern League glory is exchanged for a struggle
to make headway in the Football League 36

Chapter 4
The manager who never was 47

Chapter 5 – 1955 to 1959
Some incredible days under Benny Fenton 50

Chapter 6 – 1959 to 1968
A yo-yo club - three relegations and two
promotions in nine years 64

Chapter 7
Dick Graham on his time with the U's 88

Chapter 8 – 1968 to 1972
The old excitement is rediscovered
under Dick Graham in an era defined
by the Leeds United game 98

Chapter 9 – 1972 to 1982
Good work by Jim Smith continued
by Bobby Roberts, but horizons limited
by financial restraint 130

Chapter 10 – 1982 to 1990
Plying our trade in the bottom Divisions. Decline
and relegation from the League 144

Chapter 11 – 1990 to 1992
Happy days in the Conference 154

Chapter 12 – 1992 to 2006
Renewed ambition and steady progress 163

Chapter 13
An incredible promotion season, and a party that
started in the West Country and continued on the
Town Hall balcony 179

Chapter 14 – 2006 to 2008
Punching above our weight
in the Championship 187

Chapter 15 – April 2008
A final farewell to Layer Road 194

Chapter 16
Looking into the future 204

Chapter 17
Time moves on... 220

Introduction

26 April 2008 is a day that will be forever etched in the memories of Colchester United supporters as 71 years of footballing history at Layer Road came to a close.

Thousands of games had been played and hundreds of players had trodden the hallowed turf at the U's' first home, but it was Stoke City's Richard Cresswell who wrote his name into the history books as the final goalscorer at the cramped Layer Road stadium.

As the tears were wiped away and the fans ventured out of the ground for one last time on that balmy Spring evening, a thousand memories no doubt flooded back for those in attendance. For every supporter in the ground, Layer Road would have held a special place in their hearts and each would no doubt recollect favourite players, favourite games and the characters around them that had made it such a unique place to be. And from that was borne this book. *My Layer Road* collects together the stories, anecdotes and memories of those who lived the Layer Road experience. Enclosed in this book are contributions of fans young and old, from those that saw the early games of the 1930s to those who were given the encouragement to come along during those fantastic seasons that saw the U's elevated to the Championship just before Layer Road's stint came to a close.

Of course, not all memories relate to the games themselves. Layer Road was more than just a football ground a lot of the time. It was a social meeting space, and, as in Ray Hollingsworth's fantastic *Made in Colchester* DVD released at the end of 2008, the progress through time in this book also charts the social history of the time.

It has taken us nearly a year to put the book together and, in truth, we could have waited another year to go to print, such has been the incredible path to completion of this publication. Every time we thought we had finished writing the book, another person would be recommended to us to talk to and, having spoken to that person, they too would recommend two or three others who also had their own stories to tell!

There are some real gems contained within these pages and a few surprises along the way too, as not only do fans give their thoughts on the club's time at Layer Road, but some notable names from the management and playing side of the club do too.

Until the more recent successes in the Championship that won the U's so many friends along the way, the name Colchester United was synonymous with that game against Leeds United. The book benefits greatly from an intriguing and captivating contribution from Dick Graham about that famous game – if you read nothing else in this book, make sure you read his wonderful words. That team of 1971 has, sadly, lost several of its number over the years and throughout the course of this book, supporters recollect those that are no longer with us – both on and off the terraces.

And with that in mind, we start our story of life at Layer Road with the tale of Emily Begg's association with the club. It is one that sums up the spirit of Colchester United, their players and fans, perfectly.

Matt Hudson and Jim French

Remembering Emily

From the day her brother Daniel brought Kevin Rapley and Thomas Pinault round for lunch, Emily Begg was a Colchester United fan. Despite her tender years she was already aware of good-looking lads, and after meeting Kevin and Thomas she just had to see them on the pitch the very next game!

And so it was on 21 September 2002, aged just 10, that Emily staked her place on the Barside at Layer Road with her friend Suzanne and father Stuart, on what was to be a most remarkable occasion, both in her life and in the history of Colchester United. Stuart was a regular and was happy to explain the rules to Emily and Suzanne, who quickly learned every player by name and number and could identify any one from 400 paces!

Such was Emily's enjoyment of being at Layer Road, she never let a poor result spoil her day. Emily held the players in such high esteem that she made them cakes, individually numbered and delivered to Layer Road, and she even made a football pitch cake for Parky when he replaced Steve Whitton as manager in March 2003.

Emily never missed a home game, that was until September 2005 when she was suddenly diagnosed with leukaemia. Even though hospitalised and undergoing months of chemotherapy, Emily's interest in Colchester United never wavered. When she was allowed home between treatments she would plead with the consultants for permission to attend a game.

So with Emily in her headscarf due to hair loss and with friends Emily Kenny and Suzanne on board, Stuart drove to Swansea having organised for the girls to meet the players prior to the away match. Emily was simply delighted to be in the changing room with the lads and had her photograph taken with every player. Just imagine how thrilled she was when Wayne Brown actually gave her his shirt! Emily was made up.

However, with reality never far away, it was straight back to hospital to endure many more months of chemotherapy until Emily was pronounced to be 'in remission' at the beginning of March, just in time for the culmination of the historic 2006 season.

At Emily's first game back, the U's lost 3–0 to Southend at Layer Road with a dismal performance, yet slowly but surely under the guidance of Phil Parkinson they clawed their way back into contention for a Play-off position and possibly automatic promotion. It was almost too hard to believe it as we bought our tickets for the final game, away to Yeovil on 6 May. Anyone who made that journey will not tell of a great game, but they will tell of a great and extremely memorable day out, with the realisation of a dream come true with promotion to the Championship.

Life seemed pretty good to Emily; however, within two weeks the leukaemia had returned and she was again hospitalised for more months of intense chemotherapy, radiotherapy and even a bone marrow transplant in which marrow was donated by her brother, Alex. A massively brave battle ensued and Emily's goal was to be out of hospital and in remission in time for the home game with Southend on 25 November 2006. Emily finally came out of hospital in October and travelled with her dad and Suzanne to Coventry, where she was thrilled to be back on the terraces. Incidentally, that was the night the Colchester United team coach caught fire on the return to Layer Road, causing the players and staff to arrive back at 5am!

In spite of all the treatment, on 28 October Emily received devastating blood results, with the realisation that there was no further treatment available. Aged just 14, she knew she was now terminally ill.

The next U's game was on Tuesday 31, away to Norwich, and in spite of circumstances Emily was determined to go. Stuart had organised for Emily to meet the players at their hotel prior to the game. The players were unaware of the gravity of Emily's situation but were great with her, all posing for

photographs on request, but it was Wayne Brown who realised in his discussion with Emily just how serious things had become and he was visibly moved. Emily then went to the game, the very last time she was well enough to see her heroes.

Two days later Stuart and Emily's mum Colleen took her to Lourdes, and Stuart recalls just how excited Emily was when she received a text telling her how the boys had won away at top of the table Cardiff.

But Emily was now losing her brave battle with leukaemia and it was ironic that the very game she had targeted to attend, Southend United at Layer Road, was the next game after she lost that battle on 19 November 2006. The club sent flowers to Emily's funeral, spelling out 'CUFC' – just perfect. When the players heard that Emily had lost her battle they rallied, they wanted to do something to acknowledge Emily and so they did.

They decided to fund-raise for Emily's chosen charity, the Teenage Cancer Trust, with an ambitious target of £10,000. All of the players, apart from Wayne who just had a polish, had their heads shaved to start the ball rolling, and the headline on the back page of the *Gazette* after they had soundly thrashed Southend United 3–0 was 'We did it for Emily'. She would have been thrilled.

The very next week the players had a great time in the recording studio, re-recording *Up the U's* with local bands Koopa and Special Duties. A cycle ride was then organised by CUFC barmaid Lea Finch for the return game with Southend United, U's again winning 3–0, this time with a superb Jamie Cureton hat-trick. And that, along with many other fund-raising ideas, raised an amazing total of £24,500 by the club for the Emily Begg fund for the Teenage Cancer Trust.

It was a remarkable, yet all too short, relationship that Emily had with Colchester United, but it was a testimony to the club's community spirit and genuine recognition of a true supporter with a heartfelt passion for the club. Emily would feel honoured by what Colchester United did for her, and the club should be mightily proud of what they achieved in memory of Emily Begg.

Stuart and Colleen Begg recalling memories of their late daughter

Chapter 1 — 1937 to 1945
THE BIRTH OF THE U'S

My father was Maurice Pye, who brought together a group of Colchester businessmen with the idea of forming a professional football club. He was mayor of Colchester in 1932–33 and 1943–44, and the business people of the town who formed the club elected my father as chairman of the board of directors.

The programme for the first game as a professional club against Bath City on Tuesday 2 September 1937 contained a statement from my father.

My father's statement appeared again in the programme for the second home game, against the club's traditional rivals Ipswich Town. The U's played Bath City on the Tuesday and Ipswich Town on the Saturday.

I was nine years old when the first professional game was played. My mother always went to games with my father and naturally I went

Mrs Jean Bell, standing behind her father Maurice Pye, during the opening of Colchester bypass in 1933.

LAYER ROAD GROUND,
COLCHESTER,

September 2nd, 1937.

Left: The chairman's letter featured in the programmes of the two opening home games.

INTRODUCTORY LETTER TO SUPPORTERS FROM THE CHAIRMAN OF THE DIRECTORS OF COLCHESTER UNITED FOOTBALL CLUB, LTD.

To-day marks a very important milestone in the history of football in Colchester by the commencement of professional football in the town.

When one considers that it was only a short time ago that the suggestion of professional football was raised, it will be agreed much has been done both by the Board of Directors and football supporters to make this occasion possible.

By the generous co-operation of all concerned, including the Colchester Town Football Club, and all those interested in sport, we are able to look forward to football worthy of our town.

We were fortunate in obtaining the services of such a splendid manager as Mr. Edwin Davis, and his knowledge of football and football players has enabled us to place such a good sound side in the field to-day, and we are convinced that the players will blend into a combination which will give satisfaction to all concerned.

In the limited time at our disposal we have been unable to make improvements to the ground such as we desire for the comfort of all classes of our supporters, but we are bearing this important matter in mind and it will receive attention as early as possible.

The Board feels that the players and staff have shown such enthusiasm that their efforts will bring complete success, and all that remains is for the public of Colchester and district to give their whole-hearted support to the Club.

On behalf of the Board,

MAURICE PYE, Chairman.

The cover from the first Colchester United programme at Layer Road.

List of directors from the U's early days, from the Bath City programme.

with them. However, it took a while before I started to enjoy it. I can remember thinking 'oh, not again' on a Saturday, but once I got to understand how football was played I looked forward to it. I learned how it worked and soon became a keen follower, and to this day I still follow the team.

I would always sit in the directors' box with my parents, and I have clear memories of most of the directors. Mr Le Ball was one, and he used to keep a sweet shop in the High Street and at every match he gave me a small paper bag full of butter drops. There was Mr Jacklin, who owned Jacklin's restaurant; Leonard Boult, who was manager of the brewers Ind Coope; Mr Daniell from Daniell's Brewery; Mr Harper from the sports outfitters in the High Street and Mr G.M. Morris, who was a photographer in Crouch Street. William Allen and Ralph Wright were both butchers in the town.

We used to walk to home games at Layer Road as we lived in Irvine Road, and I remember seeing all the gardens along the route piled up with bikes. For away games we used to travel with the players. They would sit at the front of the bus and were always nice and chatty, and they would spend most of the journey playing cards for money. I had never seen so much money!

Newspaper cutting from the U's second ever home fixture, against Ipswich.

COLCHESTER DRAW WITH IPSWICH

Colchester United 3, Ipswich Town 3

COLCHESTER'S baptism into professional football was a thrilling affair, watched by 12,000 people. It is a long time since such good football was seen on the Layer Road enclosure, for many years the home of the amateur Colchester Town club, who are now sharing the ground.

It was a big task for the new team to face the champions of the Southern League in their first important home match, but they rose to the occasion splendidly after being two goals down in a quarter of an hour.

Williams had broken through the defence and beaten Dunn, and Alsop, the new Ipswich leader, had converted a brilliant pass by McLuckie. Colchester's defence had been partly responsible, Leslie playing an exaggerated third-back game, which left gaps. When this was remedied, however, the change came, and at the end of half an hour United were having their full share of the exchanges.

Cheyne, the old Chelsea player and international, was an inspiring force in the home forward line, and five minutes from half-time he slipped the ball through for Crisp to take it in his stride and reduce the lead.

Bad Quarter of an Hour

Colchester were galvanised into action by this and when a minute from half-time they were awarded a penalty for a foul on Smith. Wood scored after Houldsworth had pushed his shot on to the upright.

Ipswich had a bad quarter of an hour after the restart, their defence being even more shaky than had been Colchester's in the early stages. Leslie and Ritchie had found their true form in the half back line and kept plying their forwards with sound passes. Dunn was equal to all Ipswich shots at the home goal.

Ipswich rallied for a time, but Colchester took the lead when Cheyne converted Pritchard's pass. The United seemed safe, but ten minutes from time a penalty was awarded to Ipswich. Dunn saved Perrett's shot, but with the man following up his spot kick the scores were levelled.

Colchester make a raid—but a safe pair of hands eases the situation for Ipswich.

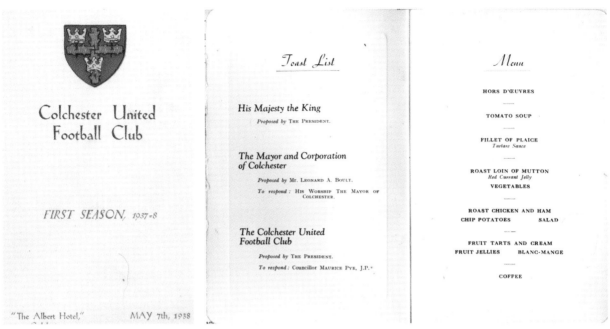

Colchester United
Football Club

FIRST SEASON, 1937-8

Toast List

His Majesty the King
Proposed by THE PRESIDENT.

The Mayor and Corporation
of Colchester
Proposed by Mr. LEONARD A. BOULT.
To respond : HIS WORSHIP THE MAYOR OF
COLCHESTER.

The Colchester United
Football Club
Proposed by THE PRESIDENT.
To respond : Councillor MAURICE PYE, J.P.

Menu

HORS D'ŒUVRES

TOMATO SOUP

FILLET OF PLAICE
Tartare Sauce

ROAST LOIN OF MUTTON
Red Currant Jelly
VEGETABLES

ROAST CHICKEN AND HAM
CHIP POTATOES   SALAD

FRUIT TARTS AND CREAM
FRUIT JELLIES   BLANC-MANGE

COFFEE

"The Albert Hotel,"   MAY 7th, 1938

The toast card from the end-of-season celebration dinner at the Albert Hotel.

The original Colchester United team photograph for their first season.

COLCHESTER UNITED FOOTBALL CLUB, 1937-38

[*Copyright Photograph by West End Studio.*]

Back Row : **Mr. C. H. S. Le Ball, Mr. L. W. Daniell, Mr. E. Davis** (Secretary-Manager), **Mr. G. M. Morris, Mr. L. A. Boult.**
Middle Row : **Mr. W. Allen** (Vice-Chairman), **Mr. W. K. Howard, Mr. P. C. Cook, J. E. Evans, G. W. Leslie, R. Dunn, J. W. Baker, J. Collins, G. T. Ritchie, Mr. W. H. Clark, Mr. B. Myers, Mr. A. E. Warner** (Accountant).
Front Row : **Councillor R. Wright, A. Wood, K. Mayes, G. Crisp, A. Pritchard, Councillor M. Pye** (Chairman), **R. Smith, J. Hodge, A. Cheyne, W. Barraclough, Councillor Wm. C. Harper.**

The decorated locomotive used to pull the train taking U's supporters to the Ipswich game at Portman Road on 5 February 1938.

At the end of the first season there was a celebration dinner at the Albert Hotel, to look back on a successful first season for Colchester United.

Ted Davis was secretary-manager and as well as him I can also remember a lot of the players quite vividly, particularly Alex Cheyne, who was one of a number of well-known players who were attracted to the club; Dunn the goalkeeper, Arthur Turner, Barrowclough and George Leslie, who was a policeman with Colchester borough police force and who had played for Colchester Town. And there was a chap called Smith who they used to call 'The Warhorse', who was always falling down. My family and I got to know them quite well and they made a fuss of me because I was very young.

One night, the Layer Road Stand roof blew off during a storm, and my father got called out in the middle of the night. Houses on the far side of Layer

An early U's share certificate, issued in 1938 by the then board of directors.

Road had been damaged and it was my father's responsibility to sort things out. My father never lost his interest in the club and continued to watch the team after he was no longer chairman.

My father was always my hero. He was just a good man, so straightforward and honest. When he was on the town council it did not matter to him what political party someone belonged to, if someone had a good idea that would benefit the town he would back it and work on it. We bought a commemorative brick at Layer Road as a tribute to my father, and it now sits proudly at the new stadium.

Mrs Jean Bell, daughter of Colchester United's first chairman, Maurice Pye, who became chairman in 1937

Reserve team fixture in the 1930s; the famous clock can be seen to the left of the goal.

A packed house for this U's winter fixture in the late 1930s.

Goalmouth action in the 1930s, as seen from the Layer Road terracing.

I was born in 1934 at 48 Layer Road, right behind the goal end. My first memory is from was when I was about three or four, when there was a fierce storm which blew the roof off the Layer Road Stand and it ended up lying in the road. Some of the debris hit our house, smashing the windows and glass and damaging a suite that stood in our front room.

A year later the roof blew off a second time during another bad storm. I think it was then that it was decided the problem was there was no gap between the back of the stand and the roof. This meant that when the wind was blowing in a particular direction it had no way of escaping and the pressure would eventually blow off the corrugated iron sheeting. This accounts for the gap which soon appeared along the back of the Layer Road Stand.

When the war broke out in 1939 an air-raid shelter was built on the pavement behind the Layer Road Stand, at a spot where the pavement is at its widest. The shelter was built to be used by everyone along that stretch of the road. The air-raid sirens went off a few times but Layer Road was never hit. I was at school at St Johns Green School when Essex Street, South Street and West Street were bombed, and I can still remember the building shaking and the blackboard coming off the wall. The bomber was a daylight raider looking for the barracks in the town. Our fighter aircraft got him on the way out.

There was a car park in Layer Road where Abberton Motors was later located. On matchdays many spectators would cycle to the games and I used to collect 2d (two old pence) from people parking their bikes in our front garden, that is until my dad found out and put a stop to it.

When I reached the age of 12 in 1946 I was allowed to go across to the ground to help the groundsman, a gentleman called Jock Duncan, who walked with a limp. I would help out in any way I could and I would often be found cleaning boots or helping to mark the pitch. The groundsman's equipment included hoses to water the pitch, and a line marker and string which were needed when marking the lines. I was allowed to go wherever I wanted in the ground and I was paid sixpence at the end of the day.

On Saturday mornings when a home match was scheduled, I would go over to help clean the ground and prepare for the game. Immediately next door to the ground was a tea shop owned by Mrs Hart and her family. Jock Duncan would give me 6d and I would go to Mrs Hart's so that she could fill a big brown teapot which I would take to the dressing rooms. The players who arrived at the ground early always appreciated having a cup of tea waiting for them.

I also spent countless hours weeding the pitch, and during the close season some players would come to the ground to do maintenance work, including joining in with the weeding. In those

A view from the Clock End in the 1930s. With no Terrace Three yet built, the houses in Layer Road can be seen beyond the stands.

days players were paid about £12 a week during the season and £8 in the close season, so any additional income was welcome. One year several of the players came in during the summer and helped to build the terraces.

Shortly before we got into the Football League it was decided that we would have ball boys around the pitch for the first time. I was one of the original ball boys along with Robert Curry (Bob Curry's son), Alan Houghton (whose mother used to wash the kit) and Peter Storey (the son or stepson of Jock Duncan). The four of us ran out with the team in full kit, one to each corner of the ground, for the game against Kidderminster Harriers. I was at the top end in the far corner. At half-time we went in for a drink and the referee asked if we could all put coats on for the second half, so for the whole of the second half we were wearing full kit and coats.

When the ball went out of the ground we had to push our way out through the crowd to find the ball and retrieve it. The ball seemed to get kicked out of the ground so often that I did not see much of the game, and I missed most of the goals in a famous 8–0 win.

One year I broke my ankle in about March. Jack Kearton was trainer and he offered to give me free treatment as the ankle recovered. However, I had to go and stay with my cousins in Southend and so Jack gave me a letter to take to with me. Southend played at the greyhound track near North Avenue at the time. When I arrived I just knocked at the door and gave them the letter, and they carried on my treatment.

Despite my connections with the club I had to pay to watch the FA Cup games against Chelmsford City, Banbury Spencer, Wrexham and Huddersfield Town. Ground admission was 6d. For the biggest games two rows of chairs were placed around the pitch. The following year we went straight into the first round against Reading. Extra seats were again put in the ground, which I think probably came from the nearby barracks.

I have watched the team ever since those days as a ball boy, apart from in 1955–57 when I did my National Service.

My father was once on the committee of Colchester Town. There is a picture from 1912–13 and he is on the right-hand side, wearing a different style of hat from everyone else. My father was friendly with Freddie Thompson, who was a window cleaner living in Butt Road and played for Colchester Town. Freddie had a piece of land three houses away in Layer Road and my father drew the plans for his bungalow – probably the first one in Layer Road.

Peter Nunn

This U's attack breaks down as the goalkeeper intercepts on the edge of the box.

Colchester kick-off this match in the late 1930s.

The U's go on the attack once again, with the Layer Road End in the background.

I can remember in World War Two a Mustang aeroplane crashed in the middle of Layer Road on its way back from a bombing raid. I was in Hamilton Road School and saw the tail fall off. Smoke was pouring off it and the plane crash-landed in the road. Jock Duncan, who was the groundsman in the club's early days, came out of the ground and tried to get the pilot out before the entire plane went up in flames.

When I came home from school, the Americans had been up and sprayed it with foam. It looked like it came out of the Arctic!

Bob Bacon

Above: Jock Duncan (far left) looks on as the pitch is prepared for action.

Left: Former groundsman Jock Duncan is pictured here (back row, third from right) on duties other than grass cutting as the ground was used as a wardens' post.

My father, Albert Quinney, used to breed rabbits in the sheds owned by Joe Clampin the gardener. That land was the bottom part of the garden and was sold to Colchester United by my father. There was only a wire fence between the field and the garden on the left.

They held a rabbit show in the Main Stand between 1944 and 1946. Rabbits were bred for meat, of course, a fact that kept my mother from working in the munitions factory during the war as she had to look after the rabbits.

The football stand was used as an air-raid wardens' post during the war. At the lower end of No. 31 Layer Road, in its garden on The Cannons side, my father and neighbours dug another air-raid shelter. The Clarke family (a wife and son Steven) joined my mother and I down in the dark depths while German planes flew over the town and the sound of Doodlebugs was heard overhead.

Betty Downing

An unusual use of the ground during the war years, as a rabbit show takes place in the main stand.

Digger Kettle goes in bravely to win this ball against Hereford United.

A packed Layer Road End looks on as the U's go for goal.

Two unidentified teams commence play under the watchful eye of the Main Stand.

A fine view of the Main Stand in the early 1940s, showing the Open End with a bank of speakers on the extreme right.

Len Cawcutt, one of the last surviving Colchester Town players, died in Norfolk in 2000. Colchester United played their last League game at Layer Road on 26 April 2008, which was a coincidence because that day also happened to be the centenary of Len Cawcutt's birth — 26 April 1908.

Dick Barton

I had a wooden football rattle in those days. I only took it to one game but I was not allowed to use it in the directors' box. I was allowed to join in the shout of 'Windy' when the opposing defence turned the ball into touch. Everybody joined in with that.

Chris Jolly worked very hard on the social side of things in the very early days. He fixed up some sort of a tannoy system with a bank of speakers and at matches he played American marches written by a composer named John Sousa. He would play marching tunes like *Stars and Stripes* and *Colonel Bogie*. Chris had a large record collection of Sousa's marches and he always played one particular march when the U's won. I think it may have been *Stars and Stripes*.

Mrs Jean Bell

Chapter 2 – 1946 to 1949

TED FENTON AND HIS FAMOUS SOUTHERN LEAGUE TEAM OF CUP HEROES

I can proudly say 'I was there' for some of the great occasions in the early days of the club:

- 1948, FA Cup Third Round vs First Division Huddersfield at Layer Road – we were in the Southern League. Ted Fenton, Len Cater, Dennis Hillman, Arthur Turner, Harry Wright, Bob Curry, etc – we won.
- 1948, FA Cup Fourth Round vs Second Division Bradford at home – we won again.
- 1948, FA Cup Fifth Round vs Blackpool away. Two old pre-war Bedford coaches from Norfolk's of Nayland, with three drivers sharing two coaches, no motorways, left Military Road at 8.00pm Friday, travelled all night, blue-and-white crépe paper suit (blew away on Blackpool's golden mile), Bloomfield Road, Stanley Mathews and Stanley Mortensen. We lost 5–0 – great day!

Tony Vaughan

The first time that I went to watch the U's play football was at Layer Road on Christmas Day 1946. The ground was about one mile from South Street, Colchester, where I lived. I was eight years old at the time and was taken to the game by my uncle, who was staying with us for the Christmas holidays. The game was a Southern League fixture against Gillingham which

Members of the 1948 FA Cup team line up in front of the Main Stand.

A training session at Layer Road during the 1948 FA Cup run.

we lost 0–1 and, to be honest, I do not remember anything about the game at all. However, it must have made a favourable impression on me because I became a regular at Layer Road from then on.

It was really a good time to be a Colchester United supporter; we were winning most games and there was always a good crowd turnout, usually around 8,000. As the U's trotted out onto the field the *Post Horn Gallop* would be played over the loudspeakers – very stirring stuff.

It only cost 9d for me to get in to watch the games, which I always did because I was doing a morning paper round that earned me six shillings a week. The ground was within walking distance for me and I usually went with a friend or two. I even went to an away game once at Chelmsford, which despite being only 22 miles away was a big occasion for me.

In the 1947–48 season Colchester United had a great FA Cup run. The media attention for that was fantastic; the papers and radio were full of Colchester stories. I remember watching the First and Second Round games against Banbury Spencer and Wrexham, but it was the Third Round game against Huddersfield that was memorable for me. Not only were Huddersfield a First Division team at the time but they also had the great Irish international Peter Doherty playing for them too.

It was a typical freezing January afternoon but I watched the game with such intensity that I did not feel the cold. When we won the game 1–0 everybody went crazy, swarming the field and patting the players on the back. I was not aware of it then but that was the first time a non-League team had beaten a First Division team in competitive football since the Football League extended to four divisions in the early 1920s.

In the next round Colchester were again drawn at home, this time the opposition was Bradford Park Avenue, who at that time were playing in the Second Division and had themselves just staggered the football world by winning their previous round game at Arsenal. Once again the impossible happened when Colchester won the game 3–2. Unfortunately I did not go to that game because I was sick, however I sold my ticket for a good profit and thus became a very young scalper.

In the Fifth Round, Colchester had to travel away for the first time and this proved to be too much for the team as they were soundly beaten 5–0 by Blackpool. In those days Blackpool were in the First Division and they had an awesome line up which included Stanley Matthews, one of the greatest players ever to play for England. Blackpool went on to reach the FA Cup Final that season, only to lose to Manchester United at Wembley.

In the 1948–49 FA Cup Colchester were drawn at home to Reading in the first round. Once again I was there as the U's

Another picture of the U's training during their famous Cup run; The Cannons can be seen in the background.

Training session at Layer Road, featuring Harry Bearryman, Bob Curry, Digger Kettle and others.

The players prepare for the new season with some fitness work at Layer Road.

trotted out onto the field; however, it was so foggy that I could not really see anything. I was positioned near the halfway line but could not see either end of the field. The game started and Reading took the lead, but I did not see the goal, and eventually the game was abandoned just before half-time.

There were more than 19,000 people in attendance for that game, a record for Layer Road. The game was replayed later that week and I went there with my ticket stub from the first game thinking that was all I needed to get in. However, I was told that I would need a new ticket for this game and as I had no money with me I had to stand outside the ground and listen to the crowd noise. Luckily for me the gates were left unattended at halftime so I was able to sneak in to watch the second half.

Malcolm Murray of Niagara Falls, Ontario, Canada

In 1944–45 I was about five or six years old and my maternal uncle lived in Layer Road at the house immediately adjacent to the southern side of the ground. Occasionally my parents used to visit him on a Saturday afternoon and, if the U's were playing at home, I used to hang about in the back garden in the hope that the ball would be kicked out of the ground into the garden. I would collect it and take it back, and I seem to remember it was worth a penny if I did so.

At the same time, my paternal uncle also lived in Layer Road directly opposite the ground, and when I was about eight or nine years old I was allowed to cycle to see him on a Saturday afternoon when the U's were playing at home. The first attraction was that, like several people along the road, he used to allow fans to park their bicycles in his front garden for a small fee and I used to 'help' him by keeping watch over them for parts of the afternoon. He used to give me a few pennies for doing that.

The second attraction was that the gates were always opened before the end of a match and the officials used to turn a blind eye to small boys who sneaked in to watch the last 10 to 15 minutes. Then, as soon as the final whistle blew I use to dash back over the road to 'help' sort out the bicycles which were all piled up together.

Terry Crossley

Bob Curry, Harry Bearryman and Andy Brown are followed by player-manager Ted Fenton as they take to the pitch for training.

It was in the Third Round of the FA Cup versus Reading on a bleak November day in 1948. The game kicked-off in good light but with an overcast sky. As the game progressed a fog descended

Harry Bearryman, Bob Curry and Andy Brown warm up in this training session.

The fans look on from what was to become Terrace Three as the U's take on Huddersfield Town in the FA Cup.

on Colchester and visibility on the pitch worsened, with the players only able to see about 20 yards ahead of them. It was then, mid-way through the first half and with the U's a goal down, that the referee decided the game should be abandoned.

The game kicked off at 3pm, and the weather was fine until about halfway through the first half when it rapidly started to deteriorate. Everyone had coal fires in those days, so the fog was more smoggy, there was no wind to take it away, and it just came down heavier and heavier.

We tried to continue to play but it got worse and worse and in the end we could not see much further than the penalty area. I could hear the opposition coming down the field but could not see them until they were right on top of me! Fortunately, the referee decided that it was time to abandon the game.

The team that we were playing was the same one that had played the previous year in the FA Cup against Blackpool, apart from Ted Fenton, Dennis Hillman and goalkeeper Harry Wright, who had a bad injury which meant that I was called up to the first team.

The club chairman Alderman Allen presenting the players to the lord mayor of Colchester before a local derby game versus Chelmsford. Seen in the picture from left to right: Harry Bearryman, Alderman Allen, Ken Whitehead, Digger Kettle, Stan Foxhall, the lord mayor, Bob Allen, Fred Cutting and Frank Stamper.
Photograph by Essex County Telegraph

The team are presented with local oysters ahead of their next Cup match

It was clear from early on that there was a huge crowd that day as when I was taking the goal-kicks I had to go into the crowd to take my run up. The fans were sat around the touchline and so it proved troublesome when taking goal-kicks and throw-ins.

It was a day with a sense of occasion because everyone had been so geared up for having a good run in the FA Cup after the previous year's successes. The fans were all excited and came from all over the place. It had the makings of a first class game until the weather came into play, and that was despite of the pitch, which was not in a very good condition and churned up very early on.

Fans had been starved of football through the war years and when we played Chelmsford in the Southern League there were 14,000 there for that game. The average gates were about 10,000.

My wages were £6 a week, plus £2 for a win and £1 for a draw, and I suppose that during the week we did not really see the rest of the players that much – some came in from London, some from Ipswich. I lived in Ipswich and I trained with Ipswich Town at Portman Road as I had been on the books there before I went to Colchester. I remember Fred Cutting used to come down from Norwich, Arthur Turner from London.

It was an enjoyable time and the Southern League was a hard League in those days. In 1948–49 we got to the Final of the Southern League Cup and I got a medal even though I did not play.

The chairman at the time was Alderman Allen and the secretary was Claude Orrin. Claude was a nice gentleman, a quiet chap and a good person to talk to. When we all met before a home game, we would go to eat at The Albert and we would have a very light meal of fish before walking up through the town to the ground.

For away games, the local ones in particular, we took a bus there and then it became a bit of a family outing along with all of the arguing and comments!

Kenneth Whitehead (with thanks to Kenneth's granddaughter, Julie Orford)

Oysters in hand, the players discuss the tactics with manager Ted Fenton.

Bob Curry and Ted Fenton discuss tactics.

I started supporting the U's in 1947. As a young lad one of my early recollections is that I once cycled to Chelmsford for a fixture in the Southern League. I went to the bus park and all of the coaches were full, so I went to North Station where they had five special trains. However, they were all full too, so I got on my bike and went all the way to the game in New Writtle Street that way. It took an hour and a half and I had to keep my head down to get there on time.

A packed Open End – tree room only! – as the fans prepare to watch the Bradford game.

I remember queuing for tickets for the Bradford game when the supporters' hut was over on the Barside, and the queue went right the way around the ground, down Layer Road and halfway up Gladwin Road. It took three or four hours to get a ticket. I saw all of the Cup games that year, starting with Banbury Spencer. They were famous because they had been reprimanded by the FA for painting their posts with black and white alternate stripes.

Another early recollection was that there was a player called Walker who played left-back. Every now and again his knee would come out of joint and he would lie down, and as the play was going on he would pop it back again and play on. It was before the day of substitutes so he had to do that!

U's fans packed tight to the touchline as the home side go on the attack again.

I suppose I have been quite fortunate that I have known quite a lot of the players over the years. I can also remember when we handed Ipswich Second Division football. I could not get to my usual place under the clock for that game, so I hung on the railing and looked over the top [where the Family Enclosure was] and watched Fenton miss the penalty and that made the difference between us going up and not.

John Simpson

Jock Duncan breaks the news that the
Bradford clash is a sell-out.

Extra seating proves useful as thousands cram into Layer Road.

My clearest early memories are of the feeling in the pit of my stomach before every FA Cup match as that was our only chance of fame. It started when the draw was made, subsided for the next few days but always returned on the morning of the match.

I can remember being mortified at not being able to travel to Blackpool to see my team take on Matthews and Mortensen, etc, but of course my time was to come some 20-odd years later in the shape of Arsenal, the top team in the country, packed with internationals.

John Foskew

When I joined Colchester in 1946, I came from Charlton who had a team in the FA Combination League.

When I got married on 3 June 1950 the directors and players were invited to the reception at Bow Council Chambers. Claude Orrin [secretary] was also invited but was unable to attend as he had been summoned to FA headquarters, where they were discussing Colchester's application to join the Football League.

We had just finished the wedding meal when Claude arrived and announced that Colchester had been elected to the Football Association League. So, in addition to the usual toasts, the whole team and directors drank to the future of Colchester United – and what a future it turned out to be!

Needless to say, a good time was had by all and this was one of many happy memories of my time at Layer Road.

Arthur Turner (Colchester United player, 1946-52)

Good news all round as Arthur Turner gets married on the day that he and his teammates find out the U's have become a football league club.

The teams line up as the U's prepare to to take on Second Division Bradford PA.

Bicycles, bottles and programmes! Every house along Layer Road used to store bikes. The bike racks were full as everyone used to travel to the ground that way.

I used to sell programmes – we used to have 50 as they did not trust us with more, and we used to run down the road to get nearest to the crowd as they came up the road. You sold more the nearer to town you were, but the problem with that was when you sold out you had further to go to get back and collect more programmes!

Another thing we used to do was collect bottles. You used to get a penny for each. The fans used to leave the bottles in the stand and we used to climb in underneath the wooden terracing and take them back for pocket money.

When I was older I became an electrician by trade and did the wiring under the stand for Ted Fenton. Many of the players at the time were customers of ours so we came to the ground to help them out. They all used to come in to our shop and buy radios and TVs, and so I got involved helping with the stands and floodlights.

When they decided to have Hospital Radio up on the gantry they needed a means of heating it quickly because in the winter it was freezing cold. Some wooden cabinet fire heaters were installed and overloaded the electricity meter so much that it burnt out!

I also had the contracts to change the bulbs on the floodlights. We would not change one bulb, we would change two as the ladder was straight and we wanted to go up there

Ted Fenton refers to his notebook to explain the F-Plan to his players ahead of their next big game.

Arthur Turner is blocked off this time as fans watch from all vantage points.

and do things properly, as there were about 36 bulbs on the floodlight. The bulbs were on a wooden tower and I made a bag that would hold 1,000 watt bulbs so that I could safely take them up the ladder.

At that time I lived in Layer Road, and there were no houses much further than the ground as they were not built until the war. The roundabout in Rainsborowe Road was where they stopped building, so people could turn around in the road and head back towards town. The U's car park was where Abberton Car Sales later appeared. It was a shame to see it go because car parking space was always needed.

Bob Bacon

My father bought No. 148 Layer Road when it was first built by Hum Builders, who built all of the houses between the two ends of Rainsborowe Road.

When my father came back from serving in the RAF he saw that other householders in Layer Road were charging to look after fans' bikes during games and decided that it would

The media capture the action from on top of the generator next to the Main Stand.

Bob Curry's first goal against Bradford is on its way into the net.

be a good thing to try and a good way for me to get some pocket money along the way. We looked after 25 bikes the very first time we tried it and we took it a bit more seriously after that! People used to come from all around, including as far away as Maldon, Abberton and Mersea. You could not get away after the game as the whole of the road was taken up by people walking back to the town centre or collecting bikes.

After the war people started to enjoy themselves again and football provided a social outlet. We attracted more and more bikes as time went on, so we widened the path down to the back of the house so more people could get down there, and then we put a fence along the side so that even more bikes could be leaned up against it.

An average matchday saw us get about 50 to 80 bikes, but in the big games it was far more than that. At that time, the big games were Chelmsford, Merthyr and Yeovil, and for those three games coaches were parked right the way back to where Kent Blaxill was later situated. At that time Boadecia Way did not exist – it was all fields.

Then things progressed a bit as my father spotted the opportunity for further business and he parked his car on the road and used to charge a shilling to store bikes in our garage if it was raining. It quickly became a two tier system and we were able to store 20 to 25 bikes in there. My mother said all the saddles would get wet if it rained, so after the game I was told I had to wipe them with towels! Then between August and October we made the most of what else was available to us. We had a long garden and in the last 50 yards there was an orchard with apple trees, so we used to pick up the windfalls and give people an apple for free as an incentive to leave their bikes.

I was not allowed to go to the game until 15 minutes after the kick-off and always left 15 minutes before the end; although my mum used to let me leave earlier than that so long as I made sure I did not stand near dad until 3.15!

David Judge

Bob Curry scores the crucial winner against Bradford, as some fans adopt any position to ensure that they can see the game.

Bob Curry watches this shot all the way into the back of the net against Bradford PA.

Ted Fenton is swamped by delirious fans as the final whistle goes against Bradford.

My parents ran the Park Hotel in Wivenhoe and at the age of 11 I saw my first-ever U's game, against Chelmsford City in the Southern League. Just a year later we had our great FA Cup run, beating Banbury Spencer, Wrexham, Huddersfield Town and Bradford Park Avenue (who had beaten Arsenal in the previous round) en route to a tie at Blackpool.

I was desperate to go to Blackpool but my parents forbade it, and instead I spent the afternoon at home wondering what was happening at Bloomfield Road. The pub was empty that afternoon, in fact all of Wivenhoe seemed quieter than usual.

I did not know the score from Blackpool until the early hours of Sunday morning, when Cedric's coach finally got back to Wivenhoe. We had lost 5–0 but I am convinced that our Cup performances were a big factor in the U's getting elected to the Football League in 1950.

Mike Mason

I first watched the U's in the Southern League days when I would cycle the 12 miles from Goldhanger, often with the Willingale twins. If it was raining their father would offer to take us and other times we would bike to D'arcy and catch the Osborne's bus there.

26 February 1949 – U's 5 Merthyr 2. For several seasons we battled it out with Merthyr Tydfil at the top of the Southern League. It was a tremendous result for U's. Arthur Turner got four goals (one pen), including a great header at the Open End when he dived in like a torpedo.

I used to stand towards the back of the corner where the Main Stand side joined the Open End. There was a corrugated iron fence at the back and we used to stand up on it to get a better view.

Cecil Chapman

Ted Fenton addresses the crowd after the historic win against Bradford in 1948.

Reading Game 1948

Later that year we decided to go to the Reading game and Ted Neville had offered to take me to the game on the back of his motorbike. I biked to Layer Road the week before the game to buy tickets for us, but the dynamo on my bike seized up at D'Arcy on the way home so I stopped at D'Arcy Lion for a pint before finishing the journey.

Travelling into Colchester on the day of the game it was foggy all the way. Just inside the turnstiles there

Ted Fenton (central) begins to be hoisted onto shoulders after the win over Bradford.

fenton's men made national headlines with their exploits, and these cuttings record the build-up to a friendly against Arsenal and the public's acknowledgements of the club's achievements.

Manager Ted Fenton (left) and Bob Curry congratulated by Colchester's Mayor and Mayoress, Councillor and Mrs. L. E. Dansie.

From the town hall balcony victorious Colchester wave to their cheering supporters.

Bob Curry meets future England boss Ron Greenwood before the Huddersfield Town game in 1948.

used to be sleepers built up and that was where we found a space for ourselves to watch the game. The fog just closed in, and it was no surprise when the game was abandoned.

The funny thing was that travelling back home on the back of Ted's motorbike, as soon as we went down the slope towards the reservoir at Layer-de-la-Haye the fog completely cleared and the sun was shining.

When I got married I went to the football less frequently, but then I got a motorbike and rarely missed a game. I would park in the car park in Layer Road and there was no need to lock up the bike.

The Willingales ran the local shop. Sam Willingale was very proud of the fact that he was a special constable. For one game he drove a group of us to a match in his car, and as we were leaving the Layer Road car park after the game there was a policeman on 'points duty' directing all of the traffic left, towards the town centre. Sam ignored the policeman and turned right without any indication. The car was not fitted with indicators but Sam should have put his arm out of the window to show he was turning right.

The furious policeman deserted his points duty and chased after us. He got hold of Sam through the driver's window and asked him what he thought he was doing, turning right without any warning. 'Don't you know you've got to signal to turn right?' he asked him. We were allowed to carry on only after a very stern lecture was given to Sam.

As soon as we were on our way again, Sam puffed his chest out and said 'He obviously didn't see my special constable's badge, did he?' We laughed about that all the way back home.

Cecil Chapman

Chapter 3 – 1949 to 1955

SOUTHERN LEAGUE GLORY IS EXCHANGED FOR A STRUGGLE TO MAKE HEADWAY IN THE FOOTBALL LEAGUE

I went to my first game in 1950 aged just seven. I have been told by my father, who still follows the U's, albeit these days by radio, that my first game ever was in September 1950 against Norwich City. I believe he and my grandfather took me to a further five or six matches that first season in the Football League.

My recollections are of standing at the front rail of the terrace. This was 'our spot', and I can clearly remember John Harrison our right full-back and Johnny Church our left-winger at the time – probably because they were always the closest U's players to me. Years later John Harrison came with his wife to my son's wedding, and knowing that he came to the U's from Aston Villa we sat him next to some of our friends from Birmingham – lifelong Villa supporters.

My favourite players at that time were Reg Stewart and Vic Keeble; although Vic was shortly to be replaced by one of my all-time favourite U's players, Kevin McCurley. I suppose most young lads like goalscoring centre-forwards and I was no exception.

Terry Lawrence

In 1950–51 Colchester United were voted into the Football League, Third Division South, along with Gillingham. I do not think I missed a home game that season, watching teams that I had previously only read about in the newspapers.

Every Saturday afternoon the BBC would broadcast a Football League game, and one Saturday, to my amazement, they announced that they would be broadcasting the game between Plymouth Argyle and Colchester United. That game was played at Plymouth on 28 October 1950 and I was listening to every word that was broadcast.

The fact that Colchester lost 7–1 was sad, but they made up for it later that season when Plymouth made the return trip and were soundly beaten 3–0. I mention this game because I still consider it one of the finest games I have ever seen, and it also produced one of the finest goals I have ever seen, a flying header by our centre-forward Vic Keeble.

The U's exert pressure at Layer Road in this early 1950s League match.

The U's prepare for action in September 1950, with a young Vic Keeble (front row, right hand side) now in their ranks.

Vic Keeble also lived on South Street, just eight houses away from our house, and he was my favourite player. I would see him on the street and he would always say 'Hello'; I just could not believe that he would even speak to me. Then, in 1952, Vic was transferred to Newcastle United for the amazing sum of £15,000. That might not seem very much now but back in those days it was a small fortune.

Vic went to Newcastle as a replacement for the great England international Jackie Milburn, who was retiring. If I remember correctly Vic played in a losing FA Cup Final for Newcastle but later on won the Cup with West Ham United. Years later I met a Geordie who was a regular at St James' Park

Bob Curry looks on as the ball is powered into the
back of the net by Vic Keeble.

fans look on from the Layer Road End as the U's take on Norwich in 1950.

Getty Images

Female supporters prepare to make some noise for the team against Norwich in 1950.

Getty Images

Men about town; the U's players in the High Street in 1950.

in those days and he reckoned Vic was the best header of a ball that he had ever seen. Whenever Newcastle got a penalty the crowd would shout 'Let Keeble take it with his head'.

Malcolm Murray of Niagara Falls, Ontario, Canada

My father was a journalist on the local papers when I was a young girl. We used to head into town and meet up in Wright's on the High Street with a number of the players, including Kevin McCurley, Digger Kettle and Vic Keeble.

It must have been around 1952–53, and the players would have been in their 20s. They made a fuss of me while they were talking to my father, but they could not stay long as they all had other jobs in the town to go to.

The games at that time were broadcast on Hospital Radio and it used to be quite a thing to go and visit folk, but also we were making the most of the opportunity to listen to the game!

Sue Hood

I remember that the FA Cup replay against Rotherham in the early 1950s was played mid-week before the lights were put up so it was an afternoon game. I was at school then, at the time when Hamilton Road was a Secondary School, so I had to play truant to go to the game. We lost 2–0 but when it was 1–0 Kevin McCurley was through on goal and was tackled from behind, a clear penalty, but Kevin stayed on his feet and then missed his shot. A player these days would have gone down I am sure.

Malcolm Murray of Niagara Falls, Ontario, Canada

Having supported Colchester United for over 60 years, I have more than a few memories of Layer Road and I would say that I have not missed more than a handful of home games in that time. Probably the worst attended season was when Her Majesty – that is the Queen not my wife – required my presence (two years' National Service, and even then I was stationed at Colchester for one of those years). It was the 1961–62 season I missed most during a posting in Kenya.

My first memories of Layer Road were of standing at the front, leaning on the rail in Terrace Four. I always got to the front despite the fact that the crowd was often double what we would record in later years.

I had the impression that we spent at least 20 years in the old Division Three South, of which 19 were spent at the bottom together with Swindon, Walsall or Torquay resulting in two teams having to apply for re-election. Looking back through the records, however, this would appear to be a false impression!

John Foskew

The goalkeeper collects safely as the U's look for a goal at the Layer Road End.

The U's are denied by the goalkeeper on this occasion as the centre-half looks on.

The fans queue down Layer Road as Ipswich come to town in 1952.

My father attended the U's first League match at Gillingham in August 1950, with my mother and his own brother while they were on holiday in Kent. My mother's recollection of that match is of standing on a log at the back and occasionally seeing the ball when it was high up in the air.

Chris Fincham

My first visit to Layer Road as a paying fan was in 1950–51 when I was in the first year at the Colchester Royal Grammar School. Several of us used to go in our purple school blazers and caps and stand right on the barrier at the north-west corner, which then was totally open. At that time it was possible to roam around the ground at will so it was possible to get close to either goal and under cover when it rained.

The wearing of our school uniforms was, I suppose, the first sign of the onset of teenage rebellion. The CRGS was a rugby school which was keen to have pupils playing or supporting that game rather than football. I remember the mantra offered by the sports master in my first year: 'Rugby is a hooligans' game played by gentlemen whereas soccer is a gentlemen's game played by hooligans'.

Terry Crossley

Supporters' club membership was among the highest in the country at this time.

My father thought that I needed to broaden my education and started to take me (reluctantly at first) to games in the 1950s. In those days the supporters' club ran a double-decker bus from Braintree to home matches, and as we lived in Coggeshall we were picked up en route.

My earliest recollections were of Percy Ames, John Fowler and Sammy McLeod but the match that has stayed in the memory was a game against Tuesday night's opponents, Northampton Town. At the time the club were running a 'penny for the ball' competition with the match ball as the prize and I had the lucky ticket; although it must have been a damn close thing as I believe Kevin McCurley scored twice in what was a 3–1 victory – and had he scored again he would have been entitled to the ball instead of me!

I know how proud I was taking the ball home on the bus, and, of course, it attracted a lot of attention from other boys in and around Monkdowns Road where I lived. For those who do not know the area this estate had been built just after the end of World War Two, and unlike housing built now the planners did not cram as much in as possible. The houses were built around a green just like the stands around a football pitch!

Captain Reg Stewart looks on as the kit is dished out at the start of the season.

The goalkeeper saves at close range from Johnny McKim's shot.

We used to play a lot of games there and, of course, what better to use than my new acquisition. The ball also saw service on Coggeshall recreation ground where there was an iron goal frame. I got a lot of enjoyment from games in those days even though the rules did not count for much.

I seem to remember a lot more than 11 players on each side and the game mostly involved chasing the ball as it gradually made its way towards the goal, with a 'goal hanger' waiting to bang it home at an opportune moment. And what happened to the ball you ask? Eventually all that kicking took its toll and the stitching split.

There was nothing left to do but deposit it in the dustbin; although if I had been a bit more sentimental in those days I would have kept a panel. But when you are young you do not think of such things.

Captain Reg Stewart and teammates holding the Essex Professional Cup after beating West Ham in May 1952. Back row, left to right: McCurley, Davidson, Bearryman, Harrison, Scott (just visible). Front row: Miller (trainer), Church, Stewart, Elder, Coombs, Pookes.

The referee whistles to signal a goal at the Open End, with the goalkeeper beaten.

My other memories of Layer Road are centred around the big games. From the 1950s I specifically remember the game against Arsenal but only because my mother would not let me go for fear that I might be crushed!

My father went and queued to get in but the gates were shut when he was about 50 spectators from the front (so I would not have seen the game anyway).

Colin Willsher

Captain Reg Stewart is presented with the Pearson Senior Cup in May 1953.

Disappointment in the dressing room as Reg Stewart contemplates a U's defeat.

Left and below: Jock Duncan hard at work as he prepares the pitch for match day.

Chapter 4

THE MANAGER WHO NEVER WAS

From the mid-1950s to the late 1980s, Ron Meades was the archetypal football journeyman.

His playing career wrecked by the intervention of the war and his managerial ambitions frustrated at every turn, Meades instead got his kicks from coaching. He helped kids and professionals alike, from Torquay to Trondheim and Cardiff to Kuwait. No session was too small and no destination too far for this enthusiast with his FA badges.

He was an unsung hero; a name unknown to the vast majority of football followers. So it is surprising to find that Ron Meades actually occupies a prominent place in football's record books. He is, in fact, the shortest-serving manager in Football League history.

In the post-war years when Ron was starting out, clubs did not chop and change managers as they do today. Sackings were relatively rare, particularly at homely little clubs like Colchester United. But somehow Ron managed to get the boot at Layer Road less than FOUR DAYS after being given the manager's job.

What on earth did Ron Meades do to deserve such a fate? The episode in the summer of 1953 has been shrouded in mystery for over 50 years, but now some of the facts can be revealed.

United fans of a certain age will recall a vaguely embarrassing close-season fiasco which the club's directors quickly sought to cover up. All that came to light at the time was the story that Colchester had torn up Ron's contract, barely 72 hours after appointing him, because of the unsatisfactory outcome of some enquiries they had made. In fact, they had been tipped off by a reporter that Meades possessed much less experience than they had been led to believe, and they were forced to act once the matter was aired in the local press due to subsequent accusations of boardroom incompetence.

To use modern parlance, Ron had allegedly 'enhanced' his CV and sweet-talked his way into a job he was clearly not qualified or ready for. At his interview, it seems the Colchester directors liked the cut of his jib and, just as importantly, thought they could save some money by asking him to both play in and manage the side.

Now a lively 88-year-old living in the Peak District, Ron laughs off the idea that he very nearly charmed his way into the Layer Road hotseat: 'I had just started coaching at that point and I must admit I was very young and inexperienced. But in those days a coach who had been on FA courses could get a job anywhere in the world and it was common to apply for all sorts of vacancies, which is what I did.

'The job was advertised in one of the papers. In those days there was a paper away from the usual dailies called the *Daily Record* and it was a sporting paper. For some reason, it had all the job adverts in there and it was sent to me through the FA.

'It's a long time ago and I can't remember the details of exactly what happened at Colchester, but I do remember the letter they later sent telling me they no longer wanted me. I was rather naïve and I just accepted it – if it happened nowadays you would obviously make a fuss about such a thing of course.'

It seems Ron was officially manager of the Third Division South club for no more than three full days in June 1953. This puts him joint-top of the list of shortest-lived Football League managers of all time. Bill Lambton is also said to have lasted just three or four days at Scunthorpe in 1959, but at least 'Iron Bill' took charge of a match, which Meades never did. The other contender for first place on the list is Dave Bassett, who was Crystal Palace boss for a mere four days in 1984.

The story of Ron's aborted reign began when Colchester advertised for a successor to Jimmy Allen, who had resigned after a five-year stint in which he took the club from the Southern League into Division Three. A 4–0 thrashing at home by Norwich saw the U's finish the 1952–53 season firmly in the League's bottom four and within days the outspoken Allen walked out, angry at fans who were calling for his head and at loggerheads with the board.

The U's supporters' club were instrumental in Allen's departure, having gone public with stinging criticisms about his 'allowing players to stroll around the town at all hours'. They called for the appointment of a young player-manager which could save at least one salary at a time of severe cash shortages at Layer Road. The board liked the idea of saving money and from the list of applicants they selected four names of potential player-managers in addition to their first choice, the Manchester United full-back Johnny Carey. When Carey turned them down flat and one of the four – Preston defender George Hepplewhite – suddenly got cold feet, they were left with a shortlist of three.

Thus, the trio interviewed in the tiny Layer Road offices were Brighton goalkeeper Harry Medhurst, formerly with West Ham and Chelsea; the Reading and ex-Arsenal inside-forward Les Henley and the lesser-known name from Wales, Ron Meades.

Says Meades today: 'For years, I was wondering whether I signed that contract but I am sure I did!

'After applying, Colchester wrote back and invited me to an interview. I remember catching a train from Cardiff to London. It was at the time of the Queen's coronation and London was absolutely packed.

'I changed trains and headed out to Colchester and they met me at the ground for the interview. When you're in the interview and someone asks you if you're a strict disciplinarian, you wonder whether they want you to be one or not and try and answer in the right way.

'However, the interview must have gone well as I can recall going down to the pitch and they took my photograph. They even showed me a club-owned house that came with the job. It was a nice looking red-brick house.

'Before I left to go home on the train I got the local paper and the news was already in the STOP PRESS section.'

Meades was described in Colchester's local Press as 6ft tall, under 12 stone and looking very fit and young for his 32 years. He had told the board he was a family man who had coaching and masseur qualifications. He claimed playing experience at Ninian Park and player-manager experience at non-League level.

Had they checked more thoroughly, however, the Colchester directors would have found that Meades had in fact joined Cardiff City as a teenager in August 1939, only to have his contract cancelled a few weeks later when war broke out. His playing career never recovered from this interruption. His managerial qualifications amounted to little more than stints at non-League minnows Treharris and Wadebridge. Moreover, his football career had been overshadowed by wartime heroics, for he had joined the RAF and fought in the Burma campaign against the Japanese.

The Colchester directors, after years of working with the grumpy Jimmy Allen, were under pressure on all fronts and the charming, fit-looking war hero stood in front of them seemed like a breath of fresh air. Meades' enthusiasm, allied to his lack of financial demands, won the day. Novice or not, they were going to take a chance on him. Club secretary Claude Orrin prepared a contract and announced that Meades had got the job. The new man signed on the dotted line and later on met some of his playing staff, several of whom were older than him.

The local press were flabbergasted. *The East Anglian Daily Times* said the appointment of this 'unknown Welshman' was a bombshell, and their reporter asked Mr Orrin: 'Do you seriously think a 32-year-old non-League player, out of League football since the war, can lead and inspire United in the Third Division?'

Startled by the unexpectedly hostile reaction to their choice of manager, Orrin and a flustered board are said to have made no reply. Orrin also refused to comment when asked what United's experienced players would think of such an appointment.

After getting little change out of Mr Orrin, the reporter from the *EADT* decided to make his own investigations into the shock appointment. He telephoned contacts in South Wales and the West Country and soon discovered that Meades had in fact mostly been a reserve player at Cardiff in the war years – hardly a glittering career – and had only coached at minor League clubs. In the past year Meades had been 'mostly based at home, while coaching locally.'

Once this information was made public the local Press and the fans made it clear they believed United's directors to have taken leave of their senses. Accusations of gross incompetence were bandied about. Public opinion quickly won the day and forced the club into a complete U-turn and the cancellation of Meades' contract. A statement was issued by the club saying that the appointment was now void 'owing to the unsatisfactory outcome of enquiries made.'

Not only was their choice of manager grossly under-qualified for the job, it was now suggested that he had exaggerated what little experience he did possess. Poor Meades was chased out of town less than four days after landing his dream job. Embarrassed director Major Gerald Benham told the Press: 'We shall have to start all over again.'

Meades accepted the turn of events with equanimity. He says now: 'I went back to Cardiff and I believe I got a letter saying that "we feel that your lack of experience is important and we have decided not to appoint you."

'If I'd had the knowledge and experience at that time, which I did gain later, I think they would have let me carry on. But I wasn't too worried by it all – you got your travelling expenses for interviews covered by the club, so I didn't feel too hard done by.

'They were in the close season so I never got to meet some of the players. I was so young and innocent football-wise at that time and I just accepted it, I suppose.

'Looking at it, I don't think they chose the right person when they appointed me – I had no experience of playing, although I knew the runnings of a football club, and when we went to Lilleshall many of us were aghast at how little we actually knew. It was only later I was to get the experience.'

So although Meades was on the Colchester 'throne' the day Queen Elizabeth was crowned, he never got to take a proper training session or oversee a single match of any description. Colchester, anxious to save face, desperately sought advice and were told by Arsenal manager Tom Whittaker about the availability of a man with an impeccable CV – former Arsenal stalwart Jack Butler, who had managed Torquay, Crystal Palace, Royal Daring of Belgium and had even led the Belgian national side at the 1938 World Cup. He was quickly contacted and accepted the job.

Butler's reputation satisfied the critics and took some of the heat off the Colchester officials. But, of course, a big name does not necessarily guarantee big success and Butler's first season ended with the U's having to apply for re-election to the League. Six months later Butler suffered a nervous breakdown and quit. Meades could hardly have done worse as it turned out!

Colchester were one of a number senior clubs at which by Meades made an unsuccesful attempt to become manager, but he did go on to enjoy a long and varied coaching career, which included stints at Torquay United in the early 1960s and postings by the FA to Africa, India, Kuwait, South America and Scandinavia.

He recalls applying to manage West Bromwich Albion and being granted an interview, but he says the job ultimately went to Vic Buckingham 'because they liked the sound of his accent'. Meades did, in fact, land a player-manager job at Ross County in Scotland, but this contract was also cancelled within a week. Ron says this was down to accommodation problems, as far as he can recall.

After all his travels Ron is most fondly remembered in Norway where he spent the 1980s coaching a series of clubs, including Karnes, Nordreisa, Kautokeino, Geitnes Midrand, Kopervik, Haugar, Hodder, Kalyan and Ullern. He made many friends in the land of the fjords, some of whom still keep in touch and remain grateful for his efforts to improve footballing standards in such outposts.

Ron Meades, with thanks to Rob Hadgraft

Chapter 5 – 1955 to 1959

SOME INCREDIBLE DAYS UNDER BENNY FENTON

When I reached the age of 13 I had a paper round at a newsagent's in Crouch Street and also worked at the Maypole in Long Wyre Street for an hour after school and Saturday mornings. This meant I was able to afford to watch the U's whenever I liked, and mostly I stood in the Layer Road Stand. During my mid-teenage years other attractions began to turn up but I do remember that the U's used to play West Ham in a charity cup match every season when Benny Fenton was the player-manager. He was what we would now refer to as a 'thorough professional', particularly in defence in the penalty area. I learned a lot from watching him which was a great help to me when I subsequently qualified as a junior referee when I turned 16.

Terry Crossley

When I first started going to Layer Road in the mid-1950s admission for boys cost one shilling, and it cost half a crown [two shillings and sixpence] for my father to enter. My friends and I used to bike to the ground from the Barn Hall estate, always in the same group of six: Richard Weldon, Jack Smith, John Tuckwell, Terry Slade, Trevor Cranfield and me. We left our bikes in the front gardens in Layer Road for about threepence each.

In those days there was just a series of poles around the ground instead of a wall. If the ball was kicked into the crowd it was just sportingly kicked back. Referees used to take some stick in those days but it was always harmless banter – never anything nasty.

I am glad that I lived through those days. If you lost, you lost, and they were better days than now.

Cliff Toft

When I was a young boy three of us used to stand in the corner of Layer Road near where the Corner Bar was later situated, balanced with one foot on a brick wall and the other on a building behind us that was not really much more than a garden shed. We were only youngsters, and at one match an older supporter said to us, 'You'll go through that bloody roof one day', but of course we never did. The building housed the supporters' club, which was essentially just a building containing a bar and some toilets. It had no windows, just a notice board with supporters' club information attached to it. It was a far cry from the place I shall take in the West Stand at the new stadium.

In the early days there were half-time scoreboards on both sides of the ground. A score would be put up next to a letter which corresponded to a fixture list in the programme.

Harry Fosker, the original 'Umbrella Man', encourages the crowd before kick-off.

Claude Orrin prepares to see the U's players onto the team coach as they depart for an away game.

I well remember times when someone would come along and put up a board showing that Ipswich Town were winning 5–0 at half-time, just to wind us up. A few minutes later the correct score would be put up and a massive cheer would erupt from the crowd. At the time we were big rivals in Division Three South. I also remember when Harry Fosker from Bergholt, the original 'Umbrella Man', would rally the crowd at half-time if we were losing.

Mike Mason

I attended games with my father and grandfather during the early 1950s, but my first real memories come from the 1956–57 season, by which time I was travelling with several mates on a Hick's bus from Braintree. I think that season we were undefeated at home and thrashed Shrewsbury 6–0 and Northampton 5–1.

That was the year Ipswich pipped us to the League title and promotion, and at a packed Layer Road Benny Fenton missed a penalty in a 0–0 draw; I think it was Roy Bailey who

The ball is unceremoniously cleared as the U's pressure the Layer Road End.

The 1957-58 squad pose for the cameras. Back row, left to right: Alan Springett, Derek Parker, Bert Hill, Tommy Williams, Ken Plant. Middle row: Russell Blake, Tony Pepper, Percy Ames, John Wright, Chic Milligan, Peter Wright. front row: Dave Carter, Ronnie Hunt, Brian Dobson, George Fisher, Edgar Rumney, Kevin McCurley, John Fowler.

pulled off the save. I can still reel off the usual team from that season by heart: Ames, Fisher, Fowler, Fenton, Milligan, Dale, Hill, Smith, McCurley, Plant and Wright.

Two seasons later I moved to my favourite spot behind the Layer Road goal, at the edge of the penalty area on the Main Stand side. I was at the back of this stand, banging on the corrugated iron fencing, when Neil Langman and Johnny Evans scored two late goals against Arsenal to secure a 2–2 draw in the Fourth Round of the FA Cup.

I was also one of the several thousand locked out of Highbury on the night of the replay. Many years later I met Tommy Docherty, who played for Arsenal in both games. He said that they were really concerned about Peter Wright, who they thought was a very dangerous winger. His remarks about Neil Langman were a little less flattering – he recalled that he was all brawn and no brain!

Terry Lawrence

Benny Fenton talks tactics before the Arsenal game to an expectant squad.

Desperate defending by Arsenal as the U's crank up the pressure.

I can remember a game at home against Ipswich. We were first and second in the division, and we needed to win to be promoted. Benny Fenton missed a penalty and we drew. There were about 18,000 people at Layer Road that day; the roof of the Bar Side Stand did well to support about 500 supporters! Ipswich gained promotion in our place and went on to great things – we stayed were we were. I was there.

Another match that stuck in my mind was U's versus QPR on a dismal midweek afternoon. It was getting dark with just a few minutes to go, and floodlights had not yet been invented. Peter Wright latched on to a ball on the halfway line and took it down the left-hand side, before cutting in and shooting from about 30 yards. The ball stayed about 6in off the ground for its entire journey into the bottom-left corner. Springett, QPR's international 'keeper, would not have seen it even in daylight! It was the best goal I have ever seen.

In the FA Cup Fourth Round in 1959 we played the mighty Arsenal at home. There was a crowd of 16,000 in Layer Road that day. United were 2–0 down with a few minutes left, when goals from Neil Langman and John Evans levelled it up for us. It was amazing! Eight of us went to Highbury for the replay in an old builder's van in the fog and frost. There were 62,686 fans in the ground. I can remember that Arsenal tried out some new shoes for that match, rather than playing in studded boots on the hard ground. It seemed to do the trick as United lost 4–0; however, it would have been seven or eight without Percy Ames.

Tony Vaughan

John Wright clutches the ball as the U's fans look on.

I suppose my most memorable match, for all the wrong reasons, was in the FA Cup at home to Arsenal when I was in my late teens. At that time I was studying an HND sandwich course at the technical college in Sheepen Road, and the engineering principal allowed the whole class to leave early one afternoon to watch the evening replay.

Special trains were laid on from St Botolph's Station and

Arsenal goalkeeper Jack Kelsey watches Peter Wright's effort pass narrowly wide of the goal.

U's players reflect with a drink after their exploits against Arsenal.

we crept up to and around North London in dense fog. They did not seem to bother much about supporters getting mixed in together then because we stood in a stand more or less on the halfway line and could not see either goal. I never did understand why the referee allowed play to go ahead.

Anyway, the players disappeared into the fog, a roar went up and an unseen goal had been scored. This happened four times, with the U's eventually losing 4–0. Apparently, according to the management, the problem was that United's boots had been fitted with the wrong type of studs, which were unsuitable for the Arsenal playing surface in those weather conditions.

Terry Crossley

I was born in Tooting, South London, in 1948, and I had two aunts and a nan who lived in Colchester. We used to visit them once or twice a year and my uncle took me to Layer Road in 1955. I can remember that he pushed me to the front in what is now the Family Enclosure and I stood on a small box. I can also recall the 'penny for the match ball' ticket and the dog with the striped coat! And from that day on the U's were

Enthusiasm from fans of all ages in the late 1950s.

A happy dressing room after beating Southampton.

my team. I only saw them once or twice a season but was tuned to BBC's *Sports Report* every Saturday afternoon to get their result. Even as an eight-year-old I would be very grumpy if Colchester United lost. My heroes at that time were Kevin McCurley, Percy Ames and Peter Wright, and I used to keep a scrapbook and cut out little reports from the London papers when they appeared, which was not that often unfortunately.

I was at the famous 0–0 draw versus Ipswich, which, if we had won, would have reversed both clubs' fortunes. I can still visualise Benny Fenton's penalty now!

I was not at the Cup game against Arsenal but pleaded with my dad to take me to Highbury for the replay. He would not take me, though, on the grounds that I was too young for an evening game on the other side of London, and I went round stomping my feet and slamming doors in protest.

I went to school in Brixton, and at the age of 12 I used to get the train to Colchester and my uncle would meet me from the station, take me to the game and then put me back on the train to go home. From about the age of 15 I used to do this on my own and that was where I met Dave Amoss, getting the 10.10pm from Colchester back to Liverpool Street and then the tube home.

Although I missed the Arsenal Cup game I can clearly remember the Fulham and Newcastle League Cup games, and the WBA, Derby, Man United and, of course, the Leeds games, all of which I went to. I also attended a few 'local' home games including Leatherhead (twice), Wimbledon (when they were amateur) and Aldershot. In fact, I saw us lose three times in a month at Aldershot; once in the FA Cup, once in the Auto Windscreens Shield and lastly in the League, when it poured with rain and made the whole month's experience make me question just why exaclty I was putting myself through it.

There was also the 30-hour round trip to Torquay in the snow where I drove from Tooting (leaving at 9.00pm on the Friday), to Colchester to get the coach, which left at midnight. It started snowing just before we left and we got stuck on a hill in Dorset at 4am, and all of the 42 blokes on the bus had to push lorries off the road and then push the coach up the hill. One by one we jumped back onto the coach as it was still moving slowly uphill. I cannot remember who the last one on was but he must have been exhausted! When we got there we were informed that the game was postponed, and I did not get home until 3am Sunday morning.

Mike Gadbury

I was born and raised in Colchester into a football-mad family; my grandparents, parents, uncles and cousins were all Colchester United fans. I watched the U's when I lived in the town between 1955 and 1972.

I was first taken to Layer Road by my mother in 1955–56 when I was about eight or nine. One of my early memories is of sitting on a small wall under a rail watching Michael Grice on the right wing. Attendances of 7,000 were the norm in those days.

In the late 1950s and early 1960s there were two or three St John blanket collections per season. Ambulance men used to carry grey blankets around the touchlines at half-time to collect any coins thrown from the crowd on the terraces. Fans would throw in their small change, but some used to miss and land on the pitch. When I was quite young I would often stand by the front rail. Sometimes you got hit by the odd stray coin when they were collecting, and I remember going on the pitch following the St John staff picking up any coins from the pitch and putting them in the blanket.

One particularly sad memory was 16 February 1957, when the U's were at home to Ipswich Town and both sides were chasing promotion to the old Second Division. As a nine-year-old I was taken to the ground with my cousin and another boy by my grandfather. We got in perhaps an hour before the kick-off, and my grandfather took us towards the open terracing at the corner of the ground opposite the Spion Kop.

There were a lot of people in the ground and my cousin and I were keen to climb up fencing at the back of the terraces to gain a better view. However, my grandfather was concerned for our safety and took all three of us outside the ground, and so we were in tears even before the U's drew that day to let our local arch rivals gain promotion.

Colin Burch

A packed Terrace Eight prepares for the game in 1955.

My first recollection of attending a match would be from around 1957, and I would have been 12 at the time. It was an end-of-season game against local rivals Ipswich. Both Ipswich and Colchester were going for promotion from the old Division Three South.

It was a packed house, with an attendance of something like 16,000 to 17,000, and the only way I could see anything was to scramble up the supporting pillars of the main grandstand near the halfway line. However, this restricted my view to just one half of the pitch.

I recall that some time during the game the U's were awarded a penalty, unfortunately for me at the end of the ground that was out of my sight. After the usual lull of anticipation prior to the vital kick I was engulfed by a huge roar, and, thinking that we had scored, I nearly fell off my precarious perch in the excitement of the occasion.

It took a few moments before I realised that the penalty had been saved and the noise had been created by what was obviously the mass of Ipswich supporters. The fixture finished 0–0, Town were promoted and the rest is history.

Who could forget the day the mighty Arsenal visited Layer Road? It was February 1959 and the U's had progressed to the Fourth Round and were drawn at home to the Gunners.

Accompanied by my usual group of friends I was one of the first to be in the queue to obtain a precious ticket. Rejoicing with prized possession in hand, I turned to see others still waiting in the long line of loyal supporters that stretched as far as the Drury Arms.

It was exactly the same on match day. There I was at the front of the queue waiting for the gates to open to claim my usual and treasured spot, just to the right of the goal at the Open End.

The U's came back from 2–0 down to earn a replay, with Neil Langman bulldozing through the middle for the equaliser. I can remember the team from memory, but this is not much of a feat as it seemed the line up was virtually guaranteed week in week out.

Ray Smith of Paignton, Devon

Layer Road has been part of my life for 51 years. I shall miss it terribly. It is homely, but it has to be accepted that for modern football purposes Layer Road is not fit for use.

I have followed the U's through thick and thin since I was aged 10, witnessing the highs and the lows including dropping out of the League and bouncing back two years later having won the Conference title and FA Trophy.

My involvement with the U's started in February 1957 when a group of boys from Myland Primary School were taken to see the home game against Newport County. We won 1–0.

Playing on the left wing was Peter Wright, like me a 'Mile End boy', who, when we lived in Nayland Road before moving to Mile End Road, lived a few doors away with his parents and his brother John who was a talented cricketer [he played for Essex].

I remember the dad in charge of us all was a Mr Cottee, father of my classmate Andrew, and he, with a couple of other dads, took us to the game. There were 14 boys and three adults. I remember that the admission cost for all of us was £1 – that was one shilling [5p] for each boy and two shillings [10p] for each adult.

Bob Russell, MP for Colchester

I remember the first game I went to with my dad, when I was 12 years old. When we got to the ground the crowd was such that we had to stand towards the back of the terracing, and being somewhat small for my age I was not able to see a thing. The suggestion was made that I should go to the front so I was carried over the heads of the crowd and down the terracing to a bench placed at the front for children.

My memory is that this was at the Layer Road End; certainly it was at a goal end because during the game I was hit on the leg by a shot at goal and it really hurt! Luckily this incident did not put me off and I became regular at Layer Road in the days of the Ames, Fisher and Fowler defensive combination. I used to cycle from my home in Eight Ash Green and leave my bike in the front garden at a friend of my dad's who lived in Layer Road. I am still a regular, and a season ticket holder, although now I live rather too far away to cycle.

Before moving to Eight Ash Green we lived in Rainsborowe Road behind the Main Stand. I can recall the day that a ball landed in our back garden. On reporting it to the club we were told that on no account should we move the ball and that someone would be round to collect it.

Ed Henshall of Baildon, West Yorkshire

- 1958 – At the age of nine my dad took me to Layer Road for the first time. This started a period of nearly six years where I went to almost every home game – both first team and reserves matches.
- 1959 – Colchester United were drawn at home to Arsenal in the Third Round of the FA Cup. Dad tells me there would be too many people in the ground and it would be dangerous so I could not go. I howled my eyes out but it did no good. United drew 2–2. As for the replay at Highbury, Dad said it would be way past my bedtime by the time we would get home so again I could not go. I howled my eyes out but it still did no good. Colchester United lost 4–0.

David Hicks

I managed to get to the front at the famous Ipswich Town game without being passed over the heads of the crowd as youngsters often were in those days. It was not until later that I started watching from further back in the stand next to my mum and dad, who both continued to support the U's well into their late 80s.

The proud manager, Benny Fenton in all too recognisable profile.

Benny Fenton lines up with his charges, including the Hunt brothers Bobby and Ronnie (front row, third from left and third from right).

At the time, I almost felt part of the match and sometimes even got to touch the ball. Despite having a 'penny on the matchball' at every game I was never lucky enough to win one.

I do not know when footballs were first fitted with valves but my early ones were always tied and laced, and my first valve-type ball was bought for me in about 1956 and was one of the first in my village; although laced-up balls very quickly went out of production. I can remember, too, that footballs had no protective coating on them, meaning that in the wet they became waterlogged and thus extremely heavy. I do not know when League clubs started playing with balls that resisted water, but I suspect that even with a ball that seemed like it was made from lead, Reg Stewart would be able to clear the Layer Road Stand with a header from just inside the halfway line! I want to ask him if it hurt him as much as it did me if I caught the lace on my forehead on a rainy day.

Another memory I have from the early days is when I discovered a bird scarer in a barn on the farm where my grandfather was foreman. I tried it out and the first swing almost broke my wrist, but I soon became quite proficient at swinging it round, and the noise it created was very impressive.

It was soon painted blue and white and was taken along with pride to home games, where, I am sorry to say, it was not always appreciated by those around me. It was also inclined to be just a bit dangerous as once it started swinging it was not easy to stop. It weighed in at just short of two pounds, so it was the heavyweight of the division! Of course, the advent of the soccer hooligan soon made it a no go, and it has remained ever since in my special treasures drawer together with an increasing number of souvenirs and programmes.

I later began work at Barclays Bank in Chelmsford and remember the horrors of having to work Saturday mornings, when I had to remain at the bank until the cheques from that morning had been balanced. I do not know if anyone noticed how hard I worked on Saturdays, but I would often leave Chelmsford as quickly as possible and catch the bus to Rivenhall, where my dad and mum would pick me up. I would be bundled into the car and there would often be a hot dinner on a plate waiting, and I would consume this on the way to the ground. We did not miss many kick-offs, despite the fact that, prior to the floodlights, matches in winter started much earlier –

Reg Stewart shakes hands as rebuilding work continues in the background.

I think it was either 1.30pm or 1.45pm. Nevertheless, I soon became addicted to following the U's.

John Foskew

When the car park was on the site where the Abberton Car Sales are now located you just parked at any angle as there were no marked bays, and as a result most of the cars were jammed in until the end of the match. You then walked to the ground and all the parents would be carrying a stool or milk crate for their youngster to stand on. Once inside, the 1d tickets to 'win the matchball' were on sale – I never did win it!

At half-time there was the mass movement from behind one goal to the other, so you could see all the Colchester United goals go in.

The best match I ever saw was the FA Cup game, Col U 2 Arsenal 2. Ten more minutes and we would have won it, of that I am sure.

David Cheeseman

In the 1950s one of Arsenal's most famous celebrity supporters was Ted Ray, who started life as a music hall comedian and later had his own BBC radio show for 12 years. Ray played comic roles in several British films including the headmaster in *Carry on Teacher*. When we played Arsenal at Layer Road in 1959 we took up our normal seats in the fourth row of the Main Stand, and I found myself sitting next to this famous comedian. The First Division aristocrats established a 2–0 lead, at which point Ted Ray leaned over to me and said 'Your little team has done really well'.

The U's fought their way back into the game, scoring two late goals and so nearly forcing a winner. I turned round to him and said 'Yes, we have done well, haven't we?' but the seat next to me was no longer occupied!

Judith Musgrove

I first started supporting the club in 1956, when you did not really need to have a season ticket. The club reserved your tickets and you collected them on arrival at the ground. If you were not attending you just told them so the tickets could be sold. But, although we never actually had season tickets but we always sat in the same place.

Judith Musgrove

During the 1950s my whole family were season ticket holders – my mother, father, my sister and myself. In those days you could buy an enamel badge and then each season add a new enamel bar to the badge. We sat on the wooden bench at the back of the Main Stand, and in fact my last season ticket at Layer Road was not too far away from that position.

I remember the following players in particular: Peter Wright, who in one game, I believe, lost his contact lens while running down the wing, and Reg Stewart, who also coached soccer in my school and taught me how to slide tackle.

Another Layer Road memory is when we drew with Arsenal at home in a Cup game, and after the interval their goalkeeper returned to the field and stubbed out his cigarette on the touchline.

I have supported the U's for around 52 years and I believe we were talking about a new stadium even as far back as in the 1950s. The new stadium is long overdue, and it looks marvellous.

Peter Seward

I would swear to this day that, in my opinion, the ground attendance record was smashed at the match against Ipswich in 1957. When I arrived at the ground at

John Wright collects this ball as Bob Dale looks on.

2.15pm the queue reached as far as Gladwin Road. Once inside the ground I saw people on the roof of the Popular Stand, up trees and standing on the toilets. I saw the first man go up the drainpipe to get onto the Popular Stand and within no time there were scores of people up there. I reckon there must have been 20,000 people in the ground that day. The game ended in disappointment, with Benny Fenton missing a penalty that would have seen us promoted instead of Ipswich. Fenton just did not really hit the penalty cleanly.

Mike Mason

I can clearly remember my first game at the age of 10 in 1957, which was the famous 0–0 draw with Ipswich Town. My 13-year-old sister, Jill, had been to Layer Road before with my father, but it was the first time I went. We stood in what became known as Terrace Three.

We arrived at the ground at 1.30pm, and as we looked back down Layer Road we saw that the queue stretched as far as Gladwin Road. As we set off walking towards the back of the enormous line two Ipswich supporters kindly pulled us into the queue so we did not have to go right to the end.

I remember Benny Fenton's penalty-kick. It must have been a dry pitch that day as I saw a puff of dust fly up as he scuffed the penalty.

Jack Manning

I went to the Ipswich Town game in 1957. I was 11 at the time and went with Mum and Dad and my younger brother, and although my parents could not get in, they waved us two boys off into the ground and said they would pick us up afterwards.

Once inside we could not get onto the terraces and our quest seemed almost hopeless. But then, just as we had given up hope of seeing the game, I remember hearing people shouting 'Let the kids through' and we were then passed overhead to the touchline so that we could see.

I remember the famous penalty vividly; a great save in the top left-hand corner by Roy Bailey. The point of that game was that Colchester, Ipswich and Torquay were vying for promotion and we were in charge at that point. However, we drew with Town 0–0 and missing out on promotion really seemed to affect the team.

Martin Broom

At the home game versus Arsenal in 1958 I remember people climbing onto any vantage point to see the action. I went to Highbury for the replay. My father worked at Woods, and we travelled on the coach arranged by them.

In my opinion the game should never have been played because of the atrocious conditions. Like most people I only saw half the game because of the fog. I always used to play in goal so that day I paid particular attention to Jack Kelsey, Arsenal's Welsh international 'keeper.

Jack Manning

I went to the Arsenal replay at Highbury in 1959. The supporters' train left from St Botolph's Station, and I remember noticing what a really long train it was.

Several players that stood out and have stayed in my memory are: Percy Ames, George Fisher, John Fisher, Parker, Chic Milligan, Hammond, Tommy Williams, Sammy McLeod, Martyn King, Bobby Hunt and Peter Wright.

Cliff Toft

When the Arsenal home game came around I was working as an apprentice in Wivenhoe shipyard earning £2 0s 2d [two pounds and two pence] a week. That was the wage for apprentices until the age of 21. I had no money to spare and so decided not to join the supporters' club, even in the knowledge that if you were not a member you would have little chance of getting a match ticket

A U's attack comes to nothing as Jack Kelsey waits to smother the loose ball.

if we were involved in a big FA Cup game. Sure enough, after that decision the inevitable happened and we were drawn at home to Arsenal, one of the most famous clubs in the country.

I was therefore desperate for a ticket but my aunt, who worked at Paxman's on the switchboard, said she thought she could get a ticket through Peter Wright if I was prepared to pay £5 for it. The ticket was Sammy McLeod's complimentary ticket, and it was spare because Sammy's family could not afford to come down from Scotland to watch the game. A deal was struck, and I had a ticket for the big game.

The day will always stick in my mind. I came into town on the bus from Wivenhoe and found a place on a level area at the back of the terracing, with quite a poor view of the pitch. However, after about 15 minutes the crowd surged forward down the terracing and I found myself nearer the front with a much better view.

There was no crowd segregation at all and we were all mingling with Arsenal fans. They all seemed to be thinking or saying the same thing: 'Who's that little b****** Sammy McLeod?' The provider of my ticket was running rings around the mighty Arsenal. Unfortunately, however, even his efforts were not enough to give United the win; although we pulled it back to 2–2 having been two goals down.

I went to the replay at Highbury, but I did not get into the ground and just walked around Highbury twice as the game went on, with 64,000 people inside and thousands more locked out.

Mike Mason

The Arsenal Cup game in 1959 really stands out – particularly the wait for tickets and parking bikes for tuppence along Layer Road. Everyone went by bike and parked opposite, and when you went back you did not give it a second thought as to whether it would be there or not.

Tickets had been sold the previous weekend and I was dismayed by the crowds and queues along the way. I parked my bike and walked back down the queue, when I stopped to talk to two lads in the queue that I recognised, and at that point a policeman walked past and pushed me into the queue. So I got the ticket, which I might not have done if I had not spotted the lads from school!

U's players look on as a chance goes agonisingly over the crossbar.

For the first 25 years of attending Layer Road I stood on what was then known as the Spion Kop. I then emigrated to behind the Layer Road End goal from where I saw some great matches, particularly the Friday night floodlit games.

The atmosphere was much better at Friday night games and there were bigger crowds. It was pay day, you see, and people who played on Saturdays were able to go. They were not all fantastic games but there was always a lot of excitement nevertheless.

Martin Broom

I went to Highbury for the replay with Arsenal. The Osborne's bus that picked up fans in Goldhanger that day was almost swamped as so many people from the village wanted to go to the game.

Joe Osborne [owner of Osborne's and stalwart of Layer Road] drove the bus himself, and he took us to see Charlie Chester [a music hall comedian and radio presenter] at Finsbury Park Empire after the game.

Cecil Chapman

As an example of how things have changed, I once saw a game delayed because Peter Wright had lost a contact lens in the goalmouth at the Layer Road End. A corner from Mike Grice had come over from the right when the incident happened. The game was delayed while the referee and several players of both sides got down on their hands and knees to look for the missing contact lens.

Mike Mason

My family lived in Clacton and I first caught the football bug when my father took me to watch Clacton Town. It was after Bob Curry had left Colchester and he was playing for Clacton Town in the Eastern Counties League in the early 1950s.

During school holidays I used to sell postcards and rock outside the Arcade on Pier Avenue with one of Bob Curry's sons. I think it was three sticks of rock for a shilling.

My interest in football led me to Layer Road, and I was a devoted follower for many, many years.

Diana Smith

As a young boy in the 1950s my late father, Frank Wenden, took me to Layer Road. I can remember sitting up in the trees at the Open End. When I was not in the trees I was on my father's shoulders or behind the goal.

Frank was a Colchester United and Arsenal fan but as a farmer he did not see as many games as he would have liked, but he never lost his interest in football. In fact he loved cricket and football. The final time I took him to see Essex play at Castle Park his eyesight was very poor. Driving home I asked him if he had enjoyed the day. He said 'I got to tell you, boy, I never saw one ball bowled, but I had a day out with you'.

We lived in Ardleigh Road, Little Bromley, and Father never drove a car. I used to love going to Layer Road; it was the highlight of the week. We used to catch the bus into Colchester and then get on a Football Special. My most vivid memory is of the 9–1 win over Bradford City in 1961. I was a rare Bobby Hunt fan and Bobby got four of the goals.

I used to have a favourite Shredded Wheat bowl with pictures of Colchester players around the perimeter, McCurley, McKim and so on; all my favourite players. I had bought the bowl from the football club, thought the world of it and always used it.

I got married at the age of 20 and had been married not many days, in fact I think it may have been the honeymoon week, when the U's caused a big row.

I came home from work late one afternoon and my wife said 'You're not going to the football?' I said 'I always go. Of course I'm going'. She said 'You are not going'. I replied 'Well I'll give you the chance to come with me'. She was getting really het-up by now and said 'You're bloody well not going'. I just said to her 'Are you coming to the game?' and left the house.

I had put on my crash helmet on and was just going out of the gate with my motor bike when all of a sudden there was a crash and broken china was falling around me. My wife had smashed my Shredded Wheat bowl on my head. I still went to the football but I was so upset that I could not really concentrate on the match.

Willie Wenden

As far as the ground is concerned, in the early days there used to be railway sleepers for terracing. And one of the features of the big Cup games was having two rows of fold-up seats stretching along the touchline.

I remember one game against Wrexham, in which Digger Kettle came up against Tunnicliffe on the wing and he lifted the player over the two rows of seats, over the wall and into the terracing! The only other player I saw do that was in the first season in the Football League when we played at Crystal Palace and Jimmy Elder put one of their players over the side wall.

The best player I have seen is difficult to say, as football has changed so much. Sammy McLeod was a little Scottish genius, while Bobby Hill was a good inside-forward and a clever ball player.

John Simpson

I was born in north London and moved to West Mersea in May 1955. I attended Primary School on the island and like most boys, started getting into football. I soon discovered that the U's were my nearest team and began my love affair with the club in the 1957–58 season. While I was to young to go, I still followed all their results intently during a very nervy end to the season as they finished 12th and just qualified for the new Division Three.

By the time I was 10, I managed to nag my parents into letting me get the football bus from Mersea to Layer Road. My temper tantrums were getting so bad, until they finally relented and at least took me to the bus station, under one small condition. I had to know somebody on the bus before they would allow me to get on. Fortunately for me, sitting in the front seat was the son of my piano teacher who took me under his wing and looked after me for the trip.

At last, my first ever match at Layer Road; September 1958 against Plymouth Argyle. Hooked for life! We won 2–0 with Johnny Evans scoring both goals. Later that season we drew Arsenal in the Cup and I remember the crowd being so big that I had to be escorted around the pitch and bundled over the wall behind the goal at the Clock End to watch the game.

Dave Amoss

Chapter 6 – 1959 to 1968

A YO-YO CLUB – THREE RELEGATIONS AND TWO PROMOTIONS IN NINE YEARS

I attended secondary school in Coggeshall, and later Stanway, and my recollections are based around the 1959–62 period. Three games in particular are most prominent in my memory, and naturally the first-ever game I attended sticks in the mind – but not for the usual footballing reasons.

It was in the 1959–60 season and the U's were playing arch rivals Norwich City, who were at the top of the League and well on their way to gaining promotion from the old Division Three.

I went with some school friends by bus from Coggeshall Square (it was packed), then on another bus from Colchester town centre (also packed) and eventually into the ground. I found myself standing on what became known as Terrace Three, surrounded by fanatical supporters, with around 15,000 in the ground.

The trouble was that most of these supporters were from Norwich, singing the praises of their team and getting really excited as kick-off time approached. My view of the playing surface consisted of the backs, heads and rattles of all of the people in front of me, and as this was my first match I was totally bewildered as to what the fuss was all about.

It did not take long to find out! The match kicked-off (though I did not see it) and Martyn King scored for the U's after 24 seconds (I did not see it either) and United went on to win 3–0.

From that moment I was hooked – attending practically all first-team games and some reserve ones too, but always watching from behind the goal at the Layer Road End and later from the Clock End at a time when you could walk round and change ends at half-time.

Norman Spencer

Martyn King scores against Norwich City in the early 1960s.

Goalmouth action from 1960 as Kevin McCurley prepares to shoot.

As a 10-year-old boy in 1960 I can remember cycling from Blackheath, across the fields through the Army grounds and paying 2p in old money to park my bike in a garage that was almost opposite where the club shop stood.

When we got to the garage we would be met by a gentleman, pay him the tuppence fee and he would take your bike, wheel it into the garage and that was the last you would see of it until you went to collect it after the game. He must have had a good system because there seemed to be hundreds of bikes. I do not know the man's name, as a 10-year-old I just wanted to get inside the ground to find my favourite spot and so never stopped to chat. I think quite a few fans in those days went to the games on bikes and so there were possibly more cycle stores near the ground; it would have been a good little earner on match days.

I went to games wearing my blue-and-white scarf and bobble hat and, of course, carrying my wooden rattle painted in blue-and-white stripes (there were so many rattles in those days). Standing on the Barside, as it was later known, I will never forget everybody shouting 'Duck' every time the ball landed on the corrugated tin roof because you would be showered in rust, and the ones who got the timing wrong would shake and do a dance to rid themselves of it.

After shouting myself hoarse and with an aching right arm I would cross the road to find my bike in the garage, amazingly without too much trouble. They were great days that I will always treasure.

There is a part of me sad to see Colchester United leave the legendary Layer Road, but the new stadium will lift the club to new levels of achievement in the football world.

William Hinson, lifelong fan, Cropenade, Brugnac 47260, France

In 1960 I cottoned on that the U's always opened the gates just after half-time and that you could walk in from then on for nothing. I used to take advantage of this whenever I was low on pocket money.

David Hicks

I spent Easter Saturday (16 April 1960) on holiday at my grandma's house in Kendal Road. Dad, a Luton Town supporter (and a referee), decided it was time for me to witness an event that would change my life forever. My first 'real' football match! The game in question was Colchester United versus Bradford City.

We boarded a maroon bus at the top of Hythe Hill, there was no one-way system in those days, and I remember going down Head Street and along Butt Road, where I saw for the first time those lovely old green floodlights.

As we approached the Drury Hotel the road was flooded with people on bicycles and people walking. The only vehicles that I can remember clearly were our bus and those parked outside the ground.

The floodlight pylons towered over the ground after their installation in 1962.

The cyclists dismounted and paid 2d to leave their bikes in the safekeeping of the front garden of the houses opposite the ground; a nice little earner for the residents in those days.

Once off the bus, we crossed the road. I was bristling with excitement. Dad bought a programme for 3d – on the front was a footballer in those famous blue-and-white stripes. Inside, both Benny Fenton and Terracite had written about the decline in attendances and the need to attract more people to the games.

I then remember going through a rather curiously built gate that was difficult to push (I had never encountered a turnstile before) and in we went. We joined a procession of people, mostly men and boys of all ages. I seemed to be the youngest and felt quite grown up among such company!

We trooped up to the steps that were situated behind the Open End goal, where a giant clock stood staring down at the proceedings below. Dad met some friends and I made myself comfortable by leaning on the white wall that stretched all around the pitch.

I remember staring at the Main Stand, a curious looking building that looked huge with a large Double Diamond sign at the top, behind the other goal. The Layer Road End was in those days crowded with U's supporters. There was a low roof and one could see the tops of the maroon buses parked outside.

We were standing quite near the corner flag and I was ever conscious of the amount of people gathering. The numbers increased all the time and the sound of all the chattering just added to my mounting excitement.

Walking around the pitch was a man selling newspapers, they were football special editions – *London News* and *Standard*. He would shout out as he walked around the touchline, and he proudly wore a U's supporters' club badge with a long row of year bars underneath.

On the pitch, unlike today, there were no players warming up before the game. Instead there was Whiskey, a little dog dressed in a blue-and-white striped coat, playing with his own special football while he was watched over by his owner, Taffy.

The kick-off time (3.15pm) approached and the *Post Horn Gallop* sounded. First out were the blue-and-white striped U's, and I instantly realised that God gives everybody a football team and this was the one cast upon me!

I cannot remember a lot of the match, to be honest. Bradford played in a sort of maroon-and-amber strip I think. I can remember Russell Blake taking a number of corners right in front of where I was standing and a large centre-forward called Neil Langman, who scored the goals in a 2–1 win.

However, my first hero was the man in the green jersey called Percy Ames. I can still see his famous swallow-dive save and remember the tumultuous applause it received.

In this early 1960s game, the muddy visitors' defence are relieved as a chance is cleared.

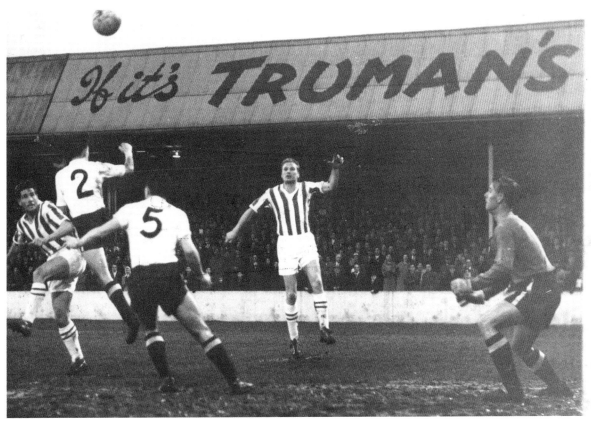

It's anybody's ball as it drops in the penalty area.

The person next to me had a large rattle that made a really loud noise which all added to the occasion, and, before my next visit, I just had to go to Wass's Toy Shop in Long Wyre Street and buy one for myself!

All too soon the game was over, the U's were victorious and, as we left Layer Road, I knew that I had changed. I was now a football supporter and life would never be the same again.

To save on the bus fare, we walked the long way back over the Abbey Field. I just did not care, I kept closing my eyes and seeing and dreaming of my new-found heroes.

By Christmas 1960 there were only two presents that I wanted. A blue-and-white striped U's shirt and a trip to Layer Road! Newport County were the visitors and 1–1 draw the result. However, I remember two goals being disallowed. We stood undercover by the side of the Main Stand, nearest the Clock End, and it was here at the tea bar that I saw my first 'naughty lady'; her picture portrait was in the calendar that proudly hung on the wall behind the counter!

We eventually moved to Colchester itself, though only for three years, and the memories of those days in the early 1960s at Layer Road often come flooding back. I can clearly remember sitting on the bus at Head Street, amazed to see the entire Exeter City team boarding complete with two large baskets of kit! They had come by train and to cut costs caught the two buses needed to get from North Station to Layer Road. We waited curiously after the game to see how they would get back. This time, they went posh – two taxis and the father-in-law of one of the players' car. And the players of today think they are hard done by!

I also remember the night that Fulham came visiting in the League Cup. Billy Stark ran rings around them, and at one point we led 5–1 before the First Division visitors restored it to 5–3.

Another visit from footballing 'celebrities' was during the dreadful winter of 1963. It was a Combination game – U's reserves versus Spurs reserves, except that on this occasion the Spurs first-team game was off and so they turned up at Layer Road with their double-winning line up; Bill Brown, Bobby Smith, Danny Blanchflower, the works! Unfortunately, none of them would sign autographs and though the U's second string gave them a good game, George Ramage had a nightmare in goal and that was that!

A more entertaining affair was the visit of an All Star XI and an amazing goal by Jackie Milburn that I have never forgotten.

Gordon Evans, Perthshire

Martyn King challenges the goalkeeper as strike partner Bobby Hunt looks on.

On 10 October 1960 the U's had been drawn to play the mighty Newcastle United in the first round of the Football League Cup. The game was unbelievable. On a dismal autumn evening, Newcastle took the field with the same XI as had played on the previous Saturday in the First Division. You would have thought that it would be no contest, but wait! The U's hit a quick-fire double and went 2–0 up inside the first 10 minutes, going on to win 4–1 with little Sammy McLeod having the game of his life. Afterwards, the Newcastle players could not believe that he normally played in the reserves! It was a bittersweet season overall, however, for the side was ageing and ended the season with relegation to Division Four.

Norman Spencer

In the 1950s and 1960s a lot of fans cycled to the match, and so the owners of several houses around the ground used let people leave their bikes in their back gardens. I think we had to pay 2d.

In 1962–63 Layer Road, like all grounds, was affected by the 'Big Freeze' and as a result there were no home games for two months. I remember the first game after the restart when the pitch resembled Clacton beach.

I used to watch most U's matches in the 1960s under the stand opposite the Main Stand, and I remember that you feared the ball landing on the roof as you were often showered with rusty flakes.

Colin Burch

Martyn King soars high as Mike Grice and Ronnie Hunt looks on with the Clock End in the background.

It seems impossible to imagine nowadays, but when I first began attending matches at Layer Road in the early 1960s, there was no segregation whatsoever between U's supporters and opposition fans. Consequently I have special memories of 90 minutes of good-natured and very amusing banter in Terrace Three with Southend fans (yes, really!) during a ding-dong 3–3 draw in October 1963. I also remember my eight-year-old younger brother being 'adopted' by Peterborough supporters in the same season. Much to his shame and embarrassment, they pinned a Posh rosette on him and even put him on their shoulders so that he would have a better view of the action. Another fond memory of those times is the opening game of the 1966–67 season, when I remember chatting amiably with Middlesborough supporters sitting next to us in the Main Stand. At the end of the match, they gave my brother a Boro balloon.

Chris Wright, Le Rouquet Nord, Maurens, France

By 1961–62 the U's had rebuilt the side with a couple of new players; Mike Foster from Leicester and Brian Abrey from Chelsea. Some players had been promoted from the reserves, such as the Hunt brothers, Bobby and Ronnie.

It was 30 December 1961 and we were at home to Bradford City, who had beaten us 4–1 in Yorkshire on Boxing Day. But this was one of those rare days on which everything that was tried on the field came off. The final score was 9–1 with Bobby Hunt and Martyn King scoring four apiece. The Bradford manager dismissed the result as a freak afterwards but I was having none of this. I was 15 years old and the U's really were the greatest team in football that I had ever seen.

Norman Spencer

Martyn King appeals for a U's free-kick beneath the imposing floodlight pylon in this 1962 photograph.

Bobby Hunt waits for a mistake from the goalkeeper as a cross drops from the sky.

My recollections from the early 1960s are of a place where I could go and enjoy a couple of hours' entertainment and find some escape from the harsh realities of a bleak, unforgiving world. To me then it was not just an opportunity to follow my team. Win, draw or lose it did not really matter to me; Layer Road was a place of sanctuary and companionship. Many people will have fond memories of Layer Road, some from the present era, some from the past and all with a personal collection of memories of hours of entertainment, pleasure and despair.

Norman Spencer

The 1960s was when I first started watching the U's, having pleaded with Mum and Dad to let me attend with my older cousins. I was immediately impressed with the striking partnership of Martyn King and Bobby Hunt. Martyn was known for his heading ability, hence the nickname 'Noddy', and Bobby was famous for his turn of speed and prolific finishing. It was an awesome pairing.

Steve Sage

Many things come to mind when I reminisce about the early 1960s, including the supporters' club badge with attachable date bar for each season that you attended. People would walk around the ground proudly displaying their long chain of enamelled metal bars from the badge in their lapels.

There was a generosity of spirit about Layer Road in those days – one example which comes to mind was the last home game of the 1959–60 season. Veteran defender George Fisher had not been retained by the club and his U's career was effectively over. However, he was restored to the first team for this final game against Accrington Stanley, who were due to be relegated.

The U's ended up winning 5–1 with the Accrington goalkeeper shaking his fist as prolific goalscorer Martyn King duly grabbed a brace. And then George Fisher was cheered off the pitch one final time, thus denying the myth that there is no room for sentiment in football.

The matchday programme in those days was a pretty Spartan affair; normally six pages with at least half dedicated to local businesses advertising their respective wares and services.

Norman Spencer

Martyn King watches the goalkeeper collect as the U's face Darlington.

Goalmouth action at the Clock End in a late 1960s fixture.

It was a very sad day when we finally left Layer Road as it had been a major part of my life since the early 1960s. According to my late father it all started with the Arsenal FA Cup tie in 1958–59, although I cannot honestly say I remember attending that game.

I have recollections of the League Cup game against Newcastle in 1960–61 and also the Fulham game in the same competition in 1963–64. I was on the Clock End and remember seeing lots of scarves being waved every time we scored on the Popular Side, and I thought how great it was and wished I had a scarf to wave as well.

Reserve team games at Layer Road were a totally different experience then but attendances were still fairly good and frequently topped the 1,000 mark. The match programme consisted of a single sheet devoid of any comment or statistic, except for detailing who was playing and who was officiating. Needless to say, the atmosphere at these games was somewhat different to that of the first team but the less defensive style of play led to many fine exhibitions of attacking football.

Norman Spencer

Players in the 1950s and 1960s seemed to have great loyalty and affection for the club and without going through a great list, some deserve further mention here.

Percy Ames: Back in those far-off days all of the players were my heroes but none more so than goalkeeper Percy. He joined from Spurs in 1955 and was quite simply immaculate, and he always had a quick quip for the crowd. His U's career lasted 10 years and he rarely missed a game up until his eventual demise in 1963 when he was replaced by George Ramage from arch-rivals Norwich City. Percy was always immaculate off the pitch, too, and I received a big shock one day when he and some other players walked in to my favourite clothes shop in town, Marks the Tailor in St Johns Street. As usual when you are young, I was completely tongue tied and said nothing. At least Percy smiled at me! Always very well turned out, he would exchange the odd comment with the spectators behind the goal.

Martyn King and Peter Wright along with Derek Parker appeal for a penalty at the Layer Road End.

John Fowler, left full-back: John was part of the large Scottish contingent to play for the U's and was consistency personified. The master of the sliding tackle, he did his job for the team in an unspectacular manner but never let the side down and had a career with the club of over 10 years.

Martyn King, centre-forward: Martyn was quite simply a goalscorer; that was the reason for his presence in the side. He was a skilful but sometimes moody player who would drift in and out of games. Just when you thought a game was entering into a quiet period or we were about to lose, he would burst into action. Although only a slightly built man, he was fearless of bigger, heavier opponents and would often outwit them with a sudden turn of pace or a quick challenge. Quite simply he was invaluable and when Martyn did not score, which was not often, then more often than not the U's would lose.

Bobby Hunt, inside-forward: here was a local boy done good. Bobby made the first team while still in his teens and is an example of what can be achieved if you put your mind to it. A prolific goalscorer with a cannonball shot, he went on to play at a higher level with Ipswich Town and Northampton Town, but I always personally felt he could have achieved even more. It was not to be, however, but Bobby Hunt is the type of home-grown player the U's with their limited financial resources need, right to the present day.

Norman Spencer

I well remember the 9–1 win over Bradford. Bobby Hunt hit a fierce drive which hit the bar, hit the 'keeper's head and rebounded into the back of the net, to much amusement on the terraces.

Bobby lived in Old Heath, and when we used to go to Middlewick Ranges we all used to go in goal while Bobby practised his shooting.

Martin Broom

Two U's players descend on the ball in front of a packed Layer Road.

Winter time reserve team action as a sparse crowd looks on.

There was a unique atmosphere in the ground way back in the late 1950s and the early 1960s. Any visiting team today will have done their homework on the close proximity of spectators relative to the playing surface. I recall many instances when a spot of good natured banter occurred between the goalkeeper and spectators. This was even more prevalent at reserve-team games where spectator noise levels were lower. In the 1960–61 season, Fulham reserves came to play the U's in a Football Combination fixture.

The chairman of Fulham was then a certain well known comedian called Tommy Trinder so the scene was set for some banter. When Fulham took to the field, I could not believe how scruffy their kit was, and their 'keeper Ken Hewkins had some boots on which had clearly seen better days. 'Are you one of Trinder's clowns?' one wag shouted out, followed by other less complimentary remarks. To my surprise, he turned around and said something to the effect that yes he was, and there were 10 other clowns that had come up from London with him.

Norman Spencer

On matchdays, I would walk from town towards the ground – the same way that many young supporters did up to the modern day. One particular day it was raining, so I took the bus and duly alighted to the top deck. A conversation, albeit one sided, was ensuing at the front and I duly listened in.

'It's not your fault Tommy, 'cos you're putting the crosses in. It's those that call themselves goalscorers who are at fault. It's not your fault Tom'.

Goalmouth action at the Clock End, with Layer Road housing in the background.

And so it went on and on and on, this person who kept trying to get the attention of the young man in the light coloured raincoat, who was desperately trying to look out of a rain sodden window and hoping that his fellow passenger would contract some kind of laryngitis – or worse!

Finally we arrived at the ground and it was then that I realised who the young man on the receiving end of all this was. The look of relief on his face was there for all to see. It was Tommy Williams, the U's' close dribbling, cross providing star right-winger. No 4x4 with tinted windows for him. Instead, he had the torture of a face-to-face journey with the most boring man in North Essex!

Norman Spencer

Pre-match entertainment at Layer Road consisted of a man who only had one arm (or so it seemed) and a dog. This was the legendary Whiskey and Taffy Richards, and after their performances (Whiskey had great technique with the ball but no positional sense!), the teams would take to the field to the strains of that well-known tune, the *Post Horn Gallop*.

The club was like a member of the family; even the newspaper sellers who would walk around the touchline with the football special edition newspapers wore their supporters' club badges with pride. One newspaper seller in particular used to strut around with a supporters' badge chain so long that I swear to this day it was almost touching his knees.

Norman Spencer

Benny Fenton was a much loved and respected man, but unlike today's managerial figures he kept a low profile. The only time I ever got to see him in the flesh was in an end-of-season friendly match, Benny Fenton's XI against a Showbiz XI.

Benny played in part of that game and it raised a lot of money for charity. Three players in the showbiz team that night who come to mind are pop singer Jess Conrad in goal (the girls were screaming) and the two wing-forwards, comedians Ronnie Corbett (5ft 1in) and Bernard Bresslaw (6ft 4in).

I have to say that the result of the match was 'fixed', something around 8–8, and when the showbiz team were awarded a penalty at the Clock End, Bernard Bresslaw took it and blazed the ball high over the bar and into the tall trees which bordered the terraces.

Norman Spencer

Peter Wright is denied as a cross is turned away from danger.

Peter Wright challenges the goalkeeper in an early 1960s match.

I am probably the one and only U's fanatic in Brisbane and have supported the club for 46 years. One of the most vivid memories I have is from way back in 1965–66 in the days when Reg Stratton was the centre-forward (a real centre-forward!).

I recall once when I was with my father and grandfather in our regular seats about five rows up from the dugouts. I cannot quite remember the incident that prompted me to launch myself out of my seat and scream that ultimate insult to the referee in those days – 'Ref you need glasses'. When I sat down I landed heavily on my grandfather's feet.

When we got home I was put over his knee and was given the slipper! The reason? Jumping on his feet? No! It was for being rude to the referee in front of the crowd!

There is something unique about this club and its fighting spirit. In years to come in our new stadium we will look back on these days as a time in our history when we built the foundations of a great future.

Tim Bloom of Brisbane, Australia

United always seemed to rise to the occasion whenever a First Division team was the opposition. I watched them beat Fulham 5–3 and they had Johnny Haynes playing for them.

Malcolm Murray of Niagara Falls

The goalkeeper is under pressure as a cross comes into the box.

In the 1960s I moved with my footballing mates from the Layer Road End to the area later known as the Barside. It was mainly evening games on Fridays and Mondays that we attended in those days because I played on Saturdays. I remember we had three or four cars between us and any number of us would go to see the U's on Mondays or Fridays, Ipswich on Tuesdays and usually take in a London game – Spurs, Arsenal or West Ham – on Wednesdays.

We really only supported the U's, but we were all football mad and if we were not playing would travel to any game – girls fortunately had not come on the scene by then.

Three players who for us stood out above any at that time were Duncan Forbes, a big hearted player who always gave his all; Derek Trevis, another captain and inspirational player; and someone I am sure many have forgotten but who on his day could be a wonderful footballer, Billy Stark.

The late 1960s saw me returning the favour of transportation to Layer Road to my grandfather. I would pick him up in Halstead and he would stand at the Layer Road End while I had once again moved with mates to what became Terrace Three.

Terry Lawrence

Peter Wright looks on as Eddie Smith attempts to head home.

Reserve team action at Layer Road.

A bandaged Peter Wright celebrates after scoring at the Open End.

In 1964 I started college and was persuaded to join the college hockey team (mainly by the promise of beer after the game). This started a period of playing hockey every Saturday (September to April) for the next 40 years. Unfortunately, my regular attendance at Colchester United matches ended.

David Hicks

I began attending matches at Layer Road as a small boy in short trousers during the exciting 1965–66 promotion season. Apart from the electric atmosphere in the ground, my abiding memory of those days was the strong smell of pipe-smoke. Very few fans appeared to be using pipes, yet the smell was certainly something that lingered heavily in the air at every game.

Rob Hadgraft.

Some classic wing play from Peter Wright.

The sights, sounds and smells of a packed Layer Road have a lot to answer for. When my family moved to Essex in 1965 I was nine years old and apparently had no interest in football whatsoever. Then over the winter of 1965–66 something strange happened. Being taken to an FA Cup tie between the U's and QPR – a see-saw six-goal thriller – turned me instantly into a football obsessive.

I can only put it down to the all-out assault on the senses of 90 minutes of tension, noise, colour and pungent pipe smoke, while gaining only tantalising glimpses of the hectic action on the pitch. Being squashed on packed terraces with a boisterous crowd whose mood veered alarmingly between ecstasy and depression might have also contributed. Subsequent visits to games against Chester, Barrow and Aldershot must have been somewhat less exciting, but they served only to reinforce my fascination. This was better than watching *Crackerjack* on black-and-white TV! It was better than the Dave Clark Five or The Searchers on *Top of the Pops*. This was real-life drama!

My first four U's games were all drawn (3–3, 2–2, 1–1 and 0–0, believe it or not!) so perhaps it was a desperate yearning for that elusive taste of victory that kept me going. My first defeat came when big bad Peterborough came to town in the FA Cup in January 1967 – and the 0–3 scoreline was a horrendous shock to the system. The U's' inability to cope with a snow covered pitch seemed like huge injustices to a young innocent's eyes!

Collecting autographs after a match became part of the match-day ritual for a couple of years. How awe-struck we were as we hung around wide-eyed outside the Layer Road dressing rooms. Only much later would we understand that these were the humblest and most austere facilities in the entire Football League. At the time we thought we were on hallowed ground!

The emerging players were studied closely for their every reaction and nuance. A few were arrogant and stand-offish but most loved the attention and were friendly. When my seven-year-old brother blurted out loudly to Terry Dyson 'My family calls you Old Man Dyson' we were frozen with horror, but luckily the veteran winger did not take offence, and Brian Gibbs and the other players naturally thought it was hilarious.

Those first few impressionable years as a football fan are never forgotten. More than 40 years later I can instantly quote facts and figures about obscure U's players like Tom McKechnie, Ernie Adams, John Mansfield and Brian Westlake and others; although I might well struggle with some of the names from more recent eras. Sadly I get few opportunities to display this rare skill!

Rob Hadgraft

Ted Phillips scoring three with his head on his debut was a memorable game. Phillips used to drink in the Prettygate and I even saw him have a beer before a game on one occasion.

Jack Manning

My first game as a supporter at Layer Road was against Oxford United in 1966–67 when a young Ron Atkinson played for them. The next season I remember trying to force my way into the Layer Road End against WBA for the FA Cup tie when there was absolutely no room.

My best mate at school was Barry Gasson who lived at No. 43 Layer Road (later the commercial deptartment office behind the club shop). Barry's dad was the club groundsman. At that time No. 43 Layer Road was a proper club residence where the groundsman lived, and we could see the pitch out of Barry's bedroom window. We would get into Layer Road during the school holidays and search under the infamous wooden planks that formed the Layer Road End terracing for money that had dropped out of people's pockets.

Another of our tricks was climbing over Barry's back fence which led onto a cinder playing surface behind the Barside Stand and getting into the games for free. No retrospective bill, please!

We used Layer Road as a playground in the holidays and I remember us collecting loads of Coke cans from the Popular Side Stand, stacking them up and then throwing a Frisbee at them. We also used to play table tennis in a room under the Main Stand. I also remember finding boxes of *Football League Reviews*, which were an insert that went into the programmes at that time.

Peter Chisnall

First evidence of the Corner Bar in the background as Martyn King rises to head the ball.

Some of the floodlit games stand out in the memory more than Saturday games, for some reason. Specifically the League Cup win over First Division Fulham that finished 5–3, Johnny Haynes and all, and the game against Newcastle in the same competition that finished 4–1. Both had that special Layer Road atmosphere.

Mike Gadbury

For a football-mad seven-year-old my first real match in a proper stadium was always likely to be the catalyst for a love affair, and it is one that continues to this day.

I was taken to Layer Road by my dad on a Saturday afternoon in 1960, and my earliest memories are of heroes in blue and white watched from the front of what was later the Family Enclosure. All us small kids were ushered down to the wall where we could smell the liniment from the players, always mixed with that smell of cigarettes and damp gabardine macs [raincoats] much favoured by our elders at that time.

Layer Road has provided some abiding memories over the past (almost) 50 years. As a 'keeper, my early idols were always the men in green (and in those days it was always green), from Percy Ames through to George Ramage, Sandy Kenyon, Tony Macedo and Mike Walker.

A few years later, and when it was common practice to bike to the ground, we used to leave our bikes with what seemed like hundreds of others in a garden opposite the ground for a few pence. Still not old enough to join the older lads in the Layer Road End, we had left our fathers to their terrace and occupied what is now the Barside Terrace. At some games you could watch while sitting on the terracing; such was the scarcity of the crowds at some fixtures.

John Grimwade

By 1968 I still attended four or five matches a season, including the Third Round FA Cup tie with West Brom which we were very unlucky to only draw. We lost the replay and West Brom went on to win the FA Cup.

David Hicks

Although I now live in south-west France, I am Colchester born and bred and have been going to Layer Road for the past 47 years (and I am still only 55!)

For the first six months of my life, I actually lived opposite the Layer Road football ground. This was because at the time I was born, in 1953, my parents were lodging temporarily with my grandparents at No. 46 Layer Road. I can clearly remember my grandfather, Walter Shephard, describing how the roof of the Layer Road End stand had virtually ended up in his front garden one night, during the great gale of January 1938. I can also remember him describing what I mistakenly believed was an extremely large hill at the far end of the ground, which (also mistakenly) I thought was called the 'Spy and Cop' – apparently named after an even larger hill captured by the British in the Boer War, the Spion Kop.

Despite my desperation to scale the Spion Kop and survey all the other wonders tantalisingly concealed behind the huge forbidding wooden gates and fences of the football ground, it was with a considerable degree of trepidation that, as an eight-year-old by then living in Prettygate, I headed to my first-ever U's match against Hartlepools in September 1961.

There were at least two reasons for my trepidation; the main one being that the only other match that I had seen in any shape or form was the 1961 Cup Final (on a black-and-white TV). I consequently imagined that all football grounds on match days bore a close resemblance to Wembley and were therefore all heaving with tens of thousands of large men shouting, waving rattles and violently throwing their cloth caps into the air every time a goal was scored. Unfortunately, my misconception had actually been reinforced by having previously glimpsed the front cover of the Colchester United matchday programme of the time, which, presumably due to a degree of artistic licence, featured a superb drawing of a U's home match in a stadium of Maracana proportions. Even at that age, I ought to have been able to work out that the football ground would consequently have had to have been designed by the inventor of Doctor Who's Tardis to have been able to fit into the available space.

Incredibly, I can still recall how I imagined my first visit to Layer Road would be, hemmed in on all sides by adults at the very back of a vast grandstand, suffering from mild vertigo. I suppose that I ought also to have been anxious about walking the mile and a half to the ground, accompanied only by a couple of equally naïve classmates. But, what the hell, this was in an era when eight-year-olds could safely roam the streets without having to be chaperoned by an adult.

I suspect that you will have already guessed that as I nervously mounted the steps at the back of the Popular Side (later the Barside) and finally caught sight of the Theatre of Dreams, my trepidation swiftly melted away to be replaced by a mild sense of disappointment. Nevertheless, Colchester won 6–1 and I was hooked.

Two weeks later my friends and I were back for the visit of Workington and we witnessed another 6–1 drubbing of the pitifully inadequate opposition. My third match was against Bradford City, just after Christmas of the same season. (Incidentally, am I alone in having fond memories of the aroma of cigar smoke that filled the air beneath the covered stands at those festive season matches?) This time, my excitement was enhanced even further by the fact that my Uncle Ray took me and we sat right at the back of the Main Stand. Even from those lofty heights I experienced precious little vertigo; although I do remember being close to tears as City equalised an early Bobby Hill goal. But normal service was swiftly resumed as the U's punished the opposition for their barefaced effrontery by scoring just the eight more in reply. The final score was an incredible 9–1.

So, my first three matches at Layer Road had resulted in 21 U's goals at a fairly respectable rate of a goal every 12 minutes 51 seconds. I knew then that I would be a lifelong supporter of what I believed was the greatest club in the world. It matters little that that initial scoring rate has slackened slightly since then. Indeed, during the entire Roger Brown reign we did not even manage 20 League goals at Layer Road and, sadly, that reign lasted almost a year!

Chris Wright, Le Rouquet Nord, 24140 Maurens, France

U's fans look on expectantly as a chance goes close.

An early season goal for Peter Wright gives the U's the lead.

In September 1962 I saw my first game under the fairly-recently installed towering green floodlights. We were extremely unlucky to lose 1–0 to Port Vale but I loved the atmosphere, which was electric. Even in those days, my parents drew the line at allowing me to roam the night streets with only a couple of equally puny small boys as bodyguards, and so I used to go to midweek games with our neighbour, Mr Paton. He stood on what is now Terrace Three, where we usually met up with his mate, Mr Skeet.

At one night game in about 1964, I clearly remember Mr Paton telling Mr Skeet that he had heard that a spanking new U's stadium was going to be built next to the by-pass [now Cowdray Avenue]. And how well-founded those rumours have proved. It was the wrong site, admittedly, and not quite the right century (or millenium), but his theory was definitely well-founded!

Bizarrely, midweek games at Layer Road were always on a Monday evening in those days – barely 48 hours after the end of Saturday's match (which might well have been in Torquay or Carlisle).

I can remember the first rickety television gantry at the ground, positioned unconventionally just to the left of the goal on the Spion Kop. One of the first televised matches I remember attending was a memorable 2–1 win in 1963 over eventual Division Three champions Coventry. John Camkin and Gerald Sinstadt were the main commentators in those early days. Like any other mature and intelligent child, I always liked to take my life in my hands and get right under the gantry to shout out witticisms. This was presumably so that the following afternoon (on Anglia TV) I could tell my parents enthusiastically 'that's me shouting out "Gerald is a twit".' It is probably a good thing that I was never heard.

One of my all-time favourite matches at Layer Road was the 5–3 League Cup thrashing of the then established top-flight team Fulham in September 1963. From what I remember, they included four legendary England international players in their line up – Bobby Robson, George Cohen, Alan Mullery and Johnny Haynes. All four of them were left overwhelmed and bewildered by the U's who actually led 5–1 at one point. Strangely, it is a match and a performance which never seems to get much of a mention.

A chance slips past the post in an early 1960s fixture.

Martyn King heads home in style as he beats a defender to the ball.

I also recall a superb game from that era in which we beat now-defunct Bradford Park Avenue 6–3 under the lights. I seem to remember that they included young future England star Kevin Hector in their side.

Chris Wright, Le Rouquet Nord, 24140 Maurens, France

I went to all the England World Cup matches in 1966 including the Final, and the next match was a pre-season trial match at Layer Road just a few weeks later. It was the first time that Layer Road stood out as perhaps not the best stadium! It certainly was not suitable for the size of the game.

I remember the queues of buses outside the ground. I often had to leave early to get on the bus and it was common for the ground to start emptying 10 minutes before the end. If you got on and ran upstairs to a certain seat, you could still see the action over the roof of the stand!

St John Ambulance men used to do collections where fans in the crowd would throw coins onto the blankets they carried around, but there were always boys scrambling behind trying to pick up the stray pieces.

Martin Broom

I must have been about 10 when I started to make regular trips to Layer Road. I used to wait expectantly by the window in the front room of our house in Margaret Road on a Saturday lunchtime for my dad to arrive home from work in his white Austin Cambridge.

The hands of the town hall clock were visible in the distance as they gradually moved around to 20 past one. If it got to 20 past, I began to worry that my dad may have had an accident, but I learned that any slight delay was due to him stopping off at the Railway Tavern or the Norfolk for a quick pint en route. The latest he ever arrived home was half past one and so he never let me down.

The goalkeeper is left on his backside as this chance finds the back of the net.

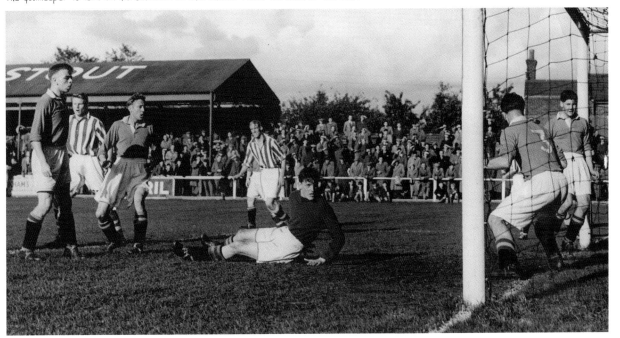

The goalkeeper collects at the Layer Road End as the U's take on Brighton in 1967.

Despite being car owners, which were fairly rare at the time, we used to make our way to a bus stop in North Station Road near the Albert roundabout and wait for green Eastern National 'Football Special' double deckers to arrive from Mile End.

Once aboard we were engulfed in the jovial conversation and the blue haze from Woodbines, rollies and pipes. There was a crackle in the air as the working men exchanged banter, uttering the names of Martyn King, Bobby Hunt and Peter Wright.

We would stop off by the market in Middlesbrough and at the top of North Hill, and by this time the bus would be packed.

I can still hear the sounds of the crowds, the programme sellers and the rattle through the turnstyles when we arrived at Layer Road. It was a special place and a special time in my life…in all of our lives in fact.

The 1960s seemed so black and white, and grey…and yet this only seemed to make the sight of our players in their blue-and-white stripes shirts all the more vivid and dramatic as they ran out on the pitch to the *Post Horn Gallop*.

Once you got a taste of it you were hooked for life.

Ray Hollingsworth

Come to think of it, if I had to choose one thing that made Layer Road football ground special it would be its capacity to transform international superstars (from Johnny Haynes to Norman Hunter via Jeff Astle and many others) into Sunday League players.

Ironically, it would actually have been good just once to have seen some big-time Charlie showing his skills and justifying his inflated wages, but I honestly cannot think of any occasion on which it ever happened; although Rodney Marsh looked quite good in a 3–1 defeat against high-flying QPR in about 1967. In fact, at one point during the game Rodney ended up next to a group of fans by the Layer Road End wall.

Quick as a flash, one of my friends invented a brilliant chant which went 'Rodney Marsh is useless, Rodney Marsh is…' etc. This was quickly taken up by all of us. However, that was not a wise idea when you were standing next to a huge, muddy puddle on the pitchside cinder track. Rodney simply smiled and with a superbly-executed sidefoot shot managed to shower all of us, plus about 15 innocents, in a gallon or two of filthy reddy-brown water. He then ran off laughing. Why he did not get the same punishment from the FA as Eric 'kung-fu' Cantona I will never know!

Since the 1960s I have seen many, many games at Layer Road and elsewhere in the UK and Europe. However, those first few years of supporting the U's will, for me, always epitomise the way that football should be – local working-class people supporting their local team, which in turn includes a nucleus of local (and loyal) players. Fans preferably standing in maximum discomfort on tightly-packed terraces in all weathers. In other words, the tribe that I proudly belong to against another tribe, as simple as that.

Chris Wright, Le Rouquet Nord, 24140 Maurens, France

Particular features of the ground that have left indelible memories include:

The way in which, whenever the ball landed on the Barside roof, everyone beneath it used to spend the next five minutes extracting rust and old birds nests from their hair.

The amazing former terracing at the Clock End which was entirely unsuitable for anyone with legs of equal length. I am sure I saw it described somewhere as being like the steps of an ancient Inca temple following an earthquake.

The 'characterful' toilets that once graced the far left-hand corner of the ground. Not suitable for fans in sandals. It should have had a preservation order on it, I thought.

Chris Wright, Le Rouquet Nord, 24140 Maurens, France

To many people Good Friday is significant for religious reasons. Until the age of 13 my memory is of a day when the TV screen was blank with dull music playing. Then, after two or three years of following United's results I was to pay my first visit to Layer Road – on a Good Friday.

In 1966, Easter was in mid-April and the Friday was a glorious Spring day. My father gave my school friend Philip Reason and me a lift to the ground from Dedham where we lived. The opponents were Luton Town, and both clubs were high in the old Division Four and looking for promotion. There was a good crowd and my friend and I managed to get a spot by the wall to the left of the Layer Road goal, a position I stood in for a few seasons before 'graduating' to the right-hand side which was the Barside equivalent of its time.

Supporters all around us had wooden rattles and a few had toilet rolls, which got thrown onto the pitch when the U's scored. Scarves and bobble-hats at that time were hand knitted by aunties rather than bought in chain stores. My hand-knitted woollen scarf, which was made for me by my Aunty Flo, eventually shrank in a hot wash and my blue-and-white striped bobble hat had to go when moths had eaten into it.

My memory of the match is of the U's being two goals down at half-time with Luton having a third disallowed just on 45 minutes as the whistle had already been blown for the interval. However, my programme for the match records the half-time score as 1–0 to Luton. I am sure the score was 2–0 to Luton at some point though, before Reg Stratton scored a brace to level the final score at 2–2.

We had arranged to be picked up in Drury Road, and I recall being asked as I passed the Drury pub car park whether I wanted to sell my programme. By this time I had decided that I was a collector of Colchester United programmes so I hung on to it.

Until 1969 and a switch to glossy paper, a new Colchester United home programme came with the smell of fresh printer's ink, and although this gradually wore off after a few weeks it is another fond memory. In the following years I amassed a large collection of Colchester United programmes, including a few early ones from the late 1930s which I still have.

I also still have the programme which I purchased at my first Layer Road game on that day. The attendance was 10,200. Both teams gained promotion to Division Three at the end of the season.

Chris Fincham

As an inhabitant of Holyhead on the Isle of Anglesey in North Wales for all of my 63 years, it would probably seem very strange if I told you that I had any connection whatsoever with the much lamented Layer Road. However, that is very much the case.

I would not even be here now had it not been for my mother, Dorothy Josephine Banfield, who lived in Layer Road (nearly opposite the ground entrance) having decided to travel to Holyhead in the 1930s, a journey of over 300 miles from Colchester. She did so on the whimsical recommendation of a friend and remained there for the rest of her life until time caught up with her when she was over 101 years old.

At roughly the same time as my mother moved to Holyhead, my father arrived from Rhosllanerchrugog near Wrexham to work in the same shop as Dorothy. They clicked and eventually I came into the world to become a lifelong Wrexham fan, but one with a deep affection for Mum's team 'across the road' in Colchester.

Neil Langman tucks home a chance as Peter Wright looks on.

I visited the ground on several occasions, remembering with affection the likes of Langman, Fisher, Wright, Ames, Plant and Martyn King (who of course was latterly of Wrexham) of the 1950s; Bobby Hunt and Stratton of the 1960s; Crawford and Svarc in the 1970s and those of the present day, not forgetting Whiskey the dog and the warm Colchester fans.

It is one of the ironies of football (and life) that when Dorothy moved to Holyhead in the 1930s the U's were a non-League team and Wrexham had established themselves in the Third Division North, whereas at roughly the same time as her passing, Colchester were leaving for pastures new and Wrexham fans were about to sample the non-League.

Mother and Layer Road are sadly no longer with us; however, their spirits live on and will always be there. I will leave you with a Welsh saying – *Hwyl a Haul*, which roughly translated means 'sunshine and happiness at the new stadium'!

Gareth Davies

I signed associated schoolboy forms for the U's and came straight from Wilson Marriage as they had a connection with the club then. They signed you on to make sure you followed through the ranks with your local club, really.

When Neil Franklin arrived he called me in and asked me to sign professional forms, but I was halfway through an apprenticeship and my dad wanted me to complete that first. So I signed part-time professional forms and I spent the rest of my time until I was 21 completing this until I went off to play for Braintree.

I had some good times at Layer Road and remember a game against Fulham reserves, my first for the club. I marked Reg Stratton who also later signed for the club. A short while after the Fulham game I came in for part-time training, which was on a Tuesday and Thursday, and there was a note on the noticeboard saying that we had signed Reg Stratton. I looked at the notice and said quietly to myself 'Well, I marked him and he didn't give me much bother, why did we sign him?' And, of course, he was standing right behind me!

I was captain of the youth team at one point and captain of Essex at the same time. The youth team went virtually unbeaten during that time and we played Ipswich in the FA Youth Cup at Portman Road. The crowd that turned up was 5,000 strong and people were queueing up and down the road to get in. However, from that team only John Mansfield really made it into the first team.

In those days, transfers were paid in cash lump sums rather than the way it is done these days with deals spread over a number of years. One year something went wrong with one of the signings Benny was making, and the part-timers were doing circuit training that day when he suddenly came and kicked over the table, threw a chair across the room and smashed the mirror on the wall. He had notes in his hand that he was going to pay for the player with, and he just threw them up in the air! They were drifting down everywhere and then Bill Light came in and dragged Benny away, and then he came back to give us part-time players a fiver to keep it quiet.

At one stage I was lined up to play for the first team as there was a bit of an injury crisis, and Neil Franklin phoned me up at work and said he wanted me there for training on Tuesday morning. In those days the right-winger was Mike Grice, who was a quiet, introverted character. He would often train on his own and liked to keep himself to himself. I attended training as ordered, and I was playing left-back in the practice game ahead of the weekend when Mike pushed the ball around me and I kicked him up in the air. He got me by the throat and told me not to do it again!

It was at that stage of my time at Layer Road that John Fowler and I once got fined for sneaking around the back of the pitch at Queens Park Rangers to go and have a beefburger before the game. Mr Franklin came around the corner and caught us and fined us both a week's pay.

I played a few reserve games and even one first-team game when Reg Stratton was taken off after 20 minutes. I came on and played centre-half, but the team we played did not bother coming over the halfway line! Sandy Kennon was in goal and he left his calling for crosses and so on very late, and so all you could do was duck and hope he did not take your head off. You do not get the impression from the stands how quick it is out there. Once I received the ball and the next thing I knew I was up in the air, and when I came down my front teeth were pushed through my bottom lip!

Bobby Hill was one of those real, rough Glaswegian Scots who loved effing and blinding. He would gamble at anything and he would always gamble on the coaches. Franklin would try to stop it because so many players were losing their money. They used to start it up as they got on the coach and by the time they got to the away match they would have lost all of their money. Even though he tried to stop them, they continued to gamble – at one point they even gambled on what record was coming on the radio next!

Hill used to live in the house next to the ground, one of the houses owned by the club. One day he was in the reserves' line up and we were playing at home. We had to be in the ground for 2pm and there was no sign of him, but at 2.45pm he came panting through the door and claimed he could not get his car started. This was odd since he lived next door! He turned out in the end to be a Jehovah's Witness going door to door, the same as Bobby Svarc. Svarc was one of those players who was pigeon chested and knock kneed but brilliant inside the box.

My dad worked for the army fire service and at the ground they used to have a concrete post and metal bar instead of a wall. He used to have to be on duty and so they used to come to the match and leave early to get to work. He and his mate managed to get under the bar and walk alongside the cinder track to get out of the ground. Unfortunately, one day my dad was so busy watching the game he ran into the linesman, who hit him in the mouth with his flag and knocked his front teeth out.

I can remember when Neil Franklin arrived as manager, he phoned everyone up at home and told them he wanted them there for a practice match. But it was so foggy you could hardly see in front of you. He insisted that we went out there and played but we could not see the ball. Not only that, we realised that if we could not see each other then he could not have seen us playing either! What he got out of that training session I will never know.

David Laitt

By the time we played West Brom in the FA Cup in 1967–68 I had my own knitted scarf and hat and was very proud of them as they lasted a good few years. I stood on the Popular Side as well, and all my dreams were being fulfilled. In 1967–68 my away travels started; I went to a Cup round against Chelmsford at New Writtle Street with over 16,000 fans in the ground!

Keith Blaxall

We were all over West Bromwich Albion in 1968, but in the end we had to settle for a 1–1 draw.

Malcolm Murray of Niagara Falls

The first-ever game I attended was on 11 May 1968. We lost 5–1 in the old Division Three against Peterborough. It was the year we got relegated; although Peterborough got relegated too because of financial irregularities.

I was nine years old and just getting into football at that time and I had always felt that you should support your home-town team, and it has worked out that way for me. My dad had been in the air force and we had been to Colchester before but got posted away.

As a kid I can remember the songs coming from the Layer Road End, particularly *Knees Up, Mother Brown*, with the fans bouncing up and down. It makes you wonder how the terraces lasted all those years with so many skinheads bouncing up and down!

Ian Craig

I remember one referee, 'Smiler' Dawes, who came from Norwich and it seemed that he was the ref at every floodlit game. He seemed to be smiling at everything and people picked up on that one. He was quite a popular chap and he knew you by name.

Martin Broom

The first match at Layer Road at which I remember any hooliganism was the FA Cup tie against West Brom in early 1968, when, according to a newspaper cutting that I have, the WBA manager Alan Ashman had to appeal to his fans to calm down.

Chris Wright, Le Rouget Nord, Maurens, France

Fans queue for tickets ahead of the West Bromwich Albion FA Cup tie.

I remember one great game in the 1967–68 season; a 1–1 draw versus West Brom in the FA Cup Third Round. We nearly knocked out the eventual Cup winners, but we were denied by a controversial goal that was disallowed for handball.

Keith Blaxall

I moved to the Colchester area from Devon. Most of my mates were Torquay United fans – I used to come up for school holidays and in the summer for three or four weeks. We used to go to Layer Road and tell Geoff Gasson, the groundsman, 'my dad has lost his lighter can I go and find it?' He would say 'go in and be quick', so we used to go in and get underneath the Layer Road End through all the rubbish under the stands, picking up the two bob bits and other coins, and by the time we got to the other corner flag we had enough money to go into the next game!

Charlie Brown

The best goals I have seen scored? Easy. They were scored by a guy called Tommy Millar, who played in the beginning of a season in the early 1960s. He kept on scoring long-range goals, and they kept reporting that he had scored 'yet again from further out'. He did it three or four games running and it became the norm that people would shout 'shoot' wherever he was on the pitch. He scored several stunning goals in only a short period of time.

Martin Broom

Excitement for the U's fans as West Bromwich Albion come to town in 1968.

I remember the wonderful evening atmosphere when we got floodlights and we began to see Friday night games. There were a couple of seasons when we played a lot of Friday night games, maybe as many as eight. The atmosphere from start to finish was always electric. No wonder teams did not like coming to Layer Road.

Judith Musgrove

For the Norwich game in 1959–60 I had to climb up the back of the stand (known these days as Terrace Four) and hang on to the panels to watch the game. Luckily, I was able to just about see Martyn King's opening minute goal, the first of a famous hat-trick.

Despite moving to Chelmsford and back to North London over the next decade, I still could not miss my U's and so I remained a regular visitor to Layer Road.

Dave Amoss

Taffy and his dog Whiskey were very popular entertainment for the big crowds. Whiskey would chase the ball, heading it all the way and would often score a goal.

Whiskey became even more popular before one game against Millwall. He popped over the wall in his normal manner, only to find that Millwall's lion mascot was already on his patch. Undaunted by this relatively huge adversary, Whiskey's territorial instincts kicked in and he attacked the stuffed lion with total fearlessness. The home crowd loved it.

Mike Mason

Winger Peter Wright is put under pressure as he tries to break into the box.

Chapter 7

DICK GRAHAM ON HIS TIME WITH THE U'S

As a result of my love of football, and a dogged determination to play football, my formal schooling came to an abrupt end at the age of 12. I had won a scholarship to Kettering Grammar School but I refused to go because on my very first day there I found that the school only encouraged rugby and that football was somewhat taboo. I was so heartbroken that instead of going to school I used to get off the train between Corby (my home) and Kettering and spend the day in the countryside. When my parents eventually discovered what was happening they allowed me to give up my Grammar School place and return to my local school in Corby.

Back at Corby I was allowed to concentrate on football and jobs like distributing the little bottles of milk around the classrooms. I did hardly any educational classroom work at all for the final two years, but I was goalkeeper for the successful school team and for Northants County Schoolboys.

~

Many years later, after a spinal injury had finished my playing career with Crystal Palace, I developed an awareness of the media when I began writing a column in the *Croydon Advertiser* with Gerry Williams. I learned a lot from that experience and was very grateful to be given the opportunity despite the fact that I had left school so young. I soon found that I had a gift for spotting a story that I thought would be of interest, sometimes, but not always, relating to football.

~

When I arrived at Layer Road even the local Press boys were suspicious of the club. I had to change that. The club was in need of good publicity and needed to develop a better relationship with the media. I made sure that I was always available to speak to the media, whatever the time of day. Over a period of time, a lot of people in Fleet Street became good friends. It was more than just a normal relationship with the media as reporters and writers could ring me at any time of the day or any time of the night. If they were struggling for a story I would probably try to dig up something for them or try and push something their way or give them an idea.

~

A famous former Charlton player named Sam Bartram used to write a Sunday gossip column for *The People*. Sam and I were both goalkeepers who had played against each other and become good friends. I would phone him up with little titbits, and sure enough, more often than not, it would be in the paper on Sunday. I never used to ask for money, it never entered my head, a story was a story and it was good for the club.

In those days as a manager you were your own media man; you did not have anyone working for you. The only person the media wanted to talk to was the manager.

~

Bill Nicholson, the manager of Tottenham Hotspur, rang me up one morning and said 'I want to ask you something, Dick.'

I thought, 'Oh good, he's going to buy one of our players!'

Bill said 'How do you attract the publicity you get?' He continued, 'Here I am, manager of one of the top clubs in the country, and when I pick the paper up all I read about is Colchester United.'

I remember on one occasion getting very upset when I learned that someone at Layer Road was trying to keep the media away from me by telling them I was not available. The information came from a good friend in Fleet Street who rang me up and said 'you're being a bit high and mighty aren't you?' He told me that he had been ringing me at the ground only to be told I was not available. I was so angry about it because something like that can break the confidence and the relationship between the club and the media.

~

When you talk about a ground like Layer Road football ground, you have got to talk about the club. You have got to talk about the players and the characters of individuals.

When I arrived in 1968, my first impression was that the club needed a good kick up the backside. It was not anyone's fault, it was just that Colchester was a lovely sleepy old town and had players to go with that sort of mood, unlike players with city teams and teams in the industrial North. It was part of my job to break that mould. Being the football manager of a town's team is a big responsibility.

~

When I first went into the dressing rooms at Layer Road I just went cold. I had created a new way of thinking about changing rooms when I was at West Bromwich, to get away from the idea that 'anything will do for the players'. I believed you have got to give players a clean and bright working environment; at The Hawthorns I had set up television sets and games tables where players could

This was a Colchester versus Ipswich challenge organised by one of the local cinemas, to see which club could get most players into a Volkswagen Beetle. Ipswich beat us by one player. I have to laugh every time I look at that photo. The man I am hoisting is Terry Dyson. I was so lucky to have some good characters and he was a lovely bloke.

play draughts or chess before a match, and I provided fruit and fruit juices for them. The idea was that everything was laid out properly and they could come in wearing their best clothes if they wanted to because the place would be clean.

When I saw the dump that the changing rooms had become at Layer Road the first thing I did was to get some tins of paint. The trainer at the time refused to help with the painting so I had to do it myself.

~

At my first board meeting the first thing on the agenda was one of the directors wanting to know who had given me permission to go and buy some paint. I stood up and said 'Look, if I haven't got the authority to go and buy a few tins of paint and go and paint the changing rooms to make them look brighter, then I'm not the man for you.' With that I walked out on them.

We had only just moved into Welshwood Park at that point and my wife Anne was still unpacking. I asked her to stop unpacking as I had just resigned. About 10 minutes later a car drew up outside. It was the chairman and the director who had raised the issue about the paint. They took me to the director's home, and I was persuaded to stay at the club.

The thing that I could not stand was that the important issues about the football club were at the bottom of the agenda, instead of the top. At board meetings by the time you got to the bottom of the agenda a couple of people would have fallen asleep! I just had to get hold of it and change it, but at the same time I had to get a successful team out onto the field.

I sold my best two players (Duncan Forbes and Derek Trevis) in order to raise enough money to rebuild the team. Brian Gibbs was the only new player to cost a reasonable transfer fee, and he cost £4,500. The rest of the new squad were mainly experienced free transfer players such as Terry Dyson (ex-Spurs), Brian Wood (ex-Crystal Palace and West Bromwich) and Tony Macedo (ex-Fulham).

~

I arrived at Colchester at a time when the public had lost confidence in the club. We had to get that back and make the club a real part of the town. That was just as important as getting the results on the field. I had to encourage my players to take part in what was going on in the town ('encouage' is a nice word to use). All of them were required to be available to attend events other than football.

~

Fans like to see their team trying; they like to see passion in their team. Football is a matter of opinion, and everybody has got their own opinions, but you cannot

In my first season at Layer Road we started very badly and Peter Smith from the Essex County Standard told me that bookmakers were offering odds of 100-1 against us getting promoted. I told Peter I was putting a fiver on us to get promotion. Fortunately I added that if we got promotion the winnings would go to Cancer Research.

Peter wrote an article about it and round about Christmas we were playing a London club and there were one or two Fleet Street people there, and Peter must have told them about the bet and one of them ran it in a national newspaper. The Football Association picked it up and gave me a very difficult time. They were going to suspend me. And at that time you could be suspended sine die.

Peter had to talk to Denis Follows of the FA himself to tell him that I was not seeking to gain financially from the bet, and I ended up with a rap on the knuckles from the FA.

The team I rebuilt during my first season in the end only missed promotion by a few points.

The filming was done for a TV programme presented by Danny Blanchflower about training facilities at various clubs. Geoff Gasson would have been watching us very closely to make sure we did not stray onto the pitch. The players seem to be enjoying it.

fool the public when somebody is not trying. The public will tolerate a person having a bad game if he is giving his best. What they will not tolerate is someone who bottles it and football is so much about character of people.

~

During all my years coaching and managing in the professional game I was never fortunate enough to have my own training and practice ground. At Colchester we used to train at the ground, often under the stand, if we could not beg, steal or borrow better facilities. It was very restrictive and it limited what we were able to do. We always had to improvise and try to keep players interested day after day so that they would not get bored and just go through the motions.

~

It was always my dream, and probably every manager's dream, to create a team of his own making, from players brought up through the club. So, to that end, I set up a coaching school in North London, close to Tottenham and Arsenal, and was getting an influx of lads into the club from that area. Gradually we had youngsters of higher quality starting to come through. But while this was going on the first team had to hold on, and neither football people nor supporters give you time. The pattern was to keep the first team in a safe position, keep the public interested, keep the media attention going and gradually bring the youngsters through.

One of the things I did to save money was to disband the Junior team. We had a team in the London Midweek League which was a good league as it gave me a chance to see my young players in action. I decided that with lads staying on at school until the age of 16, they would have less time to develop once they left. Therefore I decided that if they were going to be good enough to make the grade, they needed to come into our Reserve side in the Midweek League and raise their game to that level. The idea was to bring them on quicker, and I think it worked as a lot of them made the first team by the age of 18 or 19.

For the youngsters the Leeds United game came a year too early. If it had come a season or two later most of them would have been ready. At the time of the Leeds game they were nearly ready but needed another season.

~

Rochdale (away) FA Cup Fourth Round, 23 January 1971.

We were losing 3–1 with only 10 minutes remaining and in grave danger of being knocked out of the Cup. In those days only one substitute was permitted and I rarely used them for tactical reasons, preferring to keep him on the bench in case a player got injured.

As a football manager you go by your instincts and I looked at the Rochdale defence and thought that I needed to put a bit more pace against them. My two pacey players were Mick Mahon and Brian Hall. Off came Brian Gibbs, and I moved Mick Mahon to inside-forward, with Brian Hall moving up to outside-left with John Gilchrist coming on in his place at left-back. Brian Lewis was instructed to come in off the right touchline to give us an additional threat in the penalty box. I had often used him at Crystal Palace at centre-forward as he would often get you a penalty.

We grabbed two goals in the last 10 minutes to take Rochdale back to Layer Road for a replay just two days later.

~

On the Monday morning of the Rochdale replay we were training on the sea front at Holland-on-Sea, doing a bit of ball work, nothing at all strenuous, and a little lad with a transistor radio wandered up to us and said 'You're playing Leeds'. Nobody took much notice of him, until the penny dropped.

The strange thing is that there was a remarkable belief in that team of old professionals. It was as if they were saying, 'We are not going to let Rochdale stand in our way.' Rochdale did not stand a chance and were torn apart and swept aside.

~

In the lead up to the Leeds game we practiced a lot of crosses. With the good crossers I had in the club, and with players like Crawford and Simmons, what else would you do? I knew there was a problem with Leeds' 'keeper Sprake and central-defender Jackie Charlton. Jackie was very domineering as a centre-half and he took care of most of the crosses into the goalmouth, which meant the goalkeeper was not having to come for the ball. I reasoned that if I could get Dave Simmons to worry Charlton it would leave Ray Crawford with more freedom. I knew that if Sprake had a weakness it was that he left a lot of crosses to his centre-half.

~

One of the reasons I put benches around the pitch against Leeds United was that I had discovered on the Thursday before the Saturday match that no provision was being made for the reporters who were coming from London and other parts on the UK for the match.

~

Our match against the top club in the land had been made the match of the FA Cup Fifth Round and had caught the imagination of the whole football world. I explained to our young secretary David Havell that for the good name of the club the Press needed to be looked after.

We sat together in the club office that Thursday night arranging seats for the extra Press, many of whom were leading football writers. We did this mainly by transferring stand seats usually reserved for complimentary ticket holders to the benches on the running track around the pitch. Our Press box only held about 20 people at the most.

Many of our players gave up their own complimentary tickets. Their family members or friends together with my own sons Richard and Mark were either seated on the benches or stood on the terraces.

Virtually all of the Leeds players were internationals and I believed that they might be unprepared and unbalanced by the smallness of the playing area and the closeness of the spectators to the pitch. Probably only groundsman Geoff Gasson and I

I had promised to climb the castle walls if we beat Leeds United to reach the FA Cup quarter-finals. I had no chance! It was just one of the things you say to bring a bit of good publicity to the club

knew that the Layer Road End was not quite as wide as the other end. It meant that crosses at the Layer Road End came in a bit quicker. I was actually seriously worried about someone around the perimeter being struck by a football, but luckily it did not happen. As it worked out we hemmed Leeds in and looked after the Press at the same time. The Press praised the club afterwards for the fine hospitality they had received.

~

Playmaker Johnny Giles was marked tightly by John Gilchrist and Allan Clarke was marked equally tightly by John Kurila. I had said to my two players, 'You stay with them all through the match no matter where they go'. If a good professional knows he is being man-marked he will get away from it by taking his marker all over the field just to see how far the marker will follow him. I just said to my two players, 'Don't leave them, always be there. You're challenging them, you're worrying them'. I never instructed anyone to do anything dirty. They did it to perfection, just as I wanted and it stopped the Leeds machine. Giles was their most creative player and he found that he was doing everything under pressure. I did not know at the time, and I would not have condoned it, but John Gilchrist was having a go at Giles verbally all the time he was with him, constantly trying to agitate him. Giles wrote about it later on.

About a quarter of an hour from time Don Revie pushed Giles up front and dropped Clarke back into midfield. For some reason my instructions to my two players were not followed and if you look at the photos of Johnny Giles' goal, John Gilchrist is nowhere near Giles. In fact Gilchrist and Kurila were marking the same man, and it left Giles on his own and he just poked the ball into the corner of the net.

At that stage of the game, with the noise of the crowd and the situation of the game, I could not get messages to my players. Nobody went down injured, so I could not get Denis Mochan, the trainer, on to the pitch to pass on instructions.

~

Denis Mochan, Mickey Cook and I all showing the same serious expression in the photo showing us in the final seconds on the Leeds game. Mickey Cook was worried because he was substitute and I could have put him on for those last few hectic minutes. I think it is a marvellous photograph which I only saw for the first time quite recently. My watch shows that it was 4:42, in injury time, and it was just a case of holding on. In the latter stages every time we got the ball we would play it back in behind them, making them turn around and start again.

Ray Gamble, a former Colchester mayor and current season ticket holder, and two other distinguished visitors called on me recently. They just came round to talk about football, bringing all their books and photos. We were talking about Graham Smith's fantastic late save against Leeds. They had to agree that if it had not been for Graham's save they would not have been visiting me that day, and the Leeds game would have been largely forgotten.

Graham Smith was such a good goalkeeper on his line. We used to do a lot of reaction work in training. Having been a goalkeeper myself I knew what 'keepers needed in training, having played at a time when little specialised goalkeeper training was available.

~

Even now total strangers in Colchester talk to my wife and I about the Leeds match. This week I noticed that a taxi driver was sitting in the car outside the house talking to my wife. It turned out that he was talking about Leeds match, which he had attended. Later the same day a man came to read the electricity meter. I gave him the keys to the garage and after he had read the meter he came back to return the keys and said 'I was there, you know!' Thirty-eight years on and people still remember it and want to talk about that game as if it were yesterday. If Graham Smith had not made that save…

This was an award contested by the managers of all 92 League clubs and I was the only lower League manager to ever be nominated for Manager of the Year, as voted for by the Football Writers Association.

With Leeds United having been beaten, we were drawn away to Everton. I had to work hard to get any bonus for the players for the game at Everton. My chairman grumbled that there was nothing in the players' contracts and I had to point out that if you sign for a Fourth Division club you do not expect to get to the last eight of the FA Cup! I think we negotiated a bonus of £1.50 for every thousand on the gate. I heard from a good source that Everton may have been on £5,000 a man.

The Watney Cup is rarely mentioned these days, which is a shame as I think it was just as big an achievement as beating Leeds. With two League games left we needed as many goals as possible to qualify for the Watney Cup, with Crewe Alexandra (away) and Stockport County (home) still to be played. Qualification depended on goals scored, so it did not matter how many we conceded. At Crewe I played an all-attacking system and we won 3–0. It left us need of one goal in our final game, and Brian Gibbs scored it.

After we had beaten Luton Town in the first round of the Watney Cup, Eric Morecambe, who was a fanatical Luton fan and director came to our changing room to offer his congratulations. At the time he was possibly the most famous comedian on television.

I had not been wearing glasses for long and was standing in the changing room door. Eric stood alongside me and after he had said

I frequently used to watch our electrician named John Crisp from Mersea going up the floodlights to change the bulbs. I asked if I could go up with him. It was frightening going up there as the whole structure used to sway. The photographer deserved a medal! The pictures were taken in July 1972, and the idea was to picture me looking out across Layer Road into the future. But within two months I had resigned!

'Well done' to the team he suddenly slipped into his famous comedy act, with me playing the role of his partner Ernie Wise. Eric was fiddling with his glasses, then my glasses, and ended up hitting me on both shoulders and clapping me on both cheeks. It was straight from his TV act, and needless to say the players were virtually crying with laughter.

In the Watney Cup we beat three teams from higher Leagues including West Bromwich Albion at The Hawthorns in the Final. We had worked so hard in practice with the experimental system where you could not be offside unless you were in your opponents' penalty box. We really worked at adapting our tactics to the experimental rules, and it paid off. We had also worked hard on taking penalties and the final was decided on penalties which was only the second time that had happened in the UK. The full match was shown on BBC that evening. We scored four goals against one of the top teams in the country on their own ground, and they were trying their hardest and had a good bonus to play for.

~

I am so proud that my time at Colchester United was recognised when the refurbished Vice-Presidents' Lounge At Layer Road was renamed the Dick Graham Lounge. It gave me a similar thrill when the George Hotel named a bar the Dick Graham Sportman's Bar. To be the first manager inducted into the club's Hall of Fame was also very proud moment.

Above all, I am proud to have been the manager of Colchester United and its wonderful supporters, so much so that I have been very happy to continue to live in Colchester ever since.

Dick Graham

Chapter 8 – 1968 to 1972

THE OLD EXCITEMENT IS REDISCOVERED UNDER DICK GRAHAM IN AN ERA DEFINED BY THE LEEDS UNITED GAME

During the 1960s I would work after school and on Saturdays to save money to pay for my trips to Layer Road, often for evening games. I was at school in Brixton and would leave at 4.00pm and get to Layer Road just before the 7.15pm kick-off (as it was then).

Then came the Dick Graham era and a lot of London-based players were signed: Tony Macedo, Danny Light, Brian Wood and Terry Dyson were usually to be found on the 10.13pm back to Liverpool Street. There obviously could not have been too much time for an after match inquest in the dressing room as they never missed that last train back!

On that train one day I met Dave Amoss, another long-standing committed supporter, and we have remained good friends ever since. My uncle stopped going to Layer Road so I moved to behind the Clock End goal to stand with Dave and his friends, and right next to 'Shaky ol' 'keeper' Les Oakes. Walking behind the Main Stand and the smell of liniment must be one of those memories that many supporters have.

Mike Gadbury

My first season watching football at Layer Road ended in relegation! It all started so well. My first game was with my dad in December 1967 against Bristol Rovers and finished 2–0 to the U's, with a young Peter Barlow scoring at least one of our goals.

Soon after, it was the mighty West Bromwich Albion with Jeff Astle in the Third Round of the FA Cup. This was after the U's had knocked local rivals Chelmsford City out in the previous round at New Writtle Street in front of nearly 17,000 fans.

The West Brom game was a cracker – Layer Road was packed with 16,000 inside the ground. We were in the Barside, where the family terrace ended up. I remember being passed down to the front as the game kicked-off.

Reg Stratton put the U's one up early on and Jeff Astle equalised before half-time. The U's were the better side in the second half and Johnny Mansfield scored in the last minute only for it to be harshly ruled out.

West Brom escaped with a replay, beat the U's 4–0 at the Hawthorns and went on to win the Cup! I still have the amber-and-black Colchester rosette which was bought for me that day. In those days in the FA Cup, if there was a colour clash both teams wore their change strip.

After that game, the U's seemed to go downhill and a bad run of results ended in relegation. Dick Graham became manager, and he was a real hard nut. He bought players like Tony Macedo, Brian Gibbs, Danny Light and Owen Simpson.

The U's soon went on a winning run and crowds shot up. From playing in front of 3,000, all of a sudden there were 6,000 fans versus Port Vale, 7,000 versus Grimsby Town and then 10,000 for a Friday night match against Southend which the U's won 4–0. I can still remember the fantastic atmosphere at Layer Road that night.

The U's just failed in their bid for promotion in that 1968–69 season, but that whole period is still my favourite memory of Layer Road.

Simon Allmen

Dick Graham with Gerry Perryman, Colin Moughton and Brian Honeywood.

My first game was against Workington in 1968 and it was an evening match under lights. It was also my first visit to a professional game. I travelled from Tiptree to Colchester by bus, meeting up with my uncle at Shrub End from where we walked to the game. I was so excited and remember seeing the floodlights beaming out as we approached the ground.

Once inside we walked down the back of the Main Stand and the smell of liniment as we passed the changing rooms was a powerful and evocative smell. From there we reached the back of the Spion Kop and climbed the steps to the terracing. I have never forgotten the feeling of excitement as I looked out from the top of the terrace on that first occasion. It was a case of love at first sight.

I remained mesmerised all night, soaking in the atmosphere and enjoying every moment. The U's won 3–0 which made the night perfect, and I can still recall the Workington 'keeper Rogan chatting to us youngsters hanging on the wall behind his goal during the game.

From that day Layer Road has been a special place for me. My dad attended Layer Road from the days of entering through a five-bar gate and always talked of the magic atmosphere. As soon as I was allowed to go myself I knew what he meant, and now my son would say the same. Despite no longer living locally we remain season ticket holders and whatever the future and the new Community Stadium brings, Layer Road will always hold a special place in our hearts.

Revd Peter Ball of the United Reformed Church, Whittlesford

On 4 November 1968 I saw my first game U's game, against Workington. We went as a family group of five, and entering the ground and walking down the back of the Main Stand I was gripped by the most intense excitement I had ever known. The colour, the noise, the passion and the sweet-smelling pipe smoke swirled around the stand.

My clearest memory of the game came from an incident quite near the end. Jimmy Oliver, a crowd pleasing right-winger, shimmied through the Workington defence towards the Layer Road goal, only to be bought crashing down on the edge of the penalty box. He lay motionless on the pitch as the referee went over to speak to the linesman. With the ref deep in discussion, we had one eye on him and one eye on Jimmy Oliver, who had still not moved. Then, like a meercat sniffing the air, his head came up to see what was going on before he resumed the prone position. It was pure theatre. I think a free-kick outside the box was the eventual decision.

Jim French

By 1968–69 I had become a regular and have since racked up some 900 home games.
My favourite memories of Layer Road include:
1.   Changing ends at half-time.
2.   The *Post Horn Gallop*.
3.   The white gate that was opened to let the players out onto the pitch.
4.   The wooden planks at the Layer Road End that used to bounce up and down.
5.   The old gentleman who used to sit on a wooden box behind the Layer Road goal, retrieve the ball and throw it back to the goalkeeper. He only had one arm and whether it was rain or shine he always wore a long overcoat and a flat cap.
6.   People scaling the floodlights for a better view.
7.   The toilets at the Clock End with no roof.
8.   The club shop being where the ticket office was later situated, and the large windows being opened so items could be sold.
9.   Les Oakes booming 'shaky old 'keeper' from the Clock End.

My most memorable incidents are as follows:
1.   The dog attacking Chic Brodie, the Brentford goalkeeper, in 1970–71 at the Clock End. I was behind the goal and thought it was hilarious at the time; sadly it ended his career.
2.   The queue for tickets for the Leeds game in 1971 which stretched back to the Drury Arms.
3.   Waiting at the players' entrance after the games in the late 1960s and early 1970s to collect autographs.
4.   Seeing Kevin Keegan play for Scunthorpe in 1969–70.
5.   The 'Swansea Riot' and later crowd disturbances.

Keith Blaxall

Danny Light challenges the Doncaster
goalkeeper in the late 1960s.

The late 1960s and early 1970s were a truly memorable time; Friday night football before 7,000+ crowds, and now WE were the Layer Road Enders – in our minds the loudest and best fans in the country.

I remember that 4–0 scoreline against our big rivals at that time, Southend, on a magical Friday night in 1968, with the old wooden terracing really bouncing under the stomping feet of council estate kids, our little section being from Monkwick and Shrub End, with other parts of the town represented along Terrace Two.

John Grimwade

I remember one great game from 1968–69: Southend, Division Four, 4–0 win. It was a Friday night under the lights with 10,000 in Layer Road, with many of these fans standing behind the Layer Road goal.

Keith Blaxall

A memorable floodlit game was the 4–0 win against Southend in 1968 when Owen Simpson scored with an absolute screamer from 25 yards that I can still see today in my mind!

Mike Gadbury

I loved standing up and being able to migrate between terraces in the early days. The atmosphere at the ground was always special, particularly on Friday nights. It had a lot to do with the capacity in 1968–69 as you only needed about 6,000 or 7,000 fans to make the ground look full, and it always created a good buzz.

John Tweed

I have the following recollections of Layer Road:
1. Standing at the Layer Road End as a teenager and the crowd bouncing trampoline-like on the old wooden terracing.
2. Regularly having to crawl under the wooden terracing to retrieve my programme and various other belongings dropped through the gaps.
3. Changing ends at half-time if the U's were kicking towards The Cannons in the second half.
4. Scoring twice against Graham Smith at the Layer Road End in a kids' penalty competition.
5. A dog chasing the ball and colliding with Brentford 'keeper Chic Brodie.
7. Seeing Dave Simmons head the ball but never actually seeing it hit the back of the net against Leeds until *Match of the Day* that night.
8. In the days before local radio and the web, attending reserve matches on Saturday afternoons to find out the how the first team were getting on.

The TV gantry at the Open End preparing to record the
Leeds game for ITV's *Match of the Week*.

The TV cameras look on as a chance goes wide in the second half.

9. The curse of *Match of the Week*. Whenever Anglia TV covered a home game, I am convinced we lost.
10. When the ball hit the roofs of the stands a shower of rust falling onto the crowds below to the accompaniment of the shout 'Rust!'
11. When you could hire a cushion to avoid 'numb bum syndrome' in the Main Stand (although this was stopped after cushions were thrown at the ref during one game).
12. The evocative smell of liniment wafting out of the dressing room windows in the corridor behind the Main Stand.
13. The *Post Horn Gallop*.
14. Some great Layer Road goals: Jim Oliver scoring at the Layer Road End from somewhere over near what was then called the Popular Side, and Mick Mahon scoring against Rochdale in the FA Cup.

Nick St George

Chic Brodie was one of the most superstitious goalkeepers ever to visit Layer Road and he was also one of the unluckiest. He was, of course, the Brentford goalkeeper whose League career was effectively ended when he collided with a stray dog during the U's' Fourth Division game against the Bees at Layer Road on 28 November 1970.

The dog chased a back-pass and ended up injuring Brodie so badly that the goalkeeper was out of action for two months, and although Brodie did play for Brentford again he was never quite the same man and was forced to quit League football shortly afterwards.

Brodie was also involved in other strange incidents. During a Brentford versus Millwall game someone lobbed a hand grenade into his goalmouth (fortunately it turned out to be a replica grenade) and in a game against Lincoln the whole goal collapsed around him.

U's fans on the terraces in April 1969.

When he was a taxi driver, Brodie was involved in a collision with a Jaguar and when the driver got out to exchange details it turned out to be Sir Geoff Hurst, England's 1966 World Cup hero.

Why did all these things happen to Brodie? Was it because he was too superstitious?

He once said: 'I've always got to carry a ball out and I always carry my cap and gloves in the same hand. Then, as I go out of the dressing room into the tunnel, I always like to touch a piece of wood. I have to go out second, right after the captain, I'd knock the other players out of the way if they tried to get in front of me. It would upset me a bit if I didn't do these things, so I suppose I am a wee bit superstitious.'

Colchester's weekly newspaper, *The Essex County Standard*, did not make much of the Brodie-dog incident and threw it away in the final paragraph of their match report. *The Standard* announced: '...a thoroughly uncomfortable afternoon for Chic Brodie was complete when the Brentford 'keeper was in collision with a stray dog in the opening half and needed lengthy attention before resuming.' If Chic Brodie had been the Colchester goalkeeper and *The Standard* had also been able to establish that the dog lived in the paper's circulation area, the story might have made a page lead.

After the dog had been removed from the pitch, the U's went on to beat Brentford 4–0, with goals from Ray Crawford (two), Brian Gibbs and Bobby Cram.

Dick Barton

I can recall many Layer Road thrillers from over the years, a high number of rather dull affairs and a whole host of unusual incidents both on and off the field.

I remember Cambridge United manager Bill Leivers once ordered his entire team off the field after the U's scored because he was so furious at their poor defending. He was incandescent with rage and it was noticeable that not every Cambridge player wanted to leave the pitch. The U's players and crowd were totally bewildered, and it was some time before the game was eventually restarted.

On another day big striker Dave Simmons tried a fancy back-heel flick during the pre-match warm-up and promptly collapsed on his back. There is nothing funnier than when showboating goes wrong. We thought it was hilarious but it soon became clear that Simmons was in agony. He had to be stretchered off and his knee injury proved to be quite serious. As he disappeared down the tunnel there was a loudspeaker appeal for squad player Eric Burgess to report to the home dressing room!

One afternoon against Southport a group of us decided to taunt defender Ambrose Clarke about his unusual Christian name. Our light-hearted abuse went on for so long that poor Ambrose got visibly more and more angry. Eventually he snapped, lashed out at a U's player and was booked. If ever there was a case of the fans getting a man booked, that was it.

Around the same period, during the early 1970s, my mates and I got into the habit of helping ourselves to unused till-rolls from local supermarkets. These proved to be superb 'streamers' which could be thrown onto the field when United scored. Because of their weight and size they were far more effective than the traditional toilet roll. These days, of course, we would be thrown out of the ground for such behaviour.

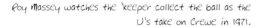

Roy Massey watches the 'keeper collect the ball as the U's take on Crewe in 1971.

Brian Gibbs challenges the goalkeeper in an early 1970s fixture.

As I went to school in Colchester but lived a long way out of town, a midweek evening match at Layer Road often meant that I had three hours to kill after school until kick-off. This sometimes led to a very early arrival at the ground after school finished. So early, in fact, that occasionally the gates were still open and it was possible to simply stroll inside. Our challenge was then to remain hidden from club staff until the crowds started arriving, in order to save paying the admission fee.

Rob Hadgraft

I do not really know why we decided to target Ambrose Clarke of Southport for our schoolboy humour. Maybe it was because he was playing left-back and we were at the very front on the Popular Side, almost within touching distance of him. Maybe it was the phoney hardness of a journeyman footballer with his droopy moustache and world-weary expression. Maybe above all else it was his silly name. Whatever the case, when we were collecting autographs behind the Main Stand after the game I remember making a very hurried exit when our victim emerged from the changing room door.

Jim French

That season featured the Leeds game. How on earth was I going to get a ticket living in South London? Somehow I did, and I arrived at the ground at 2.00pm to find that the ground was already full. I managed to get into the corner at the Clock End and I felt I was dreaming as the game unfolded. Could I really be at Layer Road watching my little team beat the 'Kings of Europe'? The outcome is history but when I got home I excitedly asked my dad if he had listened to it on the radio. He had a shop and was out doing deliveries but he said he just had to pull over and listen to the last 15 minutes' commentary and abandon his last deliveries!

Mike Gadbury

I arrived in Colchester on 9 September 1970, and I was 13 years old after coming back to live in England having been brought up in Austria. I had been following Colchester's results while still living in Vienna and on my first day in Colchester my brother and I went to seek out the place where Colchester United played.

As it happened it was not too far from where we were living. At the first game we attended we were standing at the Layer

The U's prepare for the historic game against Leeds on the beach at Holland-on-Sea. Pictured, left to right, are: Brian Gibbs, Brian Lewis, Dave Simmons, Ray Crawford, Mick Mahon, Dennis Mochan (trainer).

The ball breaks loose as the U's get close to taking the lead against Leeds.

Road End against Notts County the following Saturday, and although the U's lost 3–2 my brother and I had caught the bug, and we have followed Colchester through the good times and bad times since then.

As it turned out it was a good season to be a Colchester supporter, with the never to be forgotten 3–2 defeat of Leeds United and the Watney Cup triumph the following pre-season. I can still recall the atmosphere against Leeds United with the stands filled to capacity, people squeezed in like sardines and everybody going mad at the final whistle.

Ivars Plucis

Cup matches provide particularly fond memories from the past, and none more so than 13 February 1971 when the U's beat Leeds 3–2. My girlfriend attended her one and only match at Layer Road that afternoon.

After the marvellous, unforgettable match, later that day my girlfriend and I got engaged and we enjoyed a romantic meal at the Rose and Crown to celebrate United's victory and our engagement. I cannot remember if I gave her the engagement ring on the evening or whether I left it until Valentine's Day on Sunday 14 February. We are still together after nearly 36 years of marriage.

Colin Burch

I have been supporting the U's for 38 years. I was not able to get to so many games at Layer Road in its final days as I now live and work in the Midlands, but I still get to quite a few away games. I go to see the odd game with colleagues who support Forest, Villa and others, but home is where you are born. I do not follow any plastic Premiership corporation masquerading as a football club. Just as Colchester will always be my home, the U's will always be my one and only club.

The sight of corrugated iron will always remind me of Layer Road. The sounds I will associate with Layer Road are the incredible noise the U's supporters can make when they have a mind to and the fans banging against the corrugated iron at the Layer Road End (when we home fans were allowed to stand there). The most powerful memory of smell I will take away (it is not so evident now as there is a ban on public smoking) is the smell of stale tobacco. I am not a smoker, but the smell of stale tobacco is actually quite pleasant to me because it never fails to make me think of Layer Road!

The first game I went to, believe it or not, was the famous 'dog attacks 'keeper' game: Brentford, 28 November 1970. I was a 10-year-old behind the Brentford goal at the Rainsborowe Road End, standing with my schoolmate Mark Dow near all the Brentford fans. I do not recall any segregation at that game and there certainly was not any trouble. I remember that the dog had been running loose around the terraces, making a nuisance of itself long before it ran onto the pitch.

That game was televised, and it gave me a start to see the black-and-white footage coming up as a 'what happened next' on *A Question of Sport* recently. I did not have time to see if two small blurry figures could be seen above and to the left of Chic Brodie's goal. Mark and I were standing behind slightly to the right of goal from our perspective. Sadly, my friend Mark died of cancer while only in his 30s.

I remember running onto the pitch after the game, another thing that was tolerated in those days but is understandably banned now, and patting Mick Mahon on the back to celebrate a 4–0 win. The players seemed huge in those days, but I guess that was because I was only a little kid.

Dave Appleby, Nottingham

I remember going to Layer Road one evening to watch a training session under the lights prior to the Cambridge United game in the League Cup in 1970. It was Cambridge's first season in the League. The U's, under the watchful eye of Mr Dick Graham, were going through a corner routine at the Open End Terrace. Mr Graham was giving Brian Gibbs hell for missing the goal after a very complex move with Brian defending himself, saying that the glare of the lights made him night blind so that he could not judge the position of the incoming ball.

During this exciting period I got a job as a ball boy at Layer Road which meant retrieving the ball when it went out of the ground. In those days we were so polite and quite rightly so. I remember going to a house on the other side of Layer Road and asking if we may have our ball back as we were at home to Doncaster Rovers.

Nigel Walsh

Twiddle greets the teams onto the pitch during the famous FA Cup run of 1971.

I fondly remember the FA cup Fourth Round replay versus Rochdale in 1970–71 that finished 5–0. A wet Monday night, I stood on the Clock End and knew we had drawn Leeds in the next round. We had played superbly; Micky Mahon was at his best that day.

The day of the Leeds FA Cup Fifth Round game of that season was just magical. I got David Coleman to sign my programme after the game and he was in as much disbelief as the rest of us were that day.

Keith Blaxall

Having spoken over the years to friends who support other clubs, I have discovered that there is one thing that has always been different and unique about Layer Road in its original configuration.

Friends at other clubs religiously stood for years in the same place week in, week out until seating became the norm. Layer Road was different in that you tended to progress around the ground as you grew older. I started in the Clock End with a few friends, only scuttling for cover to Terrace Four when the weather turned really bad.

As the years passed and we got older we progressed to the Popular Side as we closed in on the hallowed Layer Road End. Once there, on those bouncy wooden boards, it took time to work your way to the back of the stand and be accepted behind the goal. At that point we felt we had come of age at Layer Road, and it was nearly five years, in my case, since my first game.

Things had then gone full circle, and for the last 10 years Terrace Three had been my spiritual home. My three daughters and my grandson have been introduced to my little piece of heaven over the years and I am eternally grateful that they have had that experience.

I have only ever sat at Layer Road once, as far as I can recall. I won a ticket as a prize in a programme competition for the Notts County game on 12 September 1970. I still have the red card complimentary ticket (Seat G108) but have never since sat at Layer Road.

I will miss the old place something rotten. She has given me every emotion it is possible to experience. Layer Road even kept me fit – evening games meant hovering by the exit at 10 past nine (after a 7.30 kick-off) and a sprint to North Station to get the 21.40 back to Ipswich to get the last bus back to Felixstowe. I would wait outside the ground at midnight for the trips to Barrow, Workington and Southport, etc, with my moped left inside the ground for safekeeping!

Keith Jenkins, aka 'Yorkshire Kipper'

My best memory from the 1970s has to be the game against Leeds United. I went to see it with my father and a friend from work and my reaction at the time was that it could not be happening. Revie's men obviously thought the same and as we know came to life in the second half, with only a superb save from Graham Smith preventing a replay and a probable thrashing from a team who were never known for the more gentlemanly aspects of the game.

After celebrating this wonderful victory I remember the excitement of queueing at the ground in the evening for a ticket for the next round at Goodison. Sadly we lost, but no matter; the team had done the supporters (and the town) proud and had made history.

Colin Willsher

I loved those heady days with trips starting at midnight so that you could arrive at Southport, Barrow, Hartlepool or Workington at breakfast time. That gave you time to explore the visual and architectural delights of strange northern outposts, grab a couple of illegal pints at lunchtime, make your way to grounds even more ramshackle than Layer Road (remember Sealand Road?), mix on the terraces with friendly (and not so friendly) opposition fans and get home at 3am on Sunday morning. Those trips were a weekend away every month or so, not just the day trip they are nowadays.

One such trip was on 18 December 1971, against Southport away. It was only my second long-distance trip on the supporters' coach, the first being Barrow the previous month. My ticket for the trip had been purchased from the supporters' hut at the previous home game against Exeter. This was my first year at work so £1.50 from my weekly wage of £5.00 was ever going to be wasted!

I wandered through an inch of snow to the bus stop in Trimley to get the Eastern Counties bus to catch the 22.00 train from Ipswich to Colchester. Alas, there was no bus. I walked back home as fast as I could, collected my racing bike, told my parents about the change of plan, ignored the parental advice, cycled in the snow down the A45 to Ipswich and made it to the station with minutes to spare.

I got to Layer Road at midnight and left my bike on the terraces for the weekend. My fellow U's fans thought I was mad (nothing new there!). It probably took me about three hours to thaw out on the trip north. Osborne's coaches were never blessed with the best heating systems for the winter.

Ray Crawford wheels away after giving the U's the lead against Leeds.

We eventually got to Southport but ended up losing the game 3–0. The return trip was the usual fun and games with a stop at The Bagot Arms on Chester Road in Birmingham (the M6 and Spaghetti Junction were still under construction I believe). We got back to Layer Road at around 2am so I crashed out at new mate Trevor's house, and as it was a fine Sunday morning (and because I had lost my train ticket) I cycled the whole way back home! It was a classic Colchester United weekend!

Keith Jenkins, aka 'Yorkshire Kipper'

Although my father took me to Layer Road in the late 1960s I can only remember the crush through the exits after the game, which I found quite frightening at the time. My first game that I am able to fully recall was under the lights for the Rochdale FA Cup replay preceding the Leeds match.

Being on Terrace Four behind the goal, the atmosphere and excitement under the lights and then knowing we were going into the next round after the fourth goal went in was fantastic. The fifth goal really gave the place a buzz and we realised we had a team that could do well.

Unfortunately I was unable to go to the replay, but, like when Kennedy was shot, I can remember exactly where I was and what I was doing when a lady shouted out the score across Port Lane.

Paul Ost

Ray Crawford heads home the U's' second from Brian Lewis' cross with Gary Sprake left nowhere in the box.

The U's put pressure on the Leeds defence in the first half of the 1971 Cup match.

A trip on the team coach to Aldershot was a competition prize in the programme one year. You had to write a match report on a game at Layer Road, and I did so and won the competition. However, I should probably now come clean. As I did a paper round, I had cobbled together the best pieces from the Sunday papers for my report. Multi-plagiarism at 14 years old!

I met Brian Smith at the ground and he introduced me to Dick Graham – how little did I know what this charming man was going to achieve for us! He then introduced me to all the players on the coach (all my heroes – I was just lost for words). Roger Joslyn took me under his wing; although I think he just needed someone to look after his Golden Labrador really! After that we had a massive steak lunch at a hotel in Farnborough and then went to the game.

I was in the dressing room before and after the game, which finished 1–1, and I got my programme signed by all the players with some nice comments (sadly when I left home in the late 1970s my brother flung out my box of U's programmes instead of the Ipswich Witches box I had told him to. Hopefully those programmes ended up in a good home but somehow I doubt it; too many Ipswich fans around!)

The team managed to sneak me into a pub on the way back so my first-ever pint was bought by Roger Joslyn. Thanks big fella!

After a day like that how could you ever think about supporting another team? Colchester United cared for me that day – I felt a real part of the club and that is something that I treasure even 40 years on.

Photographer Tony Tasker ventures onto the pitch to capture the U's delight as they extend their lead over Leeds.

And that is what supporting Colchester United means – even from hundreds of miles away in Yorkshire, the 10 years where I never saw a game as the family grew up (apart from when Scarborough made their brief foray into the League!) and my now more frequent games, I have always felt that the club cares for me as a fan, always appreciates my support and sometimes, with a classic Colchester United victory against the odds, lets me shout from the roof tops that I support the very best football club in the world.

Keith Jenkins, aka 'Yorkshire Kipper'

My father started taking me to Layer Road in 1966 when crowds were often 7,000-plus and we had to get in an hour before kick-off to get me a spot on the wall. Although it is a distant memory I do recall Tony Macedo in goal and a little later Mick Mahon swinging in corners under the bar.

I remember many big games like WBA in 1967 and a few years later the Leeds United game when I thought the hands on the old clock must have stopped as were hanging on during the last 10 minutes.

Paul Hurst

Lil Kemble was one of the U's most prominent fans, and an absolute fanatic. Lil used to clean the coaches for Cedric's in Wivenhoe, and she arranged coaches from Wivenhoe to some big away games. Lil's husband Ron used to drink in the Park Hotel and her son played in goal for Wivenhoe Rangers.

For many years I stood at Layer Road. I have always been friends with John Worsp as we both come from Wivenhoe. We used to stand with the Tiptree Jam mob, including John Wilkin, Roy Cottee and Peter Cook.

Mike Mason

My favourite supporter from the old days has to be 'Wivenhoe Lil' – I wonder if anyone else will mention her to you?

Dave Appleby, Nottingham

My first match at Layer Road was when Lil Kemble got me a ticket for the famous Cup tie against WBA in 1968. I went to as many games as I could until 1972, but then I left school and got a job so I could go to all of them after that. Up until then I could go when I liked. I used to stand in the Layer Road End until it was closed to home fans and then moved to Terrace Three after that.

Phil Gladwin

I am not originally from the area, and so my support for the U's came about because back in the early 1970s my parents owned a caravan at East Mersea. The first United game I attended was a 1–1 draw at home to Stockport, the last game of the 1970–71 season. At the age of 11 the ground seemed massive and I could not wait for the next season to start so Dad could take me to another game. As the caravan season at the time ran from March to October it meant I could only get to games at the start and end of the season.

Living in Upminster, my school friends all thought I was mad for supporting Colchester United. Most of them supported West Ham, our nearest big team. To this day I have never liked them. However, one of my West Ham-supporting friends took pity on me eventually and said Colchester would be his second team.

Colin Hutson

*The U's celebrate the third goal against
Leeds United in the FA Cup.*

Brian Hall is presented with a silver salver for making 300 League appearances by manager Dick Graham.

In around 1970 I went to a school friend's house one day. I did not like football at the time, but when Nicola said that she was watching the Leeds versus Chelsea FA Cup Final I decided to watch with her. I really enjoyed it and wanted to watch live football at Layer Road as soon as I could!

Lucy Tweed

My favourite players that stand out from my early days are Brian Hall and Mickey Cook, along with Jimmy Oliver and Danny Light.

Brian Hall always seemed very upright, even when he was in tackles, and he looked physically commanding. Full-backs get praise for going forwards these days but he did that a lot back when it was more uncommon. He also was a real gentleman and was always very pleasant. The same was true of Mickey Cook; he could not do enough for you.

The first goalkeeper I can remember is Tony Macedo and he was signed by Dick Graham. He was a very good 'keeper.

Ian Craig

I remember the Dick Graham era with a lot of fondness. In a matchday programme in 2008 there was an article on Brian Lewis, which caused me to remember meeting him in what used to be a nightclub-cum-disco known as the Affair Club in Colchester town centre. I actually played alongside Brian in a charity football match between the Affair and Tottenham Hotspur's Old Boys. He was extremely encouraging even when I made a hash of things.

One night at the Affair Club it was about one o'clock in the morning and some of us were invited to remain after the official closing time (which was illegal at the time). Brian Lewis was one of those invited to remain. He was obviously a little tipsy, and he was in a very entertaining mood and talked about some his exploits as a footballer. I cannot remember most of what he said, but I do remember him announcing that he had a little black book of players' names who he was going to 'get' when he next played them. He claimed that it was not uncommon.

Tony Bryant of Cullompton

In 1969 I changed jobs and moved to London. I would never live in Colchester again so my attendance at matches became even less frequent. In 1970 I changed jobs again and joined Cable & Wireless in May of that year. In the same department at work there was a girl called Linda, who had long, blond hair and legs that went on forever. I asked her out and got told to sling my hook! However, on Boxing Day 1970 a friend at work invited me to his for a Boxing Day party, and, to my surprise, Linda was there. I tried my luck again and bingo!

I went to see the FA Cup Third Round game away at Barnet (then in the Southern League) in January 1971. I was living in Wimbledon, and I thought sod the hockey for a week I am off to see the boys. I travelled up on the underground to Barnet. It was a bit of a foggy day but I did not mind. When I eventually got to Underhill, however, I found that the game had been cancelled. One of their directors discovered me, heard my story and immediately took me to the directors' bar, introduced me to other Barnet luminaries and bought me a beer. He then proceded to give me a ticket for the directors' box for the rearranged match later that week. I attended, gladly, and Colchester United were extremely lucky to win 1–0.

David Hicks

We knew we had our work cut out when we were drawn away to Rochdale or Coventry in the FA Cup Fourth Round in 1971. Rochdale's midweek victory over the First Division side was greeted with disappointment. Our away form in Division Four was

Dick Graham and Dennis Mochan urge on their team as the Leeds match takes shape.

unimpressive and Rochdale were a respected Division Three side, yet Dick Graham had us all believing that anything was possible and there was excitement in the air as the game approached.

A supporters' train was chartered to Rochdale and we assembled, bleary eyed, at North Station for an early start. As the train weaved its way up the country we felt a sense of trepidation like a party of crusaders venturing into hostile territory. On arrival at the Northern mill town we were ferried direct to Spotland in double-decker buses. It was a crisp January afternoon, there was some frost still on the pitch and the old ground was packed to the rafters with 13,000 fans.

Ray Crawford opened the scoring with a classic far post header but spent considerable time on the track behind the goal receiving treatment for a nasty crack on the shin; his breath and that of trainer Mochan billowed like clouds of steam in the cold air only a few yards in front of us.

We watched the first half from the Open End and switched ends at half-time to remain behind the goal we were attacking, just as if we were at Layer Road. Rochdale enjoyed the best of the middle hour of the game, building up a 3–1 lead, but then we squandered a penalty which would have made it 3–2.

Going into the last 10 minutes all appeared lost. We looked a beaten side, having given our all against 'superior' opponents, urged on by a delirious home crowd. Then, with Dick Graham willing his men to one last effort, the miracle happened in front of our eyes. As we slowly began to look threatening again, Rochdale started to crack.

Digging deep into resources of strength, character and sheer determination, we had Rochdale nervously defending on the back foot, and then, against all the odds, we snatched two late goals that even now make the hair stand up on the back of my neck. We were taking Rochdale back to Layer Road just two days later, and on home territory we knew we were in with a real shout.

More bedlam in the crowd as the U's go three ahead of their illustrious opponents, Leeds.

The journey home was the thing that football dreams are made of – the team was travelling back with us at the rear of our train. We first saw them on the platform at Rochdale. The picture in my mind is of John Kurila – a brutal defender and fearsome character, but one you would trust with your life – in a sheepskin coat, helping to manhandle the huge wicker basket containing the playing kit.

Halfway home, the chairman, a couple of directors and the team, followed by Dick Graham, walked through the train on their way to the buffet car, and each player was greeted with a tumultuous cheer as they appeared through the sliding door. Skipper Bobby Cram could barely walk and grimaced when asked if he would be fit for the Monday replay. Ray Crawford was also limping, only too happy to roll up his trouser leg and show of a fearful lump on his shin. It was hard to see how either player could be fit for the replay in 48 hours' time, but of course they both were.

Players and fans mingled in the buffet car, and Dick Graham offered to get my match programme signed by all of the players – a memento I have to this day to show that it was not all a wonderful dream, and it is a sign to me that Dick knew that we had witnessed something rare and special up in misty Lancashire that afternoon.

Chairman Bill Graver was not popular with the fans and I was young and silly enough to boo him as he walked through the train, and I got a withering glance from him in return as he turned to open the sliding door. In the hastily assembled programme for the replay Graver wrote of the game in Lancashire, 'Sitting in the directors' box at Rochdale at 4.30pm on Saturday last I certainly did not believe in fairies, but 10 minutes later I knew all the fairies who support the U's descended on Spotland and Rochdale all of a sudden, were playing 11 of our lads with a fairy on each shoulder.' Graver deserves literary immortality for that sentence. He hit the nail on the head, and no one could come closer to explaining the supernatural finale to the game at Spotland.

We arrived back at North Station at what seemed like the middle of the night, all exhausted but still glowing from the afternoon's result. The station's pedestrian exit was on the town side in those days, and I passed the wicker kit basket standing in the brick foyer at the station as I stepped out into the car park, with the lights of Colchester twinkling in the distance.

At school on Monday morning all talk was of Rochdale and of what the lunchtime FA Cup draw would bring the winners of the replay. Leeds United at home was a great draw, but also faintly chilling because of the ruthless reputation of Don Revie's team.

It was cold and wet that afternoon and evening, but the atmosphere on entering Layer Road before the Rochdale replay was a perfect balance of excitement and nervousness. Leeds United had rushed a spy down to watch the game, tucked away at the back of the Main Stand with his collar turned up against the cold, waiting to see the replay unfold. The game turned out to be the most thrilling victory I have ever witnessed by a U's side. We were rampant and unstoppable. Micky Mahon and Brian Lewis hit the heights, and Rochdale did not have the power to hold us back. I suspect their spirit had been broken in the last 10 minutes at Spotland, but I also like to believe that no team on earth could have lived with the U's that night.

Maybe every extra Cup training session that Dick Graham had insisted on and every afternoon spent sprinting up Hilly Fields paid dividends that night, or maybe it was written in the stars. Whatever the case, Rochdale buckled under the blue onslaught that overpowered them and five goals hit the back of the net.

During the first half I caught the match ball. The humble way the Rochdale left-back asked for it back made me realise that our opponents were only human and it dawned on me that they must be totally intimidated by the cauldron of passion at Layer Road that night. (Incidentally, it would be at Stamford Bridge 35 years later that I next caught the match ball.)

Standing at the front of the packed terracing I had a clear view of fans spilling out behind the Layer Road goal when a wooden barrier broke, but nothing could spoil the atmosphere that magical night. A friend working late at Blomfields in Head Street told us that she heard five distinct roars as the goals went in.

Once Rochdale had been put to the sword our thoughts turned to Leeds United, but I believe that Layer Road would never again see a performance to match the sparkling display that we witnessed against Rochdale on that soggy Monday night. I feel privileged to have been there and it was a fitting prelude to the game for which Layer Road will be remembered forever.

Jim French

Possibly the best performance I ever saw was the Cup replay with Rochdale. Afterwards, on the train home, I shared a carriage with some Rochdale fans and referee Roy Capey of Crewe who told me that he had never seen a Fourth Division team play so well, and if they played like that again, with that crowd, on that ground, they would beat Leeds. Again, the rest is history!

Gordon Evans, Perthshire

Celebrations on the pitch as the impossible became possible against Leeds.

The replay against Rochdale after drawing at their place was also a hugely enjoyable game. We beat them 5–0 and set up against Leeds, and that made all the anticipation before the game worthwhile.

John Tweed

After snatching a last-minute draw at high-flying Rochdale on the Saturday, the Monday lunchtime draw told both clubs a home draw against Leeds United awaited after the replay that evening.

Over 11,000 had packed into the ground from what I could tell, and as I squeezed in at the Layer Road End you could feel the excitement and tension rise as the game went on.

After the first goal the excitement rose, and when the second and third went in and then the fourth the atmosphere was electric; one of the best ever at Layer Road.

Chris Coe

I remember the FA Cup Fourth Round game away at Rochdale in 1971, in which we pulled two goals back in the last 10 minutes to draw 3–3. The following Monday was the Fifth Round draw; Rochdale or Colchester United versus Leeds United. Get in. Leeds were the best team in Europe at the time, and virtually every one of their players was an international. Colchester United beat Rochdale 5–0 in the replay and went through to face Leeds.

David Hicks

Prior to joining Colchester I was playing for Kettering, and I got my wife to ring Dick [Graham] as I was not sure that I was confident enough to approach him. She told him that I was not happy in non-League football and straight away he said 'Leave it with me and I'll sort it out.'

I was later told by Ted Phillips how good Dick was as a boss and that made me really keen to join Colchester. Ted spoke of how Dick's training was first class and how he had encouraged a good spirit among the lads. So it proved, as I had a fantastic season there. Dick really put us through it, however, but it got us fit and we had a fantastic season because of it.

I was 35 and a bit small, so the size of the Layer Road pitch meant that I did not have to run around quite so much! I had a good understanding with the players and Dick really got the camaraderie going.

We had the speed merchants on the wings including Mick Mahon, who was so quick he could have caught pigeons! That gave us a great outlet throughout the season and we knew we could kick it to him from the start and set him away down the wing. He was a very good player, and this was in a time where people did not pick up opponents and so it took our oppositions a while into the season to twig what we were doing!

I have played for England twice and had a good career in the game, but I got more mileage out of the famous Leeds game than the rest of the matches put together!

I remember that we were well rewarded for our Cup run that year and the U's took us out to Benidorm to thank us for our efforts. We all met up at the end of the season and Benidorm was just getting going as a resort. But to be honest, and in the nicest possible way, it was a comedy of errors when we got there. For

Dick Graham makes notes after the game, flanked by his two sons.

example, I remember Dick Graham's wife had been for a bath in the first evening and when she pulled out the plug she had heard screams and shrieks from below her. Everyone rushed out into the corridor to find John Kurila and his family soaked to the bone. It turns out that the pipes had not been fully connected and Mrs Graham's bathwater had landed on them in the room below!

Before that, my wife and Bobby Cram's wife and children had chosen to use the lift rather than the stairs to get back to their room, but rather than it going up it went down into the basement and got stuck! They had to get an electrician out at 1am and get them out. Then, the next morning Dick got us to meet for breakfast, but we found that they had not got anything to serve us with. The plates, knives and forks were all wrapped up and I think that was enough for Dick – he got us into another hotel and it was a fantastic experience from then on.

Ray Crawford

Leeds, of course, was the big one; although almost as good was the 5–0 replay win against Rochdale before over 10,000, that got us to that famous game.

John Grimwade

By the 1970s I had married and had a young family. My grandfather had died in 1970 and so he just missed what was certainly our most famous win – 3–2 against the mighty Leeds United. I watched this game from the open area (later the Family Enclosure).

I had a wonderful view of Ray Crawford's two goals, also the Leeds goals and Graham Smith's brilliant late save to win us the match. It was the biggest Layer Road crowd I had been in and it was just a fantastic occasion.

Terry Lawrence

The 1971 FA Cup Fifth Round game against Leeds United at home, who were easily the best team in England at the time, was just fantastic. There were about 16,000 in the ground. Don Revie, Jack Charlton, Paul Madeley, Johnny Giles, Alan Clarke, Norman Hunter and Peter Lorimer, etc, could not hold us. We went 3–0 up at one point; we were great.

Tony Vaughan

Strangely, I do not remember any problems with Leeds fans at the match in 1971. In fact, I do not think I remember any Leeds fans, full-stop!

Chris Wright, Le Rouquet Nord, Maurens, France

I met Don Revie in a restaurant in Spain in 1985. He confessed that the day Leeds lost to Colchester was the worst of his career! The game finished 3–2 with Graham Smith making a wonderful save in the dying minutes. It was just perfect.

Tony Vaughan

I asked my dad to try to get me a ticket for the game. Demand was massive but he somehow managed to get one ticket, which he said I could have, and he said it made up for the Arsenal games in 1959 that I was not allowed to go to.

On Friday 12 February 1971 I took my girlfriend Linda home to meet my parents. The big match was the next day. Fortunately Linda hates football with a passion and so was not bothered in the slightest about me leaving her at home while I went to the match.

On Saturday 13 February 1971 I was one of the privileged 16,000 packed into Layer Road. There are many accounts of this match so I will not add another. Needless to say, the U's win and the whole of Colchester went crazy. That was without doubt the best day in my entire life and will never ever be surpassed.

More celebrations in the dressing room after the final whistle.

I got home at 5.30pm and I was completely hoarse. Dad was still not back from playing golf, Mum had been working in the kitchen and Linda had been watching the telly. Mum took me to one side and said 'You know you said Linda doesn't like football, well she's been in and out of my kitchen all afternoon. First it's Colchester who have scored, then it's Colchester are 2–0 up and so on'. Good old BBC *Grandstand*.

That evening a couple of my mates, Linda and I went to Essex University for a gig. A couple of great bands were playing – Nucleus and Juicy Lucy. Then, suddenly, at about 9.55pm half the students that were watching the band left. The band looked bit mystified as to why their audience had vanished, but then I realised *Match of the Day* was about to start at 10pm. I said say 'come on and see what you missed' to Linda. She did not look impressed but me, my mates and Linda trooped off to a huge TV room and watched the game again anyway.

The atmosphere was as good as at Layer Road; everyone hissed when Leeds get the ball and cheered when United had it. When it was over we went back to the gig, but I suddenly realised that I was getting an extremely cold shoulder. Fortunately I managed to repair the damage over the next few weeks and Linda and I eventually got married in August 1971 (this is without doubt the second best day in my entire life). It was a lucky miss though. Layer Road nearly cost me that one!

David Hicks

When we played Leeds in the FA Cup I was living in Canada, in Montreal. Where I worked it was full of people from all nations, mostly Europeans. I was so proud that I let everyone know the result. Later a Portuguese guy came and showed me a paper from his home. The front page headlines showed the word COLCHESTER. The actual interpretation was something like 'The best of Colchester 3, the best of Europe 2'.

Malcolm Murray of Niagara Falls, Ontario, Canada

My best moment was the game against Leeds. It was my 18th birthday, and we had no chance they said. How wrong they were!

Charlie Brown

Before the Leeds United game in 1971 I said to my friend 'If I see us score one goal, I will go home happy.' I went home very happy!

Over an hour before kick-off, the ground already looked full and so when the Leeds players came onto the pitch still with their suits on, they looked dazed. The crowd booed and banged the metal sides of the stands and the visitors looked a beaten side before a ball had even been kicked.

Chris Coe

One day, when I was an eight-year-old, I was told to get ready quickly as we had to get to Layer Road. It was 13 February 1971 we were heading off for THAT game, the one in which the U's made remarkable history.

I remember my dad's friend parking at the already packed Garrison car park. We reckoned you could generally work out the attendance by the numbers of rows of cars parked there, i.e. three rows equated to approximately 3,000 fans, etc. However, on this particular Saturday I remember Dad insisting that we got there early and we parked in row two.

We saw a number of Leeds fans that had travelled down by car, wearing their white scarves, looking smug and confident. We entered the ground and I remember being pushed to the front and standing right behind the wall at the corner flag of the Main Stand and Clock End. There were some larger, older U's fans standing close behind me, and so I had that memorable aroma of cigarettes from the crowd behind me and Wrigley's spearmint gum from the chap chewing next to me.

As the game developed, I remember the comments shouted by the vociferous U's fans at Norman 'Bites your legs' Hunter and Jack 'Giraffe' Charlton. I was quite ecstatic and in awe of these icons that I had read about and seen on TV so much.

The international stars were made to look second best on the day, however. In the second half Leeds came back into the game from 3–0 to 3–2, and I remember Johnny Giles performing well in midfield, really starting to show his class. He took a corner from where I was standing and I remember leaning over to touch the number 10 shirt he wore and pat him on the back as he took the corner, which eventually ended up with Graham 'super shot stopper' Smith saving and keeping the victory safe.

On the way home I had never seen crowds like it, people cheering and jumping up and down everywhere, laughing at Leeds' humiliation. I remember travelling in a little Austin A40 slowly down Hythe Hill to the bottom where I saw cars with scarves hanging out of windows going over the Hythe Station Road level crossing and cars beeping horns and people giving 'V' for victory signs and thumbs up everywhere. It was such a memorable day. My dad even became quite optimistic about the U's' chances of actually winning the Cup that season and said 'If we can beat them, we can beat anyone!' Such was our optimism.

Later, the school playground became an enactment of the big match – Colchester United versus Leeds United was played out again and again as we relived our famous day.

Mark Osborne

At the Leeds United match in 1971, cars were parked two deep on either side of Layer Road. If you were on the inside, you would never have been able to get out!

Bob Bacon

Just before the Leeds United game in 1971, John Worsp and I joined the vice-president's club at a cost of nine guineas each.

Mike Mason

I could not get tickets for the Colchester fans' end but I had family up in Yorkshire and I managed to get a ticket through them for the Leeds end as they lived near Billy Bremner. I was sitting up with the Leeds fans in Blocks C and D and that was a good laugh, given how the game went!

I can remember the Friday before the game. We had a religious education lesson in the morning and the teacher told us that we were going to have a prayer and hope for a miracle. When we went back to school on Monday morning, the Colchester fans in class said 'you have had your miracle sir!'

Ian Craig

Celebrations in the dressing room after the game, with vice-chairman Roy Chapman overseeing from the left.

I got to know Dick Graham quite well. I was a car dealer and my ambition was to get all the U's players in Ford cars. I sold quite a few and the club used to get the manager's car from my garage. I had had an operation the week before the Leeds United game. I was on a walking stick and Layer Road was closed by the police. Through my contact with Dick, he got me a couple of tickets and he allowed my wife to drive me up to the gate. It was such a mix of emotions when we scored because I could not jump up and celebrate. I had to just sit there as the emotion built up and on the final whistle I cried because I was not able to express it during the match.

Thanks to Dick Graham I was fortunate enough to go on one or two trips with the team – I went to Aldershot and Reading on the coach, and I also went to Brentford. The Brentford game was postponed and Dick rang Chelsea to see whether we could watch. So, we sat on training benches around the edge of the pitch to watch Chelsea play.

John Simpson

My memories of the Leeds game include not being able to get anything out of my pockets. It was a bit tight but there were not as many in the ground as for the Ipswich game in 1957 and I was in my more defensive position further back in the stand.

Dick Graham climbs the wall of Colchester Castle after the U's unlikely win over Leeds.

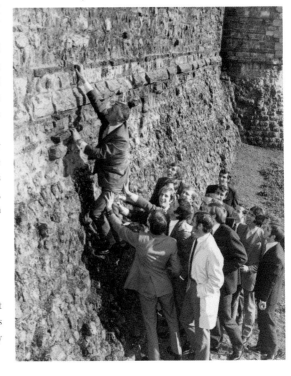

My first memory of that game against Leeds is 'Great, we've scored – at least that's given them something to think about'.
My second memory is 'Second goal, hey, we could win this!'
The third memory is 'Third goal – easy, easy!'
My fourth memory is 'Oh dear, wish I hadn't been so quick to sing "eaaasy"!'
My fifth memory is 'Oh dear, I think I'm going to be sick.'
The final whistle, the sixth memory, 'Life is perfect, now I can die a happy man!'

John Foskew

I drove to Goodison Park in my dad's Zephyr for the 1971 FA Cup Sixth Round tie away to Everton. I had to leave early because of the snow. I eventually got there about midday, and the weather was OK by then. However, Liverpool were playing at home the same day so the city was mayhem! I remember that for the pre-match warm-up United had no balls. Everton would not lend us any, and I reckon they were frightened! In the end, however, we lost 5–0 to end the great Cup run. It was still a fantastic experience.

Tony Vaughan

I can remember the long, arduous trip to Everton on a bright spring day in March. In those days it was always a trip up the A604 by local coach tour operators, and by the time you had got to Cambridge (which took about an hour and a half) it felt like you had been travelling for days! We (my dad, his mate Mick and 51 other U's fans) boarded coach number two of four travelling in convoy from the factory at Colchester Lathe Company, which was in those days in Hythe Station Road. We boarded outside The Sun pub in Hawkins Road with bags of sandwiches, drinks, sweets and reading materials (in my case, an early edition of *Shoot* magazine). I read the magazine cover to cover on that journey.

We left Colchester at about five in the morning and arrived in Liverpool listening to the sound of *Rose Garden* by Lisa Anderson and the *Pushbike Song* by the Mixtures, which were playing on the radio in the coach. We saw many other coaches on the way and

Andy Rankin saves from Ray Crawford as the U's spurn the chance to take the lead against Everton in the FA Cup.

The U's take on Everton in the FA Cup, with future assistant manager Alan Ball watching Graham Smith collect the ball.

many had *Evening Gazette* 'Specials' plastered on the back and side widows. These were pictures of the hands of Graham Smith and shots of Brian Gibbs, Mick Mahon, Dave Simmons and my favourite U's player Ray Crawford. The paper had given them away to be used for coach decorations at away games.

On the day we were well beaten 5–0 and I remember thinking that I had never seen so many people all gathered in one place, and the roar when the goals went in was unforgettable. I remember my dad shaking hands with Everton fans after the game and they acknowledged our efforts despite the defeat. It seemed strange that I was watching my beloved Colchester United play in red instead of blue, which would, of course, have colour-clashed with Everton. My dad bought a large red rosette (about 10in in circumference) with the name 'Colchester United' across the middle which I wore for the entire proceedings. (Incidentally, the tag on the front had been reversed from where it said 'Liverpool' and it had then been re-stapled and marked with 'Colchester United'!)

Everton wore their change strip of yellow tops and blue shorts and I remember Colin Harvey's white boots glinting in the March spring sunshine on that big pitch. Some Evertonians shouted out 'pretend they're 'Pool and we'll beat 'em easy!' The accents were intriguing to me, a boy of eight. We had broad, Essex or Suffolk colloquials being spoken to by broad Liverpudlians and the result was total misunderstanding and confusion.

I worked out the route to Liverpool using my grandfather's road map of the time, trying to follow the return route. We saw several Spurs fans on the journey back, and I spoke to some youngsters at a service area on a motorway returning from their match at Anfield with the Kop giants in another FA Cup quarter-final encounter. It felt as if we were mixing with the 'elite' in English football; at least for a period of time.

Nobody has ever forgotten that famous Cup run back in 1971; for me, it was just the beginning of a fascination and desire to support the U's whenever I could, home and away.

Mark Osborne

Phil Bloss scores the winning penalty against West Brom in the Watney Cup final in 1971.

U's in match action in the Watney Cup final against West Brom.

I had been asking my dad to take me to Layer Road since the Leeds game in 1971. He took my brother and me to the game against Barrow in February 1972, and we stood on what was eventually Terrace Four. I was hooked from that very first game, and, other than two years on the Barside, I was a regular on Terrace Four ever since. In 35 years watching the U's I have only had a seat a couple of times.

The final League game at Layer Road was my 691st Colchester first-team home game, to which can be added a further 170 reserve games and a total of 367 away games.

After the very first game I decided to keep a written record, first on a note pad but for last 35 years in a hard back book. As soon as I got back from a game the first thing I did was record it in my book. It is now an unbreakable habit.

I moved away from Colchester in 2000, and I have since watched football far and wide including many international games. I also write reference books on amateur athletics but my interest in the U's has never wavered, as you can see from details of away trips to play teams like Southport, Newport County and Workington. With every game comes a story or a particular memory.

Jerry Everett   *Jerry sadly passed away in December 2008.*

Layer Road memories of 1972

Certain periods of our youth remain much clearer in the memory than others. I always find the summer of 1972 easy to recall. After the ordeal of 'O' levels, Gilberd School inmates like me trudged up North Hill in our bright green uniforms for the last time that summer, some heading into the big wide world of work and others to return later to the sixth form. Appropriately Alice Cooper's *School's Out* was top of the charts.

I had managed to organise a summer stay at my grandparents' home on the edge of Colchester, which I knew would allow me to attend a number of Layer Road games at the start of the 1972–73 season. The alternative would have been a beach holiday in Spain with my more immediate family. I cannot be sure whether it was the allure of Layer Road or a teenage yearning for independence but I was happy to choose the Essex option.

Armed with my new-found freedom, plus spending money from a summer job at Tiptree jam factory, I was able to indulge in an orgy of Layer Road football, with three pre-season friendlies preceding the opening Division Four game with League new-boys Hereford.

The previous campaign [1971–72] had been disappointing, with the U's falling well short of promotion in the wake of the FA Cup and Watney Cup heroics of 1971. The manager, Dick Graham, introduced a host of youngsters to the team – the likes of Phil Bloss, Lindsay Smith, Micky Cook, Steve Foley, John McLaughlin and Steve Leslie – and over the summer of 1972 he brought in some interesting new signings too. These included Stuart Morgan, Bobby Moss, Bobby Noble and Steve Wooldridge. Dick also controversially changed the kit from all blue to all white. The famous blue-and-white stripes were now little more than a memory.

Friendlies against Orient (2–2) and AS Ostend (1–2) were followed by a rare visit from a Scottish side. St Mirren were led by Gordon McQueen, a rising star soon to sign for Leeds, and that night United's brand new floodlights were officially switched on. My clearest memory is of our new centre-half Bobby Noble (ex-Newcastle) blasting a penalty way over the bar and into the gardens at the Open End of the ground!

The League season began with a narrow win over new-boys Hereford, but Dick Graham's new-look side was not blending well and the next five games were all lost as the club sank to 23rd place in Division Four. Then came the shocking news that Dick had quit as manager, responding to criticism at the club's AGM by standing up and walking out. He never returned. Fans and players alike were stunned, but barely 24 hours later the team responded positively by thrashing Crewe 5–1.

The U's celebrate winning the Watney Cup – Micky Cook and Barry Smith are among those pictured.

It was a false dawn, however, and even the arrival of bright young manager Jim Smith failed to save the club from finishing the 1972–73 season down among the dead men. Nevertheless, it was a fascinating period in our history – after all, our playing staff included a one-eyed goalkeeper (Des Kelly), a costly ex-Fulham star who proved a complete flop (Stan Brown), a winger who scored direct from corners (Mick Mahon) and a loanee from Ipswich who lived in a caravan and was sacked after failing to turn up for matches (Mick Hill). They were happy days!

Rob Hadgraft

My first League game was Bury, which finished 0–0 game in the pouring rain. Nevertheless, I really had got the bug. My friend Nicola's dad and brother were there and we used stand by the Woodlark sign. We used to face Terrace Four and there used to be an advert for Coral saying 'Never a quarrel, bet with Coral' – it sticks in my mind to this day!

My favourite player was Brian Hall, mainly because of his lovely smile. I bought a photo of him and he really stood out. I also had a photo of Dennis Longhorn and he had a great smile too!

I started off watching the U's in 1971. I was a bit of a glory hunter to start with I suppose! I was in my early teens at that time and went up to watch the game against Leeds and it was my first and biggest event as a U's fan. I remember it all very vividly and feeling proud walking down Boadecia Way seeing such a big occasion at our local football club. I had been to Wembley in 1969 seeing rosette sellers and you could feel the occasion as you walked in.

You could see the huge TV vans outside of the ground on the Friday night and to be on telly was a big thing. When Leeds came out for their pitch walkabout, it was something special.

I went with my brother and when the first goal went in he gave me a hug and a kiss, and it was not something we normally did so we know it was a big moment; we used to fight like anything normally!

I used to love the atmosphere and the comments of the crowd, along with the smoky atmosphere from the bonfires and from the pipe smoke. You could get so close to the pitch that you could see the players' expressions, and I am sure that they, like us, enjoyed the laughing and comments, the wittiness of the fans.

Lucy Tweed

A few months after the birth of my first daughter, and in a moment of utter stupidity, I said to my wife, who had been going to Layer Road before becoming pregnant, 'Darling, if you would like to go to the game today, I'll stay at home and change nappies'. Imagine my total shock when she calmly said, 'Oh that would be nice, thank you!' And with that I missed my only home game of the season. It never happened again!

John Foskew

In September 1971 I went to the League Cup game against Blackpool away. Somebody had organised a flight from Stansted Airport. I got a ticket and left Layer Road in an Eastern National double decker about mid-afternoon. I eventually arrived at Stansted, which was a bit like Clacton Airfield in those days. I then boarded a Comet bound for Lytham St Annes. The flight time was about 30 minutes instead of the six hours it took us to get to Liverpool by car! However, we lost the game heavily. Although I did get to fly home with the players, which was great!

Tony Vaughan

All smiles as the U's receive the Watney Cup.

Of course, the highlight for any U's supporter was the never to be forgotten Cup tie with Leeds. Working in London that morning, I arrived at Layer Road just over half an hour before kick-off. Standing outside were most of the Leeds side, some of them puffing away at a fag, and they looked very nervous, especially their 'keeper Gary Sprake! The rest, of course, is history.

Loyal support followed for many years, and I must mention the wonderful job by Margaret and Tony Willoughby at Sporting U's. At every school holiday, they made my two boys very welcome on their long trips from Scotland, as they enjoyed all the events and activities that took place there. And, throughout the season, Margaret made sure that I never missed a programme – home, away, reserves, youth, friendlies, the lot – she passed them all on.

Gordon Evans, Perthshire

In 1971, on 15 May, we had an open day at the ground. The Under-30s played the Over-30s in a match that people could come in and watch for free. John Kurila came on dressed as a Mrs Mopp – he had footballs up his shirt and a bucket and cigarette!

Lucy Tweed

I have so many memories of the 1970–71 season. The FA Cup games against Ringmer and Cambridge were mere precursors of what was to come.

I actually got a mention in Frank Rowland's book *Giantkillers* as the kid he felt sorry for 'who had spent all his pocket money and paper round money' on the abortive trip to Barnet. The rescheduled game was the only match I did not get to in that Cup run.

The draw at Rochdale was a tremendous disappointment but I would not have missed that second half for anything!

With the Cup draw only seven hours before the replay on the Monday night, Layer Road was buzzing. I honestly believe that the atmosphere that night was as good, if not better, than the Leeds game – but then it was under those atmospheric old floodlights.

I was stood at the Clock End and that Mick Mahon piledriver was the hardest shot I ever saw. The 'keeper never saw it, it was that fast.

The Leeds game was so surreal. I vividly remember walking up Butt Road – it was a crisp lunchtime and this feeling came over me that we could not lose that day – I cannot explain it at all. I have never had that experience ever in my life.

I had got a ticket for my younger brother – a closet Ipswich and Leeds fan – and I told him what I felt. He laughed it off; I mean, how could little old Colchester United beat Europe's best?

The U's heroes go on an open-topped bus tour to celebrate their Watney Cup win.

The U's achievements in winning the Watney Cup are acknowledged in this newspaper advert.

The Everton game was a letdown in many respects — one step too far if you like, but what if it had been at Layer Road?

There is a fabulous last sentence in Bryon Butler's book *The Giant Killers*: 'It was a season, in the end, which history remembers for two reasons above all. Colchester, yes, but it was also the season in which Arsenal completed the League and Cup double. They pipped Leeds for the title by just one point and beat Liverpool by 2–1 at Wembley. But it took Arsenal 51 matches to make their mark…Colchester needed only one.'

My sentiments exactly!

Keith Jenkins, aka 'Yorkshire Kipper'

Looking through some stuff earlier in the week I came across an album I compiled about the fortunes of one of Dick Graham's heroes, John Gilchrist, in 1978.

As you may well be aware, in 1975 John was living on a kidney machine and Millwall, his club of 10 years previous to Layer Road, seem unprepared to do anything to arrange a testimonial.

At the end of 1977, after approaching the U's board, local referee Dave Duffett and myself got the ball rolling to arrange a sponsored walk of 30 miles to culminate at Layer Road before a match in front of Anglia TV in March to raise much needed revenue to help secure John's immediate future.

Brian Hall offered his services and joined us for the first 20 miles, and Dick Graham, Peter Wright and John Kurila joined in with a blanket collection during half-time. The money raised far exceeded our expectations.

During the time leading up to that day, great news came through that John had undergone his much needed transplant and was recovering well.

Going on from that highly successful event, Millwall then agreed to at last become involved and agreed to follow this event up by bringing down their team to play 'Dick's Granddad's' on FA Cup Final eve at the end of that season. Our aim of getting this deserving player overdue recognition for his dedicated service to Millwall and the U's was at last fully being recognised.

Once again Brian Hall, Simmo and the club pulled the stops out and it was agreed to try and get Trevor Francis, Britain's best young sought-after footballer at the time who a few months later went on to become Britain's costliest player, to come and make a cameo appearance. Much to my amazement, when we contacted him he readily agreed, and on a very wet night, for the first and only time since that side broke up, eight of the 1971 side along with Brian Wood, Keith Bertschin and Charlie Woods turned in an exciting first half where they went 2–0 ahead before the U's current team took the field and the match finished 3–0.

The veterans were naturally disappointed to have to come off at half-time!

It was one of the greatest thrills of my life to actually be able to present a cheque from the proceeds to John in person at half-time on the Layer Road pitch and meet Trevor in the changing room before the game for official photos. Incidently, the expenses we agreed to pay Trevor were handed straight back and added to the total with his own personal donation.

Speaking with John that night you would not believe he had gone through three years of ill health, not knowing whether he was going to live from one day to the next. He looked the picture of health and thoroughly enjoyed the whole event, reminiscing afterwards about that great day in 1971 when he had Johnny Giles well under control for 90 minutes.

What a fitting tribute this was for John and the rest of the 1971 heroes to appear together for the final time.

It was great to visit John in his home on several occasions afterwards and he always said that, although not bitter in any way, he had almost totally turned his back on football during those truly dark days, only for all the memories to be rekindled because of our efforts.

I could not attend that great game against Leeds but the testimonial match showed me all those years later that it was not a fluke and that these players truly deserved their victory on that historic day that John played his part in. For me the few times I saw him play he was a 100 per cent committed player who quietly and efficiently went about his job.

It was a privilege and a delight to have known John and every time I stepped through the turnstile at Layer Road I am reminded of that occasion.

RIP John, along with Bobby Cram, Brian Lewis, Dave Simmons, Les & Pat Oakes, John Claypole, etc.

Roger Herbert

Secretary Betty Scott takes a call in the Layer Road offices.

I worked at the club for about six or seven years I suppose, and I feel very honoured to have done so. I had originally moved down from London with my husband and children and had looked after them before returning to work.

I worked alongside a number of managers including Dick Graham, Bobby Roberts and Jim Smith, and it was a thoroughly enjoyable experience. I did not have much of an interest in football when I started but that soon grew over time, and obviously the match against Leeds had everyone in the town interested in Colchester United!

It was an extremely busy time and one where everyone was ringing us up looking for tickets as the best team in the land came to Layer Road. I think a lot of people did not give Colchester much hope of doing well, but they proved a lot of people wrong with a terrific performance.

It was an unbelievable day and what had made Layer Road special was the fact that it was everyone in it together, and that stood out from the Leeds match as being a day where everyone was doing their bit to create a giantkilling.

Betty Scott

As the 10-year-old son of the manager, I was very privileged and often regarded Layer Road as an extended school playground. I have a vivid memory from the Luton Town match in the Watney Cup. My mother had knitted me a very long scarf in the tradition of *Doctor Who* at the time.

I sat in the directors' box about three seats away from Eric Morecambe. After getting over the excitement of sitting near such a celebrity I settled down to the match and it turned out to be an incredibly tight and tense game in front of a large crowd. They were in the Division above us, but with my father in charge you never went to games expecting to lose.

The game was deadlocked at 0–0 and the final whistle was approaching, when we gained a penalty. For the only time I can ever recall at a football match, you could literally hear a pin drop. It was totally silent around the ground and erupted when Brian Lewis converted the spot-kick.

I went to the Final at the Hawthorns with my mother and no doubt wearing my long blue-and-white scarf along with a large Colchester rosette. Having just got off the bus at the Hawthorns we were greeted by a thug-like West Bromwich fan. He looked down at me and said 'You ain't got a bloody chance'. He was nowhere to be seen after the game!

Mark Graham

I have supported the U's for nearly 40 years, so memories of Layer Road are plentiful.

For the early 1970s, however, my memories are as much about getting to the ground and home again. Living in Felixstowe meant that for a night game, the following would happen.

I would get a lift from work to the railway station or a taxi if pushed, then I would take the train to Ipswich and then again onto Colchester, followed by the long hike from North Station to the ground.

At the sound of the final whistle, I would run down Layer Road to the Drury pub, for a pre-booked taxi for 9.15pm (7.30pm kick-offs in those days). This would take me to the bus station for my journey to Ipswich. I would have a quick bag of chips and then catch the last bus back to Felixstowe, arriving home about 11.30pm.

This was at a time when Ipswich were riding high in the old First Division and the U's in the Fourth, so I was often asked the

The U's were given this lucky mascot by supporter Bob Riddle.

question, why? The answer was that I fell in love with the club and Layer Road the first time I went there, with schoolmates in a 3–2 win against Grimsby in 1970. The next year I became a member of the supporters' club and watched us beat Leeds.

I was hooked, and what a roller coaster ride it has been since. The ground may soon be no more, but memories last forever.

Kevin Tomlinson

I will never forget the excitement and euphoria when we scored three times against Leeds United in 1971. My father took such a lot of interest in the game and was so pleased that we won. Sadly, he was seriously ill and was due to start a course of treatment on the Monday following the game, but he died on Sunday, the day after the Leeds United game. We went to see him on the evening of the Leeds game and he was so thrilled that we had won.

Mrs Jean Bell

I went to the Leeds game. I cannot remember where I stood but I know I was not up in the trees! It was one of the happiest days of my life.

Willie Wenden

Bobby Cram shakes hands with West Brom skipper John Kaye ahead of kick-off in the Watney Cup final.

Chapter 9 – 1972 to 1982

GOOD WORK BY JIM SMITH CONTINUED BY BOBBY ROBERTS, BUT HORIZONS LIMITED BY FINANCIAL RESTRAINT

There were a lot of lean years and the terrace attendances got thinner and thinner. The concrete steps at the Clock End were now falling apart and each slab seemed to slope at a different angle to the one next to it. No matter, Les Oakes was still there shouting 'Shaky old 'keeper'!

Then a fence went up behind the goal at the Clock End to segregate the visiting supporters from the faithful U's stalwarts. A solitary policeman stood guard. One day the gate burst open and the visiting thugs burst through, threatening the hotch potch of U's fans. The solitary policeman stood there doing nothing until I grabbed him and said, 'For Christ's sake, close the gate!' Luckily he sprang into action and we all got away unharmed!

Mike Gadbury

Although I joined the supporters' club the day after I was born in 1960, courtesy of my grandfather, Harold Moore, a former director and chairman, I did not actually visit Layer Road until 1973. That first trip was at the tender age of 13 and I stood in the care of our neighbour, Tony West, in what is now the Family Enclosure. I returned to that very area for the Stoke City game at the end of the final season at Layer Road.

What wonderful memories that old ground holds – one of my favourites is Colin Garwood turning on a sixpence in the 97th minute to equalise against Derby County in the FA Cup (the *Telegraph* reported 'boys threw their caps in the air, grown men gurgled with joy'!).

James Bowdidge, chairman 1991-92

Knees up Mother Brown was a favourite football chant in those days and it just involved bouncing up and down and singing. The Layer Road End was ideal for that as the wooden beams had a natural springiness that bounced you higher and higher. Millwall fans took over at the Layer Road End during one game in 1976–77.

One particular Millwall fan was jumping up and down and chanting when the wooden plank just snapped and he fell right through, only to be suspended by his armpits until his mates hauled him back out. I think it was a League Cup game in 1976 and we pulled it back to 4–4 but lost on penalties.

In those days there was no segregation, no crowd control, and Millwall stormed the Layer Road End forcing the home fans out. The broken plank was replaced for the next home game and it stood out like a sore thumb as it was a brand new bit of wood.

Peter Chisnall

The crowds in the old days were, of course, much bigger than later safety regulations would permit. The Cup matches against teams like Derby County drew 13,000-plus (and it was sometimes difficult to breathe in the crush!). Even League games drew large crowds. The final home game against Gillingham one season in April 1974 had 10,000-plus fans present.

A big change has been the terracing. The old bendy wooden slats we used to stand on were bouncy, warm and much more comfortable to stand on than today's cold, hard concrete, but after those deaths in the Bradford fire I think that everyone realised that it was better to be safe than sorry.

For many years I used to stand in the same place in the Layer Road End. Over the years I got to know the other fans who always stood in the same places around me. I was a bit of a statistician so they nicknamed me 'Facts and Figures'. It was a sad day when someone in authority decided to push the home fans out of the Layer Road End; it felt like we were being evicted from our own

Bobby Gough, Ray Bunkell and Colin Garwood watch an effort fly over the bar in the FA Cup game against Derby County.

home and the atmosphere went down noticeably after that. We did not recover for many years. I later went into the Barside but did not have emotional ties to any particular part of the ground once the Layer Road End was off-limits.

Dave Appleby, Nottingham

The most enjoyable game I saw at Layer Road was when we beat Hartlepool 6–2, with six goals coming in the first half. Talk about an open game!

The Cup match against Derby County was memorable, too, when Colin Garwood scored an absolute scorcher in injury time. This maintained our record of never having lost a competitive match at Layer Road to a top-flight side.

The Cup match against Manchester United, the game where that unbeaten record finally ended, was also highly memorable. But it took Manchester United until the 85th minute to grind us down (when Jimmy Greenhoff scored). I remember a very young Ian Allinson making a monkey out of the United skipper Martin Buchan and getting dumped on his backside the next time he got near him. I spent the match being very quiet, as Manchester United's notorious 'Cockney Reds' had infiltrated the Layer Road End and were all around me.

Dave Appleby, Nottingham

Lindsay Smith, manager Bobby Roberts, Bobby Gough and Colin Garwood at Layer Road ahead of the FA Cup clash with Derby.

Watched by manager Bobby Gough, the players train behind the main stand at Layer Road.

I have less than fond memories of being in the Layer Road End for a 3–0 Cup victory over Portsmouth and being charged by opposition fans, who had spilled out of the Clock End and poured across the pitch.

But I was downright outraged and disgusted the day that, for the first time, opposition fans were given the run of the Layer Road End (*Our* Layer Road End). This was an area that I had grown up to believe was the preserve of the most vocal and fervent U's supporters. Certainly, it always used to be standard practice for United's captains in the 1960s and 1970s who won the toss to attack the Layer Road End in the second half – because of the psychological advantage of the tightly-packed and noisy support behind that goal. I am sure that opposition goalkeepers must have found it very intimidating on occasions.

Chris Wright, Le Rouquet Nord, Maurens, France

The night matches in the 1970s were special. Especially the Cup matches against Aston Villa and Southampton. I was in the Layer Road terrace for both matches and the atmosphere, noise and support was wonderful. We were bouncing about on those wooden floorboards and climbing up the corrugated fence to be able to see. I can still remember the shiny grass when it was wet, the smoke from the generator and the mist on a damp evening.

When we played Southampton there were rumours that Chelsea supporters would be there because Peter Osgood had joined the Saints from Chelsea. Walking to the ground from Old Heath via Bourne Road for Friday night games was special. You could see the lights from a distance, the sound of the generator, people milling around and the ointment smells behind the Main Stand, and they all add to the special memories.

Paul Ost

A member of Essex Constabulary decides to watch the game with the fans!

I clearly remember the Manchester United League Cup game that I watched in the Layer Road End while bouncing on the wooden terracing. At times as the ground was so full I could not get both feet on the ground.

I remember as well the fantastic 4–3 defeat to Newcastle, which was one of those magical nights where I sang for 120 minutes of great football.

Steve Bishop

Manchester United scored near the end and the crowd started singing 'We're proud of you Col U'. It was a similar feeling to the West Brom game at the end of the second Championship season.

Lucy Tweed

My most memorable game of the late 1970s was the FA Cup Fifth Round tie at home to Manchester United. I stood on the terracing at the Clock End for the first time ever and saw U's beaten in the last few minutes by a Jimmy Greenhof goal in front of over 13,000 spectators.

Terry Lawrence

I moved to Colchester in 1982 and my first game was possibly Colchester versus Manchester United in the League Cup, with Bryan Robson and Remi Moses playing in the Manchester side. I remember that there were thousands upon thousands in the ground and you would never believe they could get that many people in. At the time I did not think it was unusual as I had seen such crowds around the country, but now, having been here a while, I know that the average crowd has been much, much lower than that. Those bigger crowds gave you an idea of what it must have been like in the big games of the distant past.

Another early memory was not so positive, however. As a Hartlepool fan I have always been keen to follow my local club. I was invited down to the club to watch Colchester versus Hartlepool by someone who worked at BBC Essex, Rachel Fletcher, and Hartlepool were at their lowest ebb at this point.

Hartlepool were 1–0 down and I was hoping that they could come back in the second half, before Colchester let rip in the second half and won 6–0. I walked out with my hood up and head down. It set the pattern for the next 10 years for me, either coming and watching the games or, from 1990 onwards, commentating for BBC Essex.

Neil Kelly of BBC Essex

A goal that stands out in the memory was from the mid-1970s. The U's were playing Charlton Athletic and I was standing, as I often did, in the corner of the open terrace behind the goal (as it was then). The U's had a winger named Phil Thomas in those days. He picked up the ball well inside his own half and skipped past half of the opponent's team on his way to the goal at the Layer Road End. When he got to the edge of the penalty area he despatched the ball past the 'keeper – sheer brilliance, and no wonder it is still etched in my memory from boyhood.

Andrew Mann of Didcot

For several years I stood on the Barside, until one late Spring game when I got sunburnt on the face and could hardly drive home! I then moved behind the goal at the Layer Road End and enjoyed jumping up and down on the wooden boards for a few more years. I have watched games from every side of the ground, finally resting on Terrace Four for 30 years.

Chris Coe

My first season supporting the U's was as a 13-year-old in the 1973–74 promotion season. I can remember walking to the Friday night games with my friends from Monkwick via Reed Hall. It was such an exciting time watching the likes of Svarc, Thomas and Leslie. The atmosphere was electric under the lights, and it certainly intimidated opposing teams. I can recall the strong smell of Germolene from the St. John's ambulance brigade as soon as I got in the ground.

I suppose I was a bit of a lad standing behind the Layer Road End, jumping up and down on the bendy wooden boards. I am surprised they did not break! When Svarc scored, everyone pushed each other down the steps, it was all terrific fun.

The banter with the away fans was always good humoured, with songs sung such as *Back to school on Monday*, *Knees up Mother Brown* and *In your Northern slums*.

Layer Road meant everything to me back then. It just felt right to be there.

I can remember seeing a tall skinhead with Crombie coat and Doc Marten boots who wore glasses. He probably was well known by older people and to me he just summed up the time. I remember wearing a parka coat with my Colchester United woollen scarf wrapped around my wrist. This was to show everyone you were hard. It was all bravado, though, but it meant so much.

On the way home you talked normally about the terrific win, we scored lots in those days and how we couldn't wait for the next match.

Mark Davies

I have supported the U's for 30 years and thought I would tell you about a great night out I had back in the 1970s. It was the League Cup Third Round tie versus Carlisle United on 9 October 1974.

I had seen the wins over Oxford (home) and Southend (away) in the earlier rounds and desperately wanted to see the Carlisle game. Dad could not make the game as he was working away so I managed to talk my West Ham-supporting friend into accompanying me on the train.

Being 15-year-olds and therefore still at school, with our parents' agreement we both informed our school that we had dentist appointments on the afternoon of the evening game! We left early in the afternoon and got our return 25p fares to Dagenham East (though money was tight and fare dodging was easy then), and got the train from Upminster to Romford, then to Shenfield and finally to Colchester.

After stopping in town for food we arrived at six o'clock-ish and were two of the first in the ground. We stood at the top of the steps which now come up in the Family Enclosure, but of course there was no fence then so it was part of the Barside.

The game was brilliant and the atmosphere electric. It was my friend's first game at Layer Road under lights and he was suitably impressed. With Carlisle being in the First Division at the time it ended with a 2–0 giant-killing. To cap it all my favourite player, Bobby Svarc, scored the first goal after running on to a bad back-pass. Towards the end a penalty converted by Steve Leslie finished Carlisle off. I seem to recall that they were a very physical team who could not handle the tight ground and its surroundings. Little was to change there over the next 30-odd years!

We seemed to take ages getting back to the station after the game, with our newly purchased Colchester silk scarves being proudly tied around our wrists. However, the train ran on time and we were back at Romford soon after 11pm, the only problem was the last train to Upminster had left at 10pm! My friend's dad had to come and pick us up, moaning all the way back that we were wasting our time watching the U's. He just did not understand.

I managed to get to the next round against Southampton (thanks Dad) and went to the Aston Villa game on my own. Although we lost to Villa it had been a great run. I cannot believe my pocket money lasted so well!

Colin Hutson

A fan's childhood memoirs, mainly from the 1970s

Layer Road is:

- the aura of floodlit games, the click of the turnstiles, the smell of liniment and the sound of the *Post Horn Gallop*.
- having to peer over the heads of St John Ambulance volunteers who have taken their seats directly in front of me.
- a roofless, terraced Clock End.
- being delighted at getting Jim Smith's autograph.

- a policeman telling me not to sit with my legs dangling over the wall in case the ball hit me and broke my legs.
- being part of a crowd which cheers as yet another ball disappears over the stand roof…and me wondering if they do ever get retrieved.
- when the pre-match entertainment is basically Twiddle with his blue-and-white umbrella.
- Mike Walker making yet another fabulous save.
- where rattles are not confined to babies and where rosettes are not only confined to gymkhanas and election rallies.
- me and fellow U's fans bouncing on springy wooden planks behind the goal at the Layer Road End.
- admiring Mickey Cook and wishing I could be like him one day.
- a packet of Opal Fruits at half-time.
- me spotting a linesman writing in his notebook during a quiet lull in play and shouting 'Oi lino…you doing a crossword or summat?' thereby provoking a wry smile from the linesman and howls of laughter from the adults standing behind me.
- not fancy, perspex 'smoke-break' shelters for dug-outs.
- me wearing my 'parka'.
- me – for some unknown reason – thinking it was Steve Dowman not Colin Garwood who scored the equalizer versus Derby!
- me reading the matchday programme and sniggering at the fact that Northampton Town's nickname is the Cobblers.
- where the warm-ups were *proper* warm-ups; none of this fancy 'stretching and running between cones' malarkey but ones where I was impressed as the players knocked inch-perfect 50-yard passes to one-another and nonchalantly brought the ball down at their feet; warm-ups where the 'keeper actually got his knees dirty before kick-off.
- the cold rising up from the terracing through the soles of my shoes and through my body.
- me thinking what a marvellous idea it is to erect fencing above the goal at the Layer Road End to help stop the ball going out of the ground.
- the ball coming to me in my seat in the Main Stand and me trying to give it back 'throw-in style' to Mick Mahon, only for the return to fall short and hit an unsuspecting bloke squarely on the head – much to the hilarity of the crowd AND the players.
- having a U's team that seems to consist solely of Steves, Micks, Mickeys or Mikes.
- taking my mum to watch Swindon Town and all game her going on about how their player called Trollope should tuck his shirt in because he looks untidy.
- when bobble hats actually had a bobble.
- where 'obscure' northern outposts such as Bury, Rochdale, Hartlepool and Scunthorpe give me more of a geography lesson than a football lesson.
- nearly getting hit by a lump of concrete thrown by Portsmouth fans and hatching my escape plan should things turn even nastier as Gillingham fans invaded the pitch.
- where Svarc and Gough were not the only bobbys I witnessed on the field of play (…not least the one who tried to arrest a Millwall player for swearing).
- discovering my mate Nigel's birthday treat is to attend a U's home match; and that, to my delight, I and some other school pals are invited along too.
- me feeling a bit sad at the U's dispensing with the programme cover that had the 'cartoon' eagle on the front…because I really liked that one.
- watching the U's give top teams like Leeds, Derby, Southampton, Aston Villa and Manchester United a real run for their money.
- enjoying some quality time with my dad and many wonderful, unique, never-to-be-forgotten memories.
- so much more than just the above.

Martyn Jones (aka Bagsy)

In the 1970s I was assistant groundsman at Philip Morant School and very few people there used to go around with Colchester scarves or hats on, but there was one young girl who did and I always wondered who she was but did not get to speak to her while she was at school.

    She used to work for Colchester United selling the lottery tickets and we went to a club party together in 1975. We got talking from there and went to games together after that. Supporting the club has been an important part of our marriage along the way.

John Tweed

Signage behind the Main Stand at Layer Road, directing fans to their familiar places on the terraces.

There have been a few changes along the way, including the seats going in the Clock End. The terracing behind the goal used to be so crooked with 2in or 3in difference in height, along with weeds and dandelions coming through. It was like Chelsea Flower Show!

I remember the game against Southampton in the Cup with Shilton in goal, and he played out of his skin that night. He put on a display that would not be matched again. Nothing could get past him! It was the best goalkeeping display I have ever seen.

Charlie Brown

Great games and very personal memories:

*   League Cup Third Round tie versus Carlisle in the 1974–75 season. The game finished 2–0. We took the top-flight club apart that night.
*   League Cup Fourth Round tie versus Southampton in the 1974–75 season, which finished 0–0. It was a very wet night and I stood on the Clock End at the back to try and get some shelter. I was under an umbrella and unfortunately it got snagged on top of the corrugated iron fence to such an extent that it tore to shreds trying to release it. I had to leave it there and got absolutely saturated walking home. It had disappeared by the next home game.
*   FA Cup First Round tie versus Dover in the 1975–76 season. The game finished 3–3. It was a bright, sunny November day and I decided to cycle to Layer Road. However, I hit a brick in Napier Road, the mudguard jammed in the back wheel and I came off. Bloodied and bruised I had to carry my bike to a friend's in Maldon Road and watched the game in a sore and battered state. I wonder what those around me thought.
*   Division Three game versus Wrexham in the 1975–76 season, a 0–2 loss. It was a disappointing game just before Christmas. Fog came down towards the end of the game, which thickened significantly at the final whistle. It was so dense in Layer Road on the way home that I failed to see the kerb, fell off the path and twisted my ankle. It was a long, painful walk all the way home.
*   FA Cup Fifth Round tie versus Manchester United in the 1978–79 season, which Colchester lost 0–1. How close were we that night to creating another upset?

Keith Blaxall

The first game against Manchester United sticks in the mind and I recall the home fans on Terraces One and Two with the London Reds on the Barside. They called in the military police as stewards, and they were sitting on the running track so everyone could watch the game. When Manchester United scored the London Reds wanted to come over the wall but the army stood up and they quickly decided against doing it! It was like a wave coming in and then out again, and it was funny to see the London Reds, so well reputed for causing trouble, beaten at their own game.

Ian Craig

From the late 1970s I started going to Layer Road with my grandparents. We used to sit in the Main Stand, just above the halfway line, in the area where the directors were later seated.

My memories as an eight to 12-year-old include:

- Friday night football under lights; Ian Allinson flying down the wing and the expectant roar of the crowd.
- Trevor Lee always seeming to get his head to the flick-on.
- Micky 'don't mess with me' Packer scoring an absolute stunner once from a throw-in and flick-up.
- A bizarre Watford goal in the Cup – I think a shot against the post rebounded off Mike Walker's back and into the goal.
- Famous visiting fans like Elton John and Ian Botham.
- The disgusting cigar smoke from a man that sat in front of us.
- The tree in the middle of the terrace behind the Clock End and the clock on a board by the Barside.
- My nan's flask with the criss-cross pattern, steaming hot tea at half-time. Can anyone remember the frisbie champions demonstration at Layer Road? How cool was that!
- Changing of ends at half-time and the fans' exodus to stand behind the goal we were attacking.
- The Pompey Chimes.
- Grandad always buying three scratchcards – I got to scratch one of them.
- The first time I held my own season ticket book, it was like someone giving me a million pounds!
- Local derbies with Cambridge United.
- The stinky loos, and parking outside the ground because my grandad had a disabled badge.
- Lunch in the café at a Saturday match or fish and chips from the chippy at the Mersea roundabout at an evening game.

Great memories! I am now 39 and my boys are eight and four. We go to every home game, and needless to say I have started off building their memories by bringing a steaming hot flask of cocoa, which they love. I hope that they have as many cherished memories of Colchester United as I have by the time they reach my age.

Aide House

The Mel Blyth and Sergeant Ruggles 'coming together' on the Layer Road pitch was perhaps one of the most notorious moments in the club's time at the old ground.

I was there with a school friend standing on the Barside Terrace, which was about three quarters full of Millwall supporters. When I think back to this era and the memories of hooliganism it makes me appreciate quite how far the game has come. Of course there are still problems from time to time but in the late 1970s and early 1980s it was widespread.

Peter Shilton pulls off another save as he keeps the U's at bay with a one-man show for Southampton.

Bobby Roberts and Ray Harford (back row, extreme left and right) line up with their squad in this pre-season photoshoot.

The build-up to the game was unsavoury. We had played Millwall in the April of the previous season (a boring 0–0), a game remembered only for the mass brawl at the old Clock End at half-time and the reported fighting in the Bay & Say pub on the Friday night.

Although I did not witness any trouble in the next encounter, there was definitely an atmosphere – so much so that watching the football received the same attention as watching the crowd around us.

The game itself went very much Colchester's way and the Millwall contingent (players and crowd) went from being highly agitated to cynically critical and resigned to a defeat.

The Mel Blyth incident was not clear at first. He had played a back-pass wide of his goalkeeper which went out for a corner. After an altercation, a policeman appeared. From where I was we thought that he was reporting an object thrown on the pitch to the referee, but as he started to lecture the player you could tell that it was going to create some headlines.

Unsurprisingly the Millwall opinion was that the policeman had no right to be on the pitch and several around us voiced this view (in graphic detail).

The expected headlines definitely materialised the next day!

David Youens

There was a lot of fuss about the Mel Blyth incident but I thought the policeman handled the situation very quietly and very well. I admired him for that.

Judith Musgrove

We had a few big Cup games in those days and that included the two-legged Aston Villa game. I went to both legs. The Newcastle replay was probably one of the best games I have seen at Layer Road. It was really end-to-end and the Geordies made it a cracking atmosphere in a huge crowd.

Les Oakes – I never stood near him but the 'keepers used to hate playing down that end because they knew that they were going to get abuse for the whole 45 minutes they were in front of him.

Ian Craig

I have been a fan of Colchester since 1976, and to this day I have a team photo on my wall from August that year from the *Evening Gazette*, with Stevie Dowman's magnificent afro hairstyle dominating the Layer Road landscape – a frizz big enough to eclipse the floodlights…

Simon Frost of Portsmouth

Could anyone who was there ever forget Mickey Packer's 35-yarder against Plymouth Argyle?

James Bowdidge, chairman 1991-92

In the mid-1970s I was taken to Layer Road by my father to see Colchester United versus Plymouth Argyle. We only missed two or three games that season. Although the quality of the football was very poor on this occasion, it was a match which will always stay in my memory because of the antics of one particular fan.

As the match progressed, it was littered with errors and compounded by some rather bizarre refereeing decisions which really benefited neither team. Plymouth had turned up looking for a nil-nil draw and were stifling any attempted creativity from the greats such as Micky Cook and Bobby Svarc. The crowd were becoming a little despondent to say the least, but one slightly more elderly fan in front of us was taking things a little more seriously than that.

Having initially cheered the home side, as the game deteriorated so did his demeanour towards the United team. From the occasional jibe towards home players who made small errors, he grew more and more angry towards the standard and the quality of the football. He 'humphed' his way through half-time and when play resumed he continued his verbal assault on the home players, now berating them at every opportunity. Things came to a head 10 minutes from the end of the match when he rather inexplicably evolved into what could only be described as Basil Fawlty's twin brother.

'Right! That's it! All of you – LEAVE THE FIELD!' he shrieked. He sent the entire home side off, much to the amusement of all the supporters in the vicinity! Whether or not any of the players heard him I do not know. But the despondence seemed to have filtered onto the pitch.

With one minute of the match remaining, United's legendary stalwart Mick Packer had had enough. Receiving the ball on the centre spot, he knocked the ball forward a couple of

A newspaper cutting reporting on the infamous moment where Sergeant Ruggles confronted Millwall defender Mel Blyth.

yards and hammered it – straight into the top corner of the Plymouth goal past the despairing dive of Jim Furnell. There was a moment's silence while the crowd digested what had just occurred before the whole of Layer Road erupted.

'I knew you could do it! I never lost faith in you!' screamed our 'loyal' fan from the row in front, with ensuing guffaws of laughter from the surrounding supporters.

So, one of the worst team performances I ever saw, the greatest goal I ever saw at Layer Road and the antics of one passionate fan have proved to be my greatest memories of this fine stadium.

Philip Carroll

The first game I attended was in 1975. My uncle took me and I vividly remember the smell of liniment while walking behind the changing rooms. The most memorable game? Derby County in the FA Cup in 1977. With no crowd segregation, I stood at the Open End among some Derby fans who gave me sweets. I was 14 at the time.

Sometimes at the Open End we would all crowd into Terrace Four if the rain got too much. I can remember how we would change ends at half-time to see the U's attacking, bouncing up and down on the wooden boards at the Layer Road End.

Derby's Leighton James apologises to a steward after running off the edge of the Layer Road pitch.

I used to watch the players train during my school holidays and buy photographs and get them signed, and Ian Allinson was my favourite.

Other things I remember include an instrumental tune that they used to play at half-time, think it was called *Pop Corn*, and the advertisements for Ronald West, rubbish removal.

I still go to matches with my son Ben. He saw his first match when he was 10.

Judith Button

Layer Road – the fantastic home of the best team in the world, Colchester United FC. For me, a visit to our home games involves a round trip of 700 miles, leaving home at 6.30am and returning at 11.30pm; as a Dartmoor U's member, every trip to Layer Road is special whatever the result and when it came to recalling my memories of the old ground it proved quite a challenge to limit the countless vivid and clear pictures of the U's in action over the years.

My first game as a spectator at Layer Road was against Chesterfield when I was nine years old; I remember the atmosphere of that first victory and that the opponents were a nasty bunch. I stood on the Popular Terrace right at the front and thought the ground was huge! I cannot remember the goals, only that we won and that we were a really good team.

In fact, the memories just pour forth. The 0–0 draw against Southampton is my first really clear memory of action; if it had not been for Peter Shilton we would have murdered them.

Ralph Wickenden of Dartmoor

My favourite player was John Williams (a solid, dependable left-back, just like me!), who lived in our village, Great Horkesley. Other favourites included Steve Wignall (a steady, solid centre-back), Lindsay Smith and Stuart Morgan (a pair of psychos – at least

Derby's Derek Hales scores at the Layer Road end in the FA Cup tie in 1977.

Another chance for Derby's Derek Hales to add to the scoring in the FA Cup game of 1977.

Bobby Gough goes close with this shot as the U's press the Derby goal.

on the pitch!), Bobby Svarc (a deadly striker), Bobby Gough (I remember a fabulous goal of his from over the halfway line, which must have been before David Beckham was even a twinkle in his dad's eye), Karl Duguid (a loyal one-club man is so rare these days) and, of course, Mark Kinsella (a player who always did something special at the precise moment when it was needed).

Dave Appleby, Nottingham

In the Bobby Roberts era, when I was aged about 10 (1979), myself and a couple of mates in the school holidays used to bike from our homes in Prettygate to Layer Road and spend the mornings in the ground. We got to know the groundsman Tom Cheney and he was always quite happy for us to be around the place as long as we kept off his sacred pitch. In fact, quite often he would get us doing little errands or jobs for him. Anyway, our one of our favourite tricks was to go looking for old lottery cards (Quicksilver I think they were called) and check that they were not winners. If we were really lucky there might have been a game on the Saturday before half term started or even a midweek match during half term, which meant that we had plenty of cards to check before the rubbish was all swept up (another job Tom let us help with). Obviously the majority of the tickets that we picked up had been discarded as losers, but occasionally we would find a winner and quickly rush into the office and see either Betty Scott or one of the office staff to claim our winnings.

Another favourite was to check for dropped coins, which for a 10-year-old would mean more penny sweets on the way home. In those days the Layer Road End was split for home and away fans with a small walkway and caged area in the middle for the police to marshal on match days. The actual standing area was made of wooden boards (a bit like large floorboards) supported on struts from underneath, rising slightly so that people could see above each other, similar to normal terracing. Anyway, we knew that during the games supporters would quite often use the flexible flooring to bounce up and down when cheering and celebrating and that a lot of the time they would lose money, sweets, programmes, scarves and hats, etc under the boards, which were open at the back giving no protection to anything that dropped. Now, in the late 1970s there was no way that if a supporter dropped anything under these wooden terraces the police at the far end (by the away supporters) would let you go under the terracing to collect anything. Most of the time the Layer Road End was packed solid anyway, so movement to the far end where the under-terrace access was located was impossible. However, on a Monday or Wednesday morning (after a game the night before) there was no-one around and we would quite happily crawl under the supports and fill our pockets with coins, sweets and programmes.

You would not believe how much money we found, and at the end of the day we would split it all up between the three of us and

Steve Wignall is felled in front of a meagre crowd at Layer Road in 1980.

head for the sweet shop (later known as Ralph & Rita's) to spend our money. We would come home very dirty as underneath the struts there was just dusty soil and quite often to get to a 10p coin we would have to lay virtually flat on our stomachs to reach it, especially if it was towards the front where the gap between the boards and the floor was very small.

Steve Wright

More great games that I remember include:
- The FA Cup First Round tie versus Portsmouth in 1980–81 which finished 3–0. The silencing of the Pompey chimes from those who were massed on the Barside.
- The Division Four match against Sheffield United in the 1981–82 season which finished 5–2. It was just a great game not appreciated by the Sheffield supporters.

Keith Blaxall

Once hooliganism really began to rear its ugly head in the 1970s and 1980s, one would have imagined that Layer Road, with its turnstiles all on one side, would have been custom-made for trouble. However, I do not recall any major incidents. As luck would have it, one of the worst matches was a 0–0 draw against Barnsley in September 1979, which just happened to be the first match to which I had dragged my future wife. Segregation must have been fairly haphazard and play was held up because of fighting on the terraces.

At one point several Barnsley fans, clearly looking for a fight, appeared beside my friends, my wife and me. After heaping abuse on the U's players and getting little reaction, they inevitably turned their attention to the Layer Road stadium itself. 'This is an effing s*** ground!' one of them shouted. This proved too much for one of my friends who reacted furiously and said 'It's alright for you, mate – you only have to come here once a season. We're here every fortnight!'

The Barnsley hooligans gave a grunt of despair and moved off! Strangely, my wife never asked me to take her to Layer Road again.

Even at the height of hooliganism, however, I seem to remember that segregation between supporters at Layer Road was organised on an ad hoc basis.

Manchester United fans occupied virtually the whole of the Popular Side for the Fifth Round Cup tie in 1979. Because of their fearsome reputation at the time I seem to remember that the army was drafted in to control them, and as a result there was no trouble.

Chris Wright, Le Rouquet Nord, Maurens, France

Rust falling from the roof went on for years. You could see the crowd move as soon as the ball hit, as everybody tried to get the rust out of their hair.

I also remember that my brother reminded me about the blankets being carried around the pitch for charity collections, with fans encouraged to throw coins into the blanket. So many coins missed the blanket and fell onto the pitch!

Judith Musgrove

A sparse crowd as the U's take on Darlington in 1982.

Chapter 10 – 1982 to 1990

PLYING OUR TRADE IN THE BOTTOM DIVISIONS.
DECLINE AND RELEGATION FROM THE LEAGUE

I always had to know United's results – no mobiles or texts in those days. If abroad I had to buy a newspaper even if it was three days old and cost a couple of quid!

Tony Vaughan

I think we all have a few fond memories of happenings at Layer Road. I will never forget the old tin roof that used to cover the Barside. Every time the ball hit it (and that was quite often) we all used to get an impromptu shower of rust particles. At the end of some games you were actually dirtier upon leaving the ground than what you were when you arrived. Oh, how we miss that rust.

Karl Groome

Many years after my introduction to Layer Road (and by now a responsible adult!) I attended post-match press conferences as part of my job as a sports reporter with *The East Anglian Daily Times*. After a demoralising 4–1 home defeat by Crewe we were left waiting in manager Roger Brown's office while he apparently gave the team a good talking-to.

Suddenly an urgent message came through asking for the office staff to get an ambulance sent to the home dressing room where a player was unconscious. The office went quiet as we all thought the same thing: 'Roger Brown has attacked one of his players!'

We hurried down to the tunnel and there we saw Richard Wilkins being wheeled out by paramedics in some sort of neck brace. Subsequently it turned out the injury was nothing to do with the manager at all and was the legacy of an incident in the match!

Rob Hadgraft

I remember when Jonathan Crisp sacked Mike Walker as manager when he had just won Fourth Division Manager of the Month and brought in the unknown Roger Brown, which paved the way for our demise to the Conference. Brown favoured the starburst corner-kick arrangement where players split out in all directions from a huddle. It was tried six times in one match without a sniff of a goal.

Peter Chisnall

My son was born on the night we beat Exeter to stay in the League in 1989. My wife was having contractions and I made her sit in the car at the hospital and wait for the result to come through on the radio! I remember saying when I heard we had won, 'Great let's go and have the baby now!' He is also a U's supporter now, and, like me, he has never lived closer than a 160-mile round trip to Layer Road.

Mike Gadbury

My first experience of watching football at Layer Road was a 1–0 victory over Hartlepool in 1984 when I was just six years old. One memory that sticks in my mind from the early days was a game that strangely I did not see much of.

It was an evening game against Darlington played in thick fog. Colchester lost the game and I can safely say that when Darlington scored at the Layer Road End I did not see the goals from where I was, I only heard a loud cheer from time to time from the away fans and presumed they had scored.

Dave Buckingham

During a five-year period I attended every home game, standing at the Open End by the white pillar whatever the weather. I would stay there for one half and then often dash to be in the Layer Road End, on the wooden terrace, in the other half. Although in doing so a 4–0 pasting of Peterborough resulted in a complete soaking and the fog against Darlington resulted in me not seeing any action at all.

One of my greatest memories of Layer Road is still the raw energy and atmosphere on the Layer Road Terrace for incredible top of the table games against Wolves and Swansea. The latter we won 2–1 to go top in September.

The Wolves game included one of the best saves I have ever seen anywhere; unfortunately it was by Kendall of Wolves down at the left-hand post. They were great days, with brilliant performances also recorded against Northampton and Hereford in the Cup. I saw Simon Lowe scoring three against Stockport and the miss by Maidstone which bounced impossibly over the bar. These are just some of the memories from on the pitch.

Off the pitch I grew up on those terraces and became a life-long fan alongside regular familiar faces including 'The Manager', an older man in a mac and cloth cap on the Open End who constantly gave instructions in his booming voice.

And while I try to forget nightmares, my worst moments included Preston outclassing us 2–0 (I particularly enjoyed our eventual revenge at home to Beck's side many years later) and a comedy moment against Scarborough at the Layer Road End when five U's players failed to clear leaving an empty net for the opponents. The behaviour of Tamworth's so-called fans was also a moment to forget as was our 100 per cent membership scheme.

Harder times followed but I still went to every match as we slipped out of the League; I remember the scenes as we completed our first escape from the drop with wins such as the one against Wrexham while under Jock Wallace's management; this was one of only two times that I ran onto the hallowed turf to celebrate.

Ralph Wickenden of Dartmoor

The U's take on Manchester United in front of a packed Layer Road in the League Cup in 1982-83.

I well remember the 'Members Only' season, resulting in low gates in 1986–87 and the Wolves fans who became members and managed to infiltrate Layer Road.

Keith Blaxall

On 6 March 1987 we played Stockport County at home. I arrived at the ground rather late. Unable to find a parking space in Rainsborowe Road, I risked parking on a roundabout, and Steve Dowman had just done the same thing. 'Don't worry mate, you'll be all right there' he assured me as we ran to the ground together. However, the £12 parking fine proved otherwise.

Stockport played as if they had spent the afternoon walking from Manchester as we romped to a 5–1 victory, with Simon Lowe notching an improbable hat-trick. I gate-crashed the vice-presidents' bar after the game, and when the players appeared John Schultz presented Lowe with the match ball and delivered a short speech saying what an important role Lowe will play for the U's (an inaccurate prediction).

But all eyes were elsewhere; on the small television in the corner of the room ITV's *News at Ten* was playing out a tragedy with shocking news about a cross-channel ferry capsizing outside Zeebrugge, with much loss of life. It was a chilling reminder that there was life and death outside of that cosy little room.

Jim French

Alec Chamberlain tips a shot over the crossbar during his lengthy spell in the first team.

The worst moment I can recall was the game which finally put us down into the Vauxhall Conference. If I remember rightly it was against Cambridge United of all teams. We certainly played them sometime in the run-in.

I folded my woolly blue-and-white scarf into my pocket and sadly walked away from Layer Road. However, that woolly scarf (very faded) survived and subsequently saw us make it all the way to the Championship.

Dave Appleby, Nottingham

The U's line up ahead of the start of the 1986-87 season.

Several times I have been among the volunteers clearing the Layer Road surface of snow on a winter Saturday morning to allow the game to go ahead in the afternoon. There were some purpose-made tools for the clearance kept in the groundsman's lock-up and these were broom handles with a curved bit of plywood on the end like a giant snow shovel.

Even more memorable was doing the same task on a weekday for an evening game when I took a day's holiday off work to help and John Schultz put his hand in his pocket and bought all the volunteers a fish and chip lunch.

Peter Chisnall

A view of the main stand in the mid-1980s.

The U's go for goal against Wolves at the Clock End.

I remember Ian Allinson saying that all footballers get stick from the crowd. When he turned round at Arsenal there was a sea of faces, but when you looked back at Layer Road you could see the individual person who had shouted out.

'Shaky ol' 'keeper' from the Clock End was legendary. Les was well known to all the locals. My favourite comment of his was in a home match against Tranmere (Jock Wallace's first game in charge, I think). A hopeful through ball was played just ahead of Mario Walsh, which was approached by the visiting goalkeeper, Eric Nixon, who gave an almighty air kick and missed the ball completely, thus providing us an easy tap in for our first goal.

Once the cheering had died down, the booming voice kicked in: 'EASILY THE GOALKEEPER'S FAULT!' The mass laughter which followed made sure Nixon suffered fully.

David Youens

The two extremes:
- The Division Four game versus Halifax in the 1988–89 season which ended 3–2 after a rollercoaster of emotions. The Darlington result on the Saturday had given us a chance of survival, but at 0–2 down against Halifax it looked all over until a great fight back with a nervous Ian Allinson penalty 10 minutes from the end sealed the win that put survival back into our own hands.
- The Division Four game versus Burnley in 1989–90 which finished 1–2. This was the saddest day. We were into the Conference and I looking around not knowing if I would ever see League football at Layer Road again.

Keith Blaxall

The fondest memories of my youth are nearly all linked to Colchester United and, more importantly, Layer Road. Growing up 10 minutes' walk from the ground, it seems inconceivable to me now that I could not have been a U's fan, but looking back now I wonder what on earth my dad was thinking. Back then, the excitement of going to see a live football match for the first time was almost too much for an eight-year-old to bear. Twenty years later, I begin to see how inauspicious my introduction to the club was.

Weeks after a Roger Brown-led Colchester were crushed 8–0 by Leyton Orient, I joined a crowd of a couple of thousand on a freezing cold evening to watch a bottom of the table U's team scrap out a 2–2 draw with Torquay United against a backdrop of fan discontent, supporter identity membership schemes and falling attendances. I watched from the Family Enclosure as we conceded a scrappy equaliser deep into injury time. Is there a better microcosm of football for a newcomer than that?

Soon, though, I was back, this time at a filled-to-capacity Layer Road to see the FA Cup Fourth Round replay against Sheffield United. Barely able to see the pitch, the one memory that stays with me is being dwarfed by the police horses patrolling the road and the sheer size of the occasion as over 7,000 fans packed the terraces.

Regular trips with my dad followed, and, with my mum and my sister also on board, we became regulars on the Family Enclosure. From then on our Saturday's were spent watching the U's slide towards relegation from the Football League.

Ben Wright

In April 1989 Colchester United were in big trouble at the foot of Division Four. It was down to the Conference for us unless we could beat Exeter at home. I travelled down for the game and we beat them 4–0. The atmosphere was electric, just as good as the famous Leeds United game. Colchester United just avoided relegation that season.

I turned 40 in August 1989. I decided to sponsor the first home match of the season against Halifax Town and took a load of my mates to the game. Playing at left-back that day was a bloke called Stuart Hicks. It was 0–0 at half time, and at the start of the second half Hicks sent a bullet of a header from the edge of the penalty area into the net.

I was up and dancing until it suddenly dawned on me that nobody else was. We had changed ends and I had just witnessed the most spectacular own goal ever. My mates proceed to give me stick unmercifully for the rest of the game (and the rest of my life, for that matter). Colchester United finished the season by getting relegated to the Conference.

David Hicks

Prior to moving to France in 2002, I think I'd seen pretty well all the usual suspects since 1961 as far as memorable matches are concerned. But way up there on my list is the now largely-forgotten (in the light of what was to happen the following season) sensational 4–0 win against Exeter on Friday 5 May 1989.

Going into the game, anything other than a victory seemed likely to result in relegation to the Conference (which was an appalling and unthinkable prospect at the time). In fact, I would like to suggest the third goal scored that evening, a victory-clinching 20-yard rising drive into the top left-hand corner of the Layer Road End goal from John Pollard, as the most memorable and important goal I've seen in 47 years. Even if it did turn out to be all in vain 12 months later.

I remember celebrating by climbing on top of a crash barrier halfway up Terrace Three and roaring. And I must have been 36 at the time!

Chris Wright, Le Rouquet Nord, Maurens, France

My earliest memories are of when my dad was a steward and he regularly took me to games. Terraces One and Two were made of wood at the time (about the time of the 1986–87 season). I used to sit in the Main Stand reasonably close to the players' tunnel, and I can still remember the smell of liniment when the players came out.

My fondest memory of all was when I was mascot. I am not 100 per cent on this but I believe it was 1 October 1988. We played Lincoln and I think the score was 3–1 to Lincoln. I was aged just eight at the time and can remember Lee Hunter taking me under his wing. It was a fantastic day for me as a youngster and one that has stuck with me.

Russell Hannan

— OUR —
Mascot

The Hannan family will be a proud group this afternoon as 8 year-old Russell Hannan fulfils his wish to be a lucky mascot for his favourite team. Russell's Dad has been a United steward for more match-days than he cares to remember!
Russell attends the Monkwick Junior School. He is very keen on football of course, and also enjoys ice skating. We hope that he and his family have a most enjoyable time today at Layer Road.

United's MASCOTS are selected by Sporting U's and receive a souvenir of the day by courtesy of Peter Joyce from
P.B.J. ARTEXING
Tel: Colchester 865928

Russell Hannan is mascot against Lincoln in October 1988.

The U's side from the fateful relegation season line up for the cameras.

Striker Simon Lowe gets the ball under control in this 1980s game.

I have great memories of the mid-1980s games, especially cycling from Maldon to Layer Road as a teenager. I can still see Perry Groves running down the wing and Tony Adcock knocking them in.

David Clark

The worst moments I can remember have to be losing the League status in 1990 against Burnley, when many fans thought at the time that there was no way back. We could remember the early 1970s when a lot of clubs, including Barrow, Workington and Southport, were not re-elected back into the League after relegation.

John Tweed

The membership scheme introduced by Jonathan Crisp made it 'home fans only' and gates dropped massively. Although I was working most Saturdays at that time, it was still devastating to see tiny crowds of between 1,500 and 2,000 fans. People were staying away because it was a hugely unpopular strategy, and sacking Mike Walker did not exactly help Mr Crisp's popularity ratings!

Ian Craig

You only really appreciate the good times if you have suffered the bad times. And as a reporter for *The East Anglian Daily Times* and *Green Un*, I occupied the Layer Road press box during those very grim days of the late 1980s when the U's slid slowly from the top to the bottom of Division Four and were demoted out of the Football League.

The Layer Road press box was not exactly the most roomy in the League, nor was it blessed with luxuries such as air-conditioning. Its senior occupant Hal Mason insisted on puffing away on his pipe, however, and we often found ourselves peering at the action through clouds of smoke and misted-up glass! Obtaining the use of a telephone could also be tricky, and even if you snared one there were always friendly freelancers like Bernard Webber begging to borrow it!

Carl Marston

On 12 April 1989 I had my one encounter with Jock Wallace, in a fish and chip shop in Hereford after a midweek 1–1 draw, with the chip shop server virtually snapping to attention as Jock barked 'plenty of salt and vinegar on mine'.

The dropped points around that time seemed like a fatal blow to our chances of avoiding relegation. Clive Stafford had gifted Hereford an equaliser in the dying minutes, and he had been in tears in the changing room after the game. Jock's response? An arm around the shoulder and the simple words 'you're in the team at Lincoln on Saturday, son'. The remaining games produced two draws followed by five wins and salvation, with Clive Stafford remaining first choice at left-back.

Jim French

My first visit to the ground was in October 1988 (21 October to be precise), when a group of friends and I decided we should finally visit the hallowed turf together for a lads' night out. Many people of our age would go clubbing, but we wanted to go to Layer Road.

Living away from Colchester, and with parents who disliked football, getting to games had previously been quite difficult when I was young. But with a job, a car (a Vauxhall Nova, with go faster stripes) and money in my pocket, a trip to see Colchester play on a Friday night was high on my priority list! So, Steve (Cambridge United and Paris St Germain fan), Tony

Match action from the U's match against Burnley in May 1990, the final home game before dropping out of the League.

A sparse crowd turned up for the match against Burnley.

More action from the match against Burnley.

The crowd looks on as the U's move closer to slipping out of the League.

(Arsenal) and I decided to travel from our homes in Hertfordshire to see the mighty Col U take on Cambridge in the East Anglian derby. Forget Liverpool against Everton, City and United, this was U's versus U's!

If I am honest, there is little that I remember about the game itself. What I do recall is that Colchester were on a miserable run of form and this was the first match since the 0–8 humiliating defeat away against Orient with Mr Colchester United himself (Steve Foley) in charge, Roger Brown having departed the manager's position the previous week. Cambridge eventually won the match 2–1, with Tony English scoring a late goal for us to at least give me something to celebrate for the journey home. Steve, though, enjoyed the beers that evening (and I was driving).

Perhaps my most vivid memories were of the cold night air on a late autumn evening; the tight, compact little ground; the wooden terracing at the away end, adjacent to where I used to stand near the Layer Road entrance and the Main Stand; the sense of expectation as I walked towards the stadium, buying the programme and the local paper, eating the hot food and savouring the atmosphere that only a Friday night game of football under lights could bring (oh how I missed those in recent years); a feeling that however long it had been since I had lived in Colchester, this was my club and my ground. I was hooked. I will never ever forget Layer Road, thanks for the memories…and long live the new Community Stadium!

Simon Frost of Portsmouth

'Why Colchester?' is definitely the most common question you get when people you meet eventually find out that you support the U's. If I could have a penny every time someone said 'Why Colchester?', we could have bought Wayne Rooney.

It all started back in October 1988 when about 10 of us were sitting on a train from Harwich to London. We had just arrived by ferry from Sweden and were on our way to see our national team play England in a World Cup Qualifier at Wembley (we drew 0–0 and defender Glenn Hysén had a great game and was sold to Liverpool).

One of the many stations that extremely slow train stopped at was, of course, Colchester. One of us, and I still do not know who was to blame, said 'Colchester, isn't that a football team?' None of us were sure. Once we got to London we decided to find out everything we could about this club that we were not even sure existed. We soon discovered that Colchester indeed had a football club and that they had recently been beaten by Leyton Orient 8–0. At that time Colchester United played in the Fourth Division and were really poor. We immediately decided that we had to get back to England soon to see this team 'in action'.

The Swedish Branch arrive in north Essex ready for the game against Hartlepool United in January 1990.

More than a year passed before we returned. Meanwhile we had great difficulties in keeping up with results. This was a few years before satellite TV and the internet, so we had to rely on sources like two-week-old issues of *Shoot* and *Match* magazines and the odd phonecall to English newspapers: 'What, calling from Sweden and you want the results from the Fourth Division? Get lost!' That is exactly what I was told once when I phoned up the sports desk at *The Sun* in 1988.

We were back on British soil at New Year 1989–90 for our first Colchester game. At least some of us were there. Anders and I stayed at our hotel rooms with terrible hangovers. Who the hell decided New Years Day was a great day for football?

The rest of the boys, seven or eight of them I think, managed to get to Colchester and see the U's beat Hartlepool 3–1. This was also to become the last game any of us would see the U's win for a while. Before, during and after the game they met loads of people who thought it was great that there were people who came all the way from Sweden to see their really bad team. Hey, they said it, not me! So the boys immediately decided that we had to go back to Colchester again in the near future.

A few months later, at Easter 1990, it was time for our second visit to the hallowed turf. Colchester played Southend. Colchester were bottom of the Fourth Division and lost 0–2, and later that season the U's were relegated to the GMVC or the Blue Square Premier as it is called nowadays.

Great, now it got even harder for us to catch up with results from England. The Swedish papers did not cover the Conference that well; in fact most people in Sweden had never even heard of the Conference.

By now we had become rather addicted and trips to UK became more and more frequent. During the first trips we hardly ever saw Colchester win at all. Even during the first year in the Conference when Colchester only lost one home game all season, we still managed to pick that game! Yeovil Town won 1–0.

The following season, 1991–92, it changed slightly, both for Colchester United and our little group. We set a new record of four visits to England and the U's won the Conference and also the FA Trophy at Wembley. After the Wembley game we met a bloke at Gatwick Airport wearing a Colchester United top. He lived in the United States – and I thought we were the weirdest people on earth!

As the Fourth Division was scrapped, Colchester were the first club to make it straight from the GMVC to the Third Division. We were back in the League and our travels did not decrease. We made another four trips that season.

Now it is 2008 and we have actually followed our beloved Colchester United for more than 19 seasons, and we still try to get over as often as possible. I still do not really know why, though. But when you have started to follow a team it is bloody hard to give it up.

But if I wanted great football and fancy grounds I would be at Arsenal, Chelsea or Man U. So it must be the people and the atmosphere. Small and often neglected grounds, but with a crowd that really cares passionately about their team, town and colours. That is what football is all about…for me anyway.

Paul Andersson

We won 1–0 at Layer Road (with a goal in the final minutes) to virtually end your Football League status at the time! I have a very vivid memory of celebrating after the final whistle as we were kept behind. The goal meant we could still be promoted – which we were – and so of course it was sheer ecstasy.

I looked across to the left (to the opposite stand to the Barside) and noticed two Colchester United fans that I recognised. They were two guys who wore denim with literally hundreds of Col U badges and stuff on and they always had scarves. I knew they were real supporters as I had seen them at various motorway service stations over the years as we travelled to different games.

The two guys were just standing there as we sung about non-League and promotion. They just looked at us…then cried.

I doubt I will ever forget that.

Tenerife Shrimper

Layer Road has provided some great memories for this particular Southend supporter and I do not just mean the odd victory over our local rivals. During the 1970s and 1980s Southend played many home games on a Friday night, leaving Saturday free for my dad and I to take in another game. Regular venues were Ipswich, Norwich, Colchester, Chelmsford and Orient, and although my school friends were visiting the London glamour clubs such as Tottenham, West Ham and Arsenal, I feel that my footballing apprenticeship was much more interesting.

Layer Road during the 1970s was always remembered as the place mighty Leeds were brought to their knees, and right up to my very last visit I do not think that ghostly feeling ever went away.

There were some good players, too, an early favourite of mine was Trevor Lee, a powerful forward player with an Afro haircut that would put any glam rocker to shame! Then there was Roy McDonough who scored goals for both Southend and Colchester during a number of spells. He went on to manage the U's during their successful Conference season, and I believe that to this day he holds the Football League record for being sent off more times than any other player. Another goalscorer was the ill-fated John Lyons, who took his own life at a tragically young age.

In goal during those early visits was Mike Walker. My wife once told me how she took a slight fancy to a Spurs goalkeeper at the very first football match she ever saw – it made me feel very old telling her I had watched his dad play!

Then there were the games I watched. There were some memorable games with Southend including the Shrimpers' 4–3 win in the League Cup, a 3–3 draw at the start of the 1984–85 season and a 2–0 win that as good as relegated the U's to the Conference as well as just about securing promotion for Southend.

One of my favourite matches was from the 1988–89 season. Colchester had endured a poor season and their League status was in doubt. A run of results towards the end of the season had lifted them, but when Halifax Town arrived at Layer Road only a victory would do. The Shaymen had former Manchester United and Ireland goalkeeper Paddy Roche in their line up. As the match progressed it seemed as if Colchester would never get past the Town 'keeper as they trailed 0–2. But then they had a stroke of luck as the Irish 'keeper caught the ball but landed awkwardly, badly damaging his ankle. The stricken 'keeper was carried from the field and replaced by a big cumbersome central-defender as there were no 'keepers on the bench in those days. The U's saw their chance and roared back to win 3–2, and can I remember the place going crazy as the winning goal went in. League football was secured albeit only for another 12 months. As for Paddy Roche, he never played League football again!

In fact, in some 40 visits to Layer Road I never saw a goalless draw.

I also remember the 3–3 draw with Southend at the start of the 1984–85 season. Tony Adcock scored a hat-trick for Colchester and former Ipswich and England man Trevor Whymark was on target for the Shrimpers. The game had been marred by crowd trouble, and as the game ended the police took the unusual step of keeping the home supporters in the ground while the visiting Southend fans were escorted out of the stadium.

As I started to leave, a surge from the back of the stand caused us at the front to become crushed. I called to a police officer to help me lift my girlfriend of the time over the wall and onto the perimeter track and what seemed to be safety, and as he did so his now agitated police dog tried to bite her! She never went to another Essex derby again!

But for all the wonderful players, great games and fantastic memories, this book is about the ground. Layer Road is, as the Shrimpers fans would say, falling down, but it is a ground full of character and the sort of place a *REAL* football fan could watch a *REAL* game of football.

My special memory of Colchester United's home is a 3–0 win over Peterborough Reserves. The final game, the final goals and a special chance to watch football from the terraces with my young son Alfie, just as I had with my late father many years ago. Thank-you Layer Road, you will never be forgotten.

Brian Jeeves, Southend United fan

On 5 May 1989 the U's played their final home game of the season, against Exeter City at home. The rampant U's were on a run of five consecutive wins, including the famous and pivotal win at Darlington, as Jock Wallace and Alan Ball guided the team away from relegation trouble.

After the final whistle I lingered a while before walking out along the front of the Main Stand. Looking up into the stand I saw Jonathan Crisp sitting in the

Trevor Morgan puts this one wide and the U's' stay in the League draws to an end.

The membership card scheme introduced by Jonathan Crisp was far from popular.

back row staring impassively out onto the pitch as the crowds made their way home. I like to think I caught his eye, but there was no flicker of emotion on his face. He might as well have been carved from stone with no sign that he was deriving any pleasure from what was his finest hour. Maybe he wanted to appear enigmatic, or perhaps he had a premonition of the dreadful year which lay ahead.

A year to the day later, on 5 May 1990, we all witnessed the U's losing 1–2 to Burnley to complete a season that many of us believed would be Colchester's final League game ever.

I spent the second half at the back of the terrace at the Open End, immediately behind the domain of Les Oakes. If Les was there that afternoon then even he was silenced, which perfectly summed-up the mood. After too many defeats the fight had been knocked out of us, and fans and players alike had accepted our fate. As we trudged out of the ground that afternoon we had no idea that Conference and FA Trophy glory were less than two years away and that our best days lay ahead.

Jim French

If the going got tough and the football got dull, we could always resort to our favourite parlour games. This might include naming a team made up of players who had been to prison, or maybe even an 'Ugly' XI. Some of the other themes we dreamed up are best not repeated here for the sake of political correctness!

Not that the football was always dull, of course. I recall covering the club's record 8–0 defeat at Leyton Orient (manager Roger Brown refused to comment after that one), a shock Cup win at Fulham (caretaker-manager Steve Foley conducted his press conference wearing just a skimpy towel), and the League debut of Dave Barnett (someone mentioned he was a born-again Christian just moments before he battered an opponent and was red-carded).

I also recall interviewing an excited Perry Groves after he signed for Arsenal, taking a phone-call from a bewildered coach Stewart Houston who wanted to publicise his anger at being sacked, and I remember the day I upset Roger Brown, who accused me of smirking at him. At least he did not challenge me to a bare-knuckle duel, which allegedly did happen to vociferous fan Les Oakes!

Rob Hadgraft

HAPPY DAYS IN THE CONFERENCE

Two games stick out in my mind when I think back to Layer Road, one in each of my spells at Colchester. The first one was in the year we won the Conference and FA Trophy in the 1991–92 season. It was an amazing season with a group that had probably the best team spirit I have ever experienced in my whole career.

The game I remember from that season was against Kettering in our penultimate League game. It was a Tuesday night and the atmosphere was electric. Night games at Layer Road were always good with a lot of teams not enjoying the small ground and basic changing rooms!

Kettering were a threat to us, even though our last game against barrow was one we were expected to win. We ran out 3–0 winners and I scored the third after having a bit of a bad time in front of goal.

We won the last game 5–0 with the big yank (Mike Masters) getting a hat-trick and completing the double at Wembley a week later. They were really special times with a great set of lads.

I also recall a funny story from when Roy McDonough applied for the manager's job. All the team at that time were desperate for him to get the job because he was so popular among the lads. We all thought it would be a jolly up, which it was most of the time without interfering with our performances. The squad knew how to enjoy themselves with Eamonn Collins, the social director, leading Benno, Sheeds and myself astray!

The day we were waiting for Roy to be appointed we were playing Halstead in a pre-season friendly. Roy told the first-team squad that they were not playing but we had to show our face at the game. By now, we knew Roy was going to get the job so we decided to spend the day drinking in Halstead starting at lunchtime.

Eamonn lived in Halstead at the time and was familiar with most of the landlords, so we ended up in The Bull which was at the bottom of the High Street and on the way to the ground. On hearing confirmation that Roy had got the job in the afternoon, we started on the champagne to celebrate in style.

By early evening we were all worse for wear when we decided to show our new manager how happy we were with his appointment. We knew Roy would be coming down the High Street about 6.30pm on the way to the ground so we had a lookout at the top of the High Street to give us the signal he was coming.

All of the first-team squad assembled outside the pub loaded with bottles of champagne and when Roy drove past we started spraying it all over the road and his car, his face was a picture! Needless to say he stopped the car and popped in for a pint!

Steve McGavin

In the Conference years I remember that we had a trip down to Farnborough in the FA Trophy. Farnborough's normal gate was about 600, so you can imagine the chaos that ensued when 2,000 travelling fans turned up. We were all herded into the stand behind the goal and to one side of the Main Stand.

With the exuberance of the Colchester United fans at its peak, singing, dancing and full of expectation, the crowd surged forward a little and broke the makeshift perimeter fence, which was made up of pieces of 4x2 timber nailed together. Before the game could go ahead this had to be repaired, so the groundsman went to fetch his toolbox which consisted of one hammer and a couple of nails.

As he prepared to fix the damaged fence, he placed his nail in the prime position, held the hammer aloft and struck the head of the nail. But then, oops, the hammer handle snapped in half. So then we had a groundsman with a broken fence, a broken hammer and nowhere to hide. He shrugged his shoulders, gave us a toothy grin and walked away with his head hung low and with the sound of 2,000 U's fans singing to him. It was priceless.

Karl Groome

During the 1980s and 1990s I attended fewer games; although I sat in the Main Stand for the first time ever that season thus completing a 'full house' of supporting the U's from all corners of the ground. I went to Wembley with the U's, too, and I also saw the memorable home games against Altrincham, Wycombe and Barrow which helped us back into the League.

Terry Lawrence

I also have two great memories of the Conference days. Clearing snow off the pitch to try and get the Orient Cup game played, only for it to be called off due to frozen terraces. And I remember like many others being on the edge of the pitch before the great celebrations after beating Barrow to get back to the League (helping to remove the great wooden terracing so we could get back to the League as well).

Steve Bishop

During the Conference years I was lucky enough to go on the team coach to Boston, where we won 4–0 during the promotion year. I have many fantastic memories from that season, including meeting Ray Hollingsworth at a number of Conference outposts! The Macclesfield semi-final will always be very special, too. That was the time my little old Colchester United reached Wembley. I never thought that would ever happen and when it did I stood there feeling utter elation. To get there twice more in quick succession was amazing.

Then came the Barrow game and another unforgettable day. Mike Masters was the hero and the U's were back in the League.

Mike Gadbury

Job done! The U's with their silverware from a memorable season.

Roy McDonough goes for goal with this header against Wivenhoe in the FA Trophy.

The worst opposition goalkeeping performances at Layer Road? Certainly John Osborne looked overwhelmed and hopeless in the West Brom Cup match in 1968. But even he looked world class compared with Paul Hyde in the vital 3–0 win over Wycombe in the Conference in December 1991. From what I remember, he was totally responsible for all three U's goals. In fact, I recall that towards the end of the match the Wycombe subs were warming up in front of us and, as Hyde went down to field a soft shot, one of them put his hands over his eyes before turning to the U's fans and laughing. That incident still makes me smile. It was the sort of incident that would probably never happen in the higher Leagues.

In fact, Paul Hyde single-handedly got us back into the League as it was he who let in our 'keeper Scott Barrett's last-minute punt in the away match that same season. Without Paul Hyde in their goal, Wycombe would have finished four points clear of us!

Chris Wright, Le Rouquet Nord, Maurens, France

The following years saw Layer Road turned into a fortress as we stormed through the GM Vauxhall Conference, a period of our history that, due to the free-flowing football of our collection of rejects, youngsters and journeymen, may never be beaten. School holidays and weeknights at that time were spent on the concreted patch behind the Family Enclosure, participating in as many 'Sporting U's' activities as my parents could take me to before running up the steps to see what reserve or youth-team game was also scheduled that night.

During this time I was picked as mascot for the FA Cup tie against Birmingham City, just a day after my ninth birthday. The game was featured on that evening's *Match of the Day* highlights and one of my most cherished possessions will always be the battered VHS tape that shows me passing the ball back and forth to Eammon Collins as the players prepared for kick-off. However, you might not spot me if you do not know where to look! But trust me, I am there, on the pitch at Layer Road playing football with my childhood heroes.

I have actually been lucky enough to play on the hallowed turf three times, representing the mighty Philip Morant School, Reed Hall Sentinels and the Colchester United Supporters' Association. As an awestruck 12-year-old U's fan warming up at the Clock End, I made sure I smacked the ball high into the net so that I could say forever that I had scored at Layer Road.

Fourteen years later I was one of the fully-grown adults representing the CUSA, belting penalties into an empty net at the Layer Road End and then celebrating in front of imaginary away fans.

Ben Wright

I can recall the doom of relegation to the Conference and also the joy of promotion two years later when I stood on the pitch and saw Tony English pick up the trophy after a 5–0 win.

Paul Hurst

I have had about 50 or 60 years of connections with the club. It started when I was about five as a little boy and went on until I left the club in the 1990s.

The number of anecdotes accumulated over such a period of

The legendary Les and Pat Oakes, along with Tim Amoss, ahead of the game against Carlisle in 1997.

Massed ranks of U's fans celebrate the victory over Witton.

time is endless, with so many managers and players having passed through in my time at the club.

I was involved with the board when we went through the Conference years, and while it was fantastic to be so dominant at the time it was the camaraderie about the other clubs that made it such an enjoyable experience. They were without exception very nice people and you enjoyed your day whatever the result.

We were very successful in those days, and in the promotion season Layer Road was something of a fortress. In the last home match of the season we had to win against Barrow and duly did so by a comfortable 5–0 scoreline.

In my mind, though, the turning point in the whole of that season was the goal scored at Wycombe by Scott Barrett. It was a complete freak of a goal and it gave us the advantage that we needed by the time the final game. A draw at Adams Park would have meant they would have gone up and not us, so it turned out to be a very important strike.

There have been so many highlights along the way and it makes it hard to just pick one. But while there was plenty of excitement along the way, relief was the main emotion when we got the victory we needed against Barrow. Promotion had been within touching distance, and, although we won comfortably, they are the sort of games you can dominate and end up losing 1–0.

We followed that up with a trip to Wembley and the fans, who had been 12th man throughout the season, made it a fantastic experience once again. It was quite extraordinary how many fans we had. The journey to London was an amazing experience, with all of the bridges on the A12 festooned by people in blue and white. It was to be the first of two visits to Wembley during my time on the board and not many chairmen of lower League clubs can say that!

The U's celebrate winning the FA Trophy on their first visit to Wembley in 1992.

Barrow's resistance is broken again as the U's find the back of the net.

Halfway there as the teams come off at the end of the first half.

The floodlights tower over the ground as the U's move closer to a return to the football League.

The U's celebrate one of Mike Masters' goals as promotion draws closer.

In the period that I was there, one of the strengths of the club was Marie Partner. She was superb, and if anything had to be done she did the hours and was always so reliable. If she was asked to do something you knew it would be done.

Gordon Parker

Older, and perhaps a little wiser, the so-so and not so good times were watched from the Clock End Terrace. Relegation from the Football League and a change to Terrace Four brought a change of luck in the club's fortunes. The last game I watched from there introduced another generation (my eldest daughter) to Layer Road and our religion, with promotion back to the Football League confirmed and Barrow well beaten.

Back in the League, and with a bit more cash in my pocket, quite a few games were viewed from the Main Stand; although sitting down at Layer Road never did seem right to me.

John Grimwade

As it turned out, the games in the Vauxhall Conference were normally very entertaining and the trip to Wembley to win the FA Trophy was also a memorable day out.

Dave Appleby, Nottingham

During the Conference years I saw quite a few away games because there were lots of Conference sides within a short distance of where I lived. I went to Layer Road for the last home match in May 1992 and saw us beat Barrow 5–0 to return to the League. I also went to Wembley to see us win the FA Trophy.

David Hicks

Most of all I will remember the fans who helped to bring Layer Road up to scratch. I was one of those few who spent every day painting and digging, and I even helped to take out the wooden terracing at the Layer Road End when our Football League return was under threat.

David Welham

I remember Scott Barrett scoring in the penalty area for the equaliser against Kingstonian in the FA Trophy, when I just knew we were going to Wembley. I also fondly recall Mike Masters' spectacular goal against Barrow to seal the Conference title.

James Bowdidge, chairman 1991–92

The fans flood onto the pitch as promotion is sealed.

I have fond memories of being on Terrace Three for the Conference matches. Being relegated to non-League seemed to stir the town and gave the club something to focus on. There was lots of excitement then, not unlike our first season in the Championship. Getting to Wembley helped give the old home a real feeling of excitement and renewed confidence about the club's future.

Paul Ost

In the second season in Conference, my brother was fourth official for the first game versus Macclesfield in the FA Trophy. He introduced me to Paul Taylor who was referee that day.

My brother was also refereeing a youth game at Layer Road one Sunday morning a while later. I had gone up there to watch him referee and it transpired that one of the linesmen had not turned up. I was also a qualified referee, however, and so I volunteered and got to run the line, and that is a special memory too.

When we played Wycombe in the Bob Lord Trophy I was surprised the game even took place. Only 10 to 15 Wycombe fans were there and it was cold and foggy, and in Terrace Three you could not see the far end of the ground. During the first half our goalkeeper, Scott Barrett, paid for all the Wycombe fans to have a cup of coffee!

For the crucial game against Barrow I went up to the ground early, about 12.30pm, and there was already a queue from the ticket office down to the club shop to get in. It was pay on the day, you see, and everyone was eager to get in. Once inside you really could not move on the terraces.

In the season that we were relegated from the League things looked so bleak, but it was the days in the Conference that really got me hooked for the second time and I have been a regular ever since.

In the first year in the Conference Ian Atkins did a good job, but he cost us by sitting on narrow leads for too long in the games against part-time teams. The goal difference proved crucial, so in the second season in the Conference, to do the non-League double and go and see the U's at Wembley was phenomenal.

Ian Craig

I remember the 1991–92 win against Barrow, 5–0. It was a great day all round. No one was bothered about the Wycombe result; we were going up. I remember towards the end Warren Donald was pushed upfront to try to get him a goal as he was the only player who had not scored all season. I remember him being set up six yards out and screwing the ball past the post of an empty net right in front of me.

Captain Tony English lifts the GMVC Trophy at Layer Road.

U's fans on the pitch at the end of the game against Barrow as the club returns to the League.

The champagne flows in the Layer Road dressing room.

Captain Tony English lifts the GMVC Trophy at Layer Road.

It was a very happy and moving day on the Clock End, so much so that when Mike Masters scored the second goal the spontaneous response from the crowd created a surge and I moved from a few steps from the back to a few from the front behind the goal. I was not able to regain my position and watched the rest of the game from down the front. Happy memories of life on the terraces.

Keith Blaxall

There was a banner in the crowd on the day we won the Conference, which said: 'A football team is for life, not just a day out at Wembley'.

Nick St George

The second and final time I ran onto the hallowed turf to celebrate came after the promotion game against Barrow, a match where I was in a direct line with Masters' first screamer!

Ralph Wickenden of Dartmoor

'If we ever see League football again at Layer Road, I will eat my hat' said a former chairman after the Football League Ground Inspection Committee visited in February 1992, declaring the ground unfit for a return to the League. Gordon Parker and I set about organising the huge programme of works necessary to ensure that return, culminating in the 'Back to the League Appeal', which saw a massive, community-wide effort to bring Layer Road up to the required standard.

Builders took time off work to lay concrete; someone sat in a bath of cold baked beans in the middle of the pitch to raise sponsorship and I even went on a sponsored diet! My regular climb to the commentary box kept everyone updated, and, with all that volunteer work, by raising well over £100,000 the ground passed inspection with flying colours.

When I took over the club in 1991 we had less than two years left on the lease from Colchester Borough Council, a legacy of the Crisp administration, at an annual rent of something like £140,000 – a fortune in those days and quite unaffordable. But, with amazing support from the council we were granted the 10-year lease we needed to meet Football League regulations and they even gave us a grant to cover the rent. We never did get the former chairman to eat his hat, but we let him off as he was as thrilled as any of us at the outcome.

While I loved my time as chairman, watching all those sterling deeds on the pitch, it was the so often the unseen work behind the

Roy McDonough and Gary Bennett with the U's silverware.

The U's players embark on their tour around the town to celebrate promotion.

Photographers get their shots of the masses on the pitch.

scenes, like getting the ground up to standard, extending the lease and restructuring the finances, of which I was always most proud. Without these things, none of us would have seen League football return to Colchester regardless of the heroics on the pitch.

James Bowdidge, chairman 1991–92

In 1992 I spent two of my weeks' holidays working at the ground with many others to make sure that the U's were allowed back in the Football League. Over the years the club has been run as a small and friendly club, so not only do you get to know a lot of the fans but the friendly players and staff too. I will miss Layer Road a lot because over the last 40 years that I have been going I have made many friends, seen many a funny sight and seen a lot of great games.

Phil Gladwin

Managers in arms; Dick Graham congratulates Roy McDonough on his success.

RENEWED AMBITION AND STEADY PROGRESS

One year we were due to entertain Hartlepool United at Layer Road. Due to the strange history that surrounds Hartlepool resulting in their nickname of the Monkey Hangers, my work colleagues and I planned a little surprise for the teams as they ran out.

We managed to obtain a toy chimp from a toy box, a length of rope and a banner which read, 'The Monkey was innocent!' As the teams ran out onto the pitch we unfurled the banner and ran up the monkey on our makeshift gallows. As the monkey swung in the breeze, much to our surprise the visiting fans gave us a round of applause.

Karl Groome

Steve Wignall was one of my favourite managers to work with and one who was exceptionally successful in getting the U's promoted. He was a mild mannered and lovely man to work with. I remember Tony Lock, who could never get a run in the side, came on as sub in one match and scored the winner. In my report on the game, I wrote, 'maybe he'll get a start next time'.

Steve tore into me afterwards and said 'You don't pick the team, I do!' He had never lost his cool before with me, but it reminds you what is at stake for managers and how much pressure they are under. We do sometimes forget that, as journalists, because we are always looking for an angle.

Neil Kelly of BBC Essex

All my great memories with over 30 years on the terraces and later the family seating were eclipsed when I sneaked into the ground under the pretence of showing my girlfriend the new family end seating (about 1994, I guess). On the old Barside I proposed to her. She accepted and we now have two avid Colchester United season ticket holders of our own.

Steve Bishop

My first memory of Layer Road is of my dad paying through a window to get into the Family Enclosure and then walking round the back of the soccer centre to get into the ground. It was before the roof had gone up over part of the terrace and I remember really enjoying it. I was ready to go home at half-time, however, as I did not understand why we had to stay after the players had gone off already!

The place has obviously changed since then. I remember the Clock End being built, around the time that Scott McGleish was on loan and did his back flip goal celebration. There was just a huge mound of earth behind the goal for ages!

I have managed to watch games from every part of the ground, apart from the away end of course, and I spent the last seven seasons or so standing in Terrace Four, which was a mixture of all sorts of supporters.

Duncan Stonehouse

Carl Marston selects his favourite match from his last 16 seasons as the U's' correspondent for *The East Anglian Daily Times***:**

Ian Holloway, who was the manager of Bristol Rovers at the time, proved to be the master of under-statement following his side's dramatic 5–4 defeat at Layer Road on 8 January 2000.

Colchester United marked their first game of the new Millennium with one of the most amazing games of football ever staged at their famous old ground. It will always remain my favourite Layer Road match. The headline in the following Monday's *EADT*, exclaimed 'United's new year epic!', alongside the banner 'nine goals and a last-gasp Colchester win.' But beaten manager Holloway did not get carried away. 'It was a good game for the neutral,' conceded Holloway, who is now the boss at Leicester City.

Well, it was a GREAT GAME for everybody except the few hundred Rovers fans who had made the 200-mile trip eastwards and for Holloway and his players. The new Millennium had peaked after just eight days!

And so where to start? Steve McGavin and Karl Duguid both bagged a brace, each of them netting candidates for goal-of-the-season, but it was Lomana Lua Lua who made it such a special day. Lua Lua, already installed as the darling of Layer Road, leapt off the substitutes' bench to provide this Nationwide Division Two clash with one final twist, an 89th-minute winner.

For Rovers, Jason Roberts boosted his tally for the season to 18 goals with a brace, while a diminutive striker by the name of Jamie Cureton had a day to remember and also a day to forget! Current Norwich City striker Cureton, who ironically made Layer Road his home in the 2006–07 season (scoring 24 goals for the U's to win the Championship's Golden Boot), converted a penalty and missed another. His 65th minute spot-kick misery was to prove crucial because had he scored then Rovers would have been 4–2 up and coasting.

Substitute Nathan Ellington halted a superb U's fight-back with an 86th minute equaliser, to make it 4–4, but Steve Whitton's entertainers were to have the last laugh, Lua Lua in particular.

It was 1–1 at the break, with little suggestion of what was to come. Blink and you would missed a goal.

All of the goals were major talking points. Roberts put Rovers 2–1 up, courtesy of a dreadful back pass by U's centre-half David Greene, and Ipswich Town loanee Titus Bramble's afternoon was summed up by his mis-timed tackle on David Pritchard in the box. Bramble was booked for the challenge, which meant that he faced a suspension, and Cureton dispatched the penalty to hand the visitors a 3–1 lead. Bramble later hobbled off injured.

The first goal-of-the-season contender arrived just after the hour mark, with McGavin curling a delightful long-range shot into the far corner of the net. Cureton then struck the bar from his second penalty and Duguid made him pay by firing home an 80th minute equaliser for 3–3.

By now it was end-to-end, thrills-and-spills stuff. Duguid blasted the U's 4–3 up with a stunning right-footed pearler from just outside the box, only for Ellington to seemingly rescue a point for Rovers.

Cue Lua Lua! The Congalese striker had hardly touched the ball before he somehow managed to deceive three defenders and squeeze a shot past 'keeper Lee Jones.

The noise was deafening.

A view of the main stand, so often packed to capacity.

In fact, it was later confirmed that the roars which greeted Lua Lua's winner, and then the final whistle, could be heard by shoppers in the town centre outside Marks & Spencer. U's supporters will have to scream a little louder if they want to be heard by Saturday afternoon shoppers next season. Cuckoo Farm is perhaps a little out of ear-shot, even for them!

Match details:

Date: 8 January 2000

Score: Colchester United 5 Bristol Rovers 4

Goals, U's: McGavin (37 & 62), Duguid (80 & 82), Lua Lua (89). *Rovers:* Roberts (12 & 47), Cureton (59 pen), Ellington (86)

U's squad: Brown, Dunne, Keith, Greene, Skelton, Bramble (sub Arnott, 69), G. Johnson, D. Gregory, McGavin (sub Opara, 90), Dozzell (sub Lua Lua, 67), Duguid.

Attendance: 4,482

Carl Marston

One game that stands out, putting aside the Cup games and the promotion-winning games, was the unforgettable match against Bristol Rovers which was the first game in 2000. Most of us were struggling with hangovers and too much food in our bellies on New Year's Day. This was just another game, it seemed, but that is the magic of watching live football.

Neither side were necessarily promotion chasing outfits, but the game came to life in the second half and you would not have wanted to be anywhere else that day. The U's won 5–4, and Lua Lua was sublime and unplayable. They just could not get the ball off him. It was a cracker that no one anticipated; even at half-time the fans were thinking it was a decent but not amazing match. They knew though, by the final whistle, that they had seen a fantastic game of football.

Neil Kelly of BBC Essex

As Layer Road has been my second home since I was knee high, the place has so many memories. Some of my favourites are:

The 5–4 win over Bristol Rovers with, unless it just felt like it at the time, three last-minute goals.

A 7–1 thumping of Lincoln City in 1996, when Tony Adcock, Steve Whitton, Paul Abrahams and Chris Fry all scored, with two penalties from John Taylor when he wore a 'Robbie Fowler' nose plaster. I was in the Main Stand for that game after winning some tickets. It was my first time anywhere else in the ground other than the Family Enclosure so it was pretty special for me!

The 5–1 win over Macclesfield, which showed how far we had come. My memories of the game are that it was before names appeared on the backs of the shirts. We were in the thick of the play-off chase and Aaron Skelton scored a trademark belter from about 35 yards. Mark Sale scored a great volley in that game as well and the feel-good factor was flowing through the whole team. It was the game when I think everyone started to believe we could get promotion from Division Three.

I have got good memories from all parts of the ground, despite the fact that back in my younger days standing in Terrace Three or Four you had to rely on someone telling you what was happening in the far corner.

There was often a really special atmosphere at Layer Road. We all know it was not the smartest of grounds and away fans turned their noses up at everything, but it has been home to my team and it has been home to me and my mates. As much as I know we need a new ground, I will miss the old place. I probably was not alone as a little tear rolled down my cheek when the final whistle blew on the 'Layerdrome'.

Duncan Stonehouse

Due to my work, shortly after our promotion back to the League I was exiled to sunny Dartmoor and since then I have become a fanatical follower of the U's. I have a home season ticket and have increased my away support. My memories have also been enhanced by the fact I teach 11 to 18-year-old Devon football fans so as you can imagine Kinsella's winning goal against Argyle on the first day of the season while playing with 10 men was particularly sweet (as was the Play-off Final win against Torquay, and a 0–0 draw at West Country Yeovil although these were away from Layer Road).

Ralph Wickenden of Dartmoor

David Greene acknowledges the fans after the U's reach the Play-off final with victory over Barnet in 1998.

The drinks are on Carl Emberson as the U's head to Wembley.

Great games that I remember include:
- A 1996–97 game against Peterborough in the Auto Windscreen Shield which finished 3–0. Paul Abrahams' golden goal took us to Wembley.
- A 1997–98 game against Barnet in the Division Four Play-off which finished 3–1. A tense night of great excitement in which David Gregory's goal in extra-time to send us to Wembley again.

My all-time best team across the years:

Goalkeeper	Mike Walker
Defenders	Micky Cook, Wayne Brown, Steve Dowman, Brian Hall
Midfield	Colin Garwood, Mark Kinsella, Steve Leslie, Mick Mahon
Strikers	Bobby Svarc, Bobby Gough
Substitutes:	
Goalkeeper	Graham Smith
Defenders	Bobby Cram, Tony English
Midfield	Steve Foley, Richard Wilkins
Strikers	Tony Adcock, Brian Lewis
Manager	Dick Graham

Steve Leslie is my all-time favourite player; sheer quality, an eye for a goal and Colchester through and through, I consider it a privilege to have seen him play.

Very personal memories include:

A 1996–97 match against Peterborough in the Auto Windscreens Shield. It was probably the strangest experience that have ever had, when Paul Abrahams scored the winning golden goal it took a few seconds for it to sink in that we had won and then that we were actually going to Wembley. It must have taken me a little longer to realise what had happened because I looked around me and I was the only person still standing on the terrace for at least 10 yards either way. Everyone was on the pitch jumping up and down and celebrating a great night.

Keith Blaxall

Two of my fondest Layer Road memories are the Auto Windscreen semi-final golden goal win against Peterborough and the semi-final win against Barnet in the Play-offs, and I think that was the noisiest I ever heard Layer Road. The Barnet manager tried to get their fans going at half-time but they were just drowned out.

Paul Hurst

Steve Wignall is triumphant as the U's book a place at the Twin Towers in 1998.

Jose Antunes Fumaca (left) in action against Manchester City, the only game of his shortlived U's career.

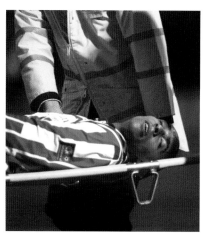

Jose Antunes Fumaca is stretchered off the pitch after his collision with Manchester City's Andy Morrison.

An off-the-wall yet totally genuine suggestion for the best performance by a U's player at Layer Road might be the Brazilian Jose Antunes Fumaca against Manchester City on 20 March 1999.

Fumaca was absolutely dazzling for what seemed like half an hour (but might have been much less) before being knocked unconscious going for a sensational header. The header clipped the bar, we lost 1–0, Fumaca ended up in hospital and was never heard of again at Layer Road. A difference of a centimetre or so and a fully-conscious Fumaca would have scored and gone on to become a Layer Road legend. Imagine Lua Lua and Fumaca playing alongside each other for the U's. It would have been Martyn King and Bobby Hunt all over again!

Chris Wright, Le Rouquet Nord, Maurens, France

One of the best and worst parts of my job is having to carry out interviews at the end of a game. It is the best part because of the access it provides to managers and players when they are on real highs, but it is also really difficult as well because within half an hour of gut-wrenching results which can cost a side a place in the Cup or threaten them with relegation or the manager with his job, you have to ask the difficult questions.

You are obliged to ask some fairly searching questions sometimes. What has been great about being here has been the access to the key people and the fact that they will talk, regardless of the result.

I stood there interviewing people and knew how significant some of their answers would be. I remember interviewing Steve Whitton, and although he did not always enjoy it he never complained. I remember interviewing him after the Blackpool game, talking to him knowing that the match has just cost him his job, and it reminded you that people's livings and livelihoods were at stake. All I can do is be as professional as possible and be as searching as possible as well.

Neil Kelly of BBC Essex

On Easter Monday 2003, I finally managed to take my youngest son to a match at Layer Road. Colchester, on a huge roll under recently-appointed Phil Parkinson, were playing Luton.

If only, like his dad, my boy's first match could result in a thumping 6–1 victory for the U's. The final score was U's 0 Luton 5. Needless to say, he has not asked to go again. Although, the upside of this (and correct me if I am wrong) is that I cannot think of any other home League match in which the U's have lost by five clear goals. All of which must make me one of the very small number of people who have witnessed both the U's greatest-ever League victory and the biggest-ever League defeat at Layer Road.

Chris Wright, Le Rouquet Nord, Maurens, France

The best time I had in my career was the time I spent at Colchester United. Layer Road was not only our home ground for games but was also my everyday place of work for over six and a half years.

My very first memory of Layer Road is from the early part of 1977, when I was taken to United's FA Cup tie against Derby County, which we drew before losing the replay. I was only seven and had no inkling that the place would become the main part of my football life years in the future.

David Gregory and Joe Dunne acclaim the supporters after reaching Wembley in 1998.

I have got to be honest and say that that game was only one of two – the other being the defeat against Manchester United – that I attended as a youngster. That was all to change in December 1995, however, when I became a U's player under the management of Steve Wignall.

It was not long before I was loving the games and the atmosphere at Layer Road as I became a regular in the U's midfield. There were plenty of noteworthy matches for me there but I do not think I would be short of correct answers if I asked which was my most memorable.

We were 1–0 down from the first leg of the Division Three Play-off semi-final, thanks to Greg Heald's effort for Barnet at Underhill. Guy Branston, who returned to Leicester after the first leg following his loan spell, did his bit and more for us by getting sent off with Barnet's Sean Devine in that first leg. Devine had been in excellent form for the Bees but was obviously suspended for the second leg due to his red card, giving us a bit of an advantage. We got back on level terms with an early penalty, my first spot-kick for the U's after taking over the role earlier in the season, but we went behind again just before half-time.

David Greene headed us level again on aggregate and the game went into extra time with us knowing we had to score or Barnet would go through on the away goals rule.

In the first-half of extra time Steve Forbes dribbled his way into the penalty area and toed the ball towards me before he got tackled. I hit it first time with my left foot and watched it hit the net before embarking on a run to the corner by Terrace Three. I have seen photographs and to say I looked a bit demented as I ran off would be an understatement!

Barnet were already down to 10 men and we held out pretty comfortably to book our second Wembley appearance in just over a year. Thoughts of erasing the memory of defeat against Carlisle the previous year came later that week but when the final whistle went against Barnet, it was pandemonium.

We were all engulfed by supporters and the emotion of it all was clear to see, with tears on the faces of fans of all ages. We managed to fight our way to the changing rooms but it was just as manic in there, with camera crews and journalists trying to get footage and interviews. We then went back out and up to the directors' box to acknowledge the supporters, before retiring back to the dressing room for the first of more than a few drinks.

There were plenty of other games that stick in the memory – against Wigan when I scored my first-ever U's goal, the 5–4 win against Bristol Rovers and a 4–3 win against Hull City all spring readily to mind. But the night of 13 May 1998 will still stand out above all the others.

David Gregory

I once offered to help to do up the dressing rooms and ended up with pneumonia! It all started with managing director Steven Gage when he was at the club in around 1999. He came to a CUSA meeting and asked for help to do up the dressing rooms. I volunteered my dad and he was promised help, and he got the wonderful Bill Chatten to work alongside him. I came down and helped him too when I was not at work, by filling in the baths, ripping everything out and ferrying it all into skips.

It prompted an even closer involvement with the club afterwards as Dad then stayed on in other positions. The work on the dressing rooms made a big change between home and away and you can see what it used to be like and what the playing staff had to work in. That was one of the good things that Mick Wadsworth did at Layer Road, ensuring the players' environment was improved. As with a lot of things at the time it was done by volunteers and people working for free, although Dad did get a season ticket as payment! As for me, all that fetching and carrying in the open air gave me pneumonia for my hard work.

Even my son Ben became involved, so it was a bit of family affair at the time. It became the story of my life with Colchester United and I got involved with the supporters' association soon after and eventually I ran the Corner Bar and organised the away travel.

CUSA asked the club if we could have the Corner Bar. The original CUSA before we reformed had owned that space and given it to the club and it used to be a supporters' bar many years previously.

I was not on the committee then but had worked in pubs before and volunteered to run the bar. We ran it from then until the end of Layer Road's existence. My very first customer was Alan White's dad and he and Alan became real regulars. The bar grew in popularity from there. We got real ale in and got another type of clientele, and it was always special because people from all parts

Dave Blacknall and his assistant show off their work on the Layer Road pitch.

of the ground came together there and met up before the game. It was always a friendly place if the players did come up and see us, and it was almost never a place for criticism. Most of the comments you heard were never overly critical or negative about the team. It was all long-time fans who just wanted to support the boys and the club.

We eventually had to extend into the old kitchen as the bar was getting so popular. We used to have the odd away supporters pop in and say 'Hi' and they also enjoyed the atmosphere. Stoke fans came in a couple of times and we also let them in on the last day. Swedish U's fans had also popped in and it had been a good mix of people, with the Northern Ireland supporters and our northern exiles coming in too, of course.

It was a very special place decorated with banners and pennants from other clubs, and those of us that worked up there did it for the love of the club. We also sold programmes and took travel bookings at the same time.

The Corner Bar summed up Layer Road in one room. It was a great space to bring everyone together and the friendships you built through socialising were built to last.

We also assisted groundsman David Blacknall with equipment, trailers, ground maintenance gear and so on. We have also bought physiotherapy equipment including heart rate monitors, ice baths and so on, with some of that coming from the membership fees. We have always tried to work very closely with the club with any profit from food etc being transferred to the club, sometimes in sponsorship of the youth team, for example. In the final season at the ground, for example, we sponsored five players.

We also paid to improve the ladies' toilets. People at first did not think it was necessarily the best idea, but the fact is we needed to have fairly pleasant toilets to encourage women and children to the ground. It was all about using money to improve the fans' facilities within the limitations of Layer Road.

Jeanette Westlake

The turnstiles await their first visitors on a matchday.

The Layer Road floodlights rise into the sky.

The new floodlights are installed at the Layer Road End – the towers were eventually taken to the new stadium.

A view of the front of the ground at the Barside corner; the windows above lead to the Corner Bar.

This way to a vocal afternoon out!

The steps leading out of the Barside.

My first experience of corporate hospitality came in what was later to become the Corner Bar. I was talking to Big Roy as he leant up against the bar telling stories that I could not possibly repeat!

Towards the end, the one thing I do miss very much is indeed the Corner Bar. It became a special place for many fans to socialise before and after the match. Being able to look out onto the wonderfully kept hallowed turf before kick-off, meeting friends and talking football gave supporters a real feeling of belonging and camaraderie.

I was fortunate enough to have experienced every area of the ground at some point or another. I particularly enjoyed being in the TV gantry on many occasions, recording various games and events and seeing the match from a different perspective. Even on a cold, wet and windy night, climbing those steps and walking across that roof was special. It was hallowed ground wherever you went.

Paul Ost

I have been selling programmes since 1998 and in that time I have seen plenty of things behind the scenes. You get to meet a lot of people along the way when you are selling the programmes, and, in a way, you are privileged because you get to see a bit of what goes on behind the scenes.

Ian Craig

The first eight years of watching the U's for me was spent in the Family Enclosure with friends that lived close to the ground, as I did. During the Conference days I remember celebrating a goal while holding a hot dog, when suddenly the hot dog flew up in the air and on its return I managed to catch it – although it was by then minus the onions! I also remember soaking a few fans with an exploding can of coke during the same season.

The following season everything changed for me as I joined Hospital Radio Colchester as a commentator in the box on the roof of the Main Stand, and that was the beginning of a 16-year love affair with the Layer Road commentary box.

My first game in the commentary box was the 3–0 win over Chesterfield in September 1992, the perfect debut for what lay ahead. The commentary box in 1992 was shared between radio commentators and the tannoy announcer. I remember the ceiling was sinking because of the ramshackle TV gantry above but amazingly nobody ever came through the ceiling to join us.

One of the great commentary box memories for me was describing the winner by Paul Abrahams in the Auto Windscreens Shield against Peterborough and the amazing pitch invasion that followed. It was a great sight to see the fans from the Barside and the rest of the ground rushing towards the Main Stand.

I returned to Hospital Radio in 2001 and continued just like the years before based in the famous box. It is that very box that I will miss most about Layer Road. I have spent many hours in there on a matchday before taking the unique walk along the roof in the dark after the floodlights had been turned off. There

Steve McGavin scores for the U's in the 5-4 win over Bristol Rovers in January 2000.

Steve McGavin curls in his second of the match.

Karl Duquid scores in the second half of the win over Bristol Rovers.

Karl Duquid scores his second.

are many members of the visiting media that have been guided along the roof and down the ladder by me in the darkness – it could only happen at Layer Road.

Dave Buckingham

My first visit to Layer Road was for a Friday night game in September 1997 against Scarborough. It was a 1–0 win thanks to a Tony Locke volley about four minutes from the end. The crowd was about 2,700 strong and I stood in the Family Enclosure with my dad.

Other matches that I recall from those early days are a 1–0 win against Chester in December in front of only around 1,700 fans and a match against Scunthorpe who fought back from being 3–0 down to get a 3–3 draw.

One of my most memorable matches was the Play-off semi-final against Barnet when we were 1–0 down from the first leg but came back to win an exciting encounter 3–1, with David Gregory getting the crucial goal in extra-time. At the end of the match everyone was on the pitch singing and chanting in a good natured way.

Lomana Tresor Lua Lua scores a dramatic late winner against Bristol Rovers.

Lomana Tresor Lua Lua celebrates his winning goal in the game against Bristol Rovers in January 2000.

The most extraordinary match I ever witnessed at Layer Road was the 5–4 win against Bristol Rovers. It was 1–1 at half-time and we were soon 3–1 down, but then we came back to win an incredible match in which Jamie Cureton missed a penalty for Rovers.

Trevor Wade

The 1990s saw a return to the League again and I remember being on the pitch (along with most supporters I guess) at the end of the game against Barrow. From that point forward we started to build slowly and there were also the Wembley appearances to enjoy (although the Carlisle result was not what we had hoped for).

Under Peter Heard's stewardship the club consolidated and we had our first multi-million pound player – what a turn around from those dim distant days of my first visits to the ground, when decent players joined to secure housing for their families and nothing was paid to them between the end of one season and the start of the next.

Recent memories include the epic game against Bristol Rovers that we won 5–4, and the match was played during Titus Bramble's loan spell and he hit an opposing player who I thought might have expired on the pitch!

Colin Willsher

In my second spell at Colchester United we did not have the best team and Steve Whitton and Geraint Williams did well keeping us in the division. I think back now to some of the players that Steve inherited and I do not know how we won a game! We were pretty strong going forward with Lua Lua, Doogie and myself up front getting plenty of goals.

That leads me to the game against Bristol Rovers, possibly one of the greatest games at Layer Road. The game was non-stop with penalty misses and loads of goalmouth incidents besides the goals. I scored two, Doogie got two and the enigmatic Lomana came off the bench to seal the winner. What a game it must have been to watch!

I could have picked many other games; Wycombe at home 3–0 in the Conference, me playing for Wycombe winning at Layer Road 2–1 in the FA Cup and getting slaughtered by the Barside (thanks boys!), but overall I have lots of great memories to cherish.

Steve McGavin

My first game was on a Friday night at home to Rochdale in Nationwide Football League Division Three on 21 March 1997. I had never really taken any interest in going to support a team, though I had developed a love for football after watching the Italia '90 World Cup tournament. During early 1997 I had

Steve McGavin in action in front of the main stand.

been watching *Anglia News* regularly. Not that that was particularly unusual except that I lived in Basildon. They would often show clips of some lanky striker in a blue-and-white shirt making a nuisance of himself. That lanky striker turned out to be the legend that is Mark Sale.

One Friday afternoon my dad, who is not a football fan, said we were going up to Colchester to watch the game that evening. Having never been there, we set out early with a large road map and no idea what to expect. Colchester is only 45 minutes north of Basildon, however, so we got there without much of a problem. We did stop twice to ask for directions when we got near the town, though, and the first person we stopped had never heard of Colchester United and the second told us we were going the wrong way (he was wearing a U's shirt and walking in the opposite direction).

We approached the ground from Boadecia Way and drove past the stadium. The floodlights were the first part of the ground I saw and as we drove past I commented on how small the ground was.

We managed to find a parking space on the housing estate somewhere nearby and walked up Layer Road for the first time, a walk I would be doing many times over the next 11 years. Outside the ground was a bloke selling programmes, and I just had to have one. What a bad move that turned out to be! I now have a stack of programmes from every game I have been to since.

The ground seemed even smaller when we joined the queue to get into the Family Stand. We eventually got through the old blue turnstile and found a small café area with white plastic seating serving tea in polystyrene cups (which I took home and still have).

We made our way into the Family Stand. The ground seemed really small, the roofing was low and you stood really close to the pitch. But the ground looked great under the floodlights and there was a good atmosphere before the game. I stood on the terracing reading the programme and someone asked me what I thought the score would be. I explained it was my first game and I did not know what to expect. He made some comment about being unlucky if I got addicted to watching the U's. It would be my first experience of the friendly nature of the majority of U's fans, something I have enjoyed sharing with away supporters on many occasions since.

I do not remember the game being a classic, particularly the first half. However, in the second half the game went from end to end. Rochdale even had the ball in the back of the net but the linesman stood with his flag pointing towards Carl Emberson's area. The winning goal was scored by Paul Abrahams, who had recently scored a goal against Peterborough to send the U's to Wembley, and his low drive from the edge of the area squeezed under the Rochdale 'keeper and into the goal in front of the Clock End.

The ground erupted as the players celebrated. Paul Abrahams was announced as the goalscorer and the crowd erupted again.

From that point onwards I was hooked. Everything about the experience was brilliant. I had a programme to read and to act as

The sun sets over Layer Road as the fans wait for the second half to begin.

The U's take the lead as Rowan Vine smashes home this effort in the first half against Coventry in the 2003 FA Cup.

a reminder of the night. The smell from inside the ground and even the smell of tea in the small café, the atmosphere, the expletives sang by the Barside and winning all made it a great night and afterwards I could not wait to go back.

James Nason

I have heard a story that Paul Parker (who played for England at the San Siro in a World Cup semi-final) found himself as a Fulham player sitting in the shabby surroundings of Layer Road dressing-room after a 2–1 defeat on a wet January Tuesday night and thought, 'how on earth can it have come to this?' He hung up his boots shortly afterwards!

Chris Wright, Le Rouquet Nord, Maurens, France

My favourite place for working at Layer Road was behind the dugouts from 1992 to 2000. That was great because it was like having someone pitchside, because you had a great view of the whole of the pitch and the interaction of the players, managers and officials. The disadvantage was you got just a bit too close and there are a couple of examples that come to mind.

Colchester were at home to Scunthorpe and Richard Money was the manager of Scunny at the time. We had tried to buy

Rowan Vine is the hero after the U's beat Coventry City in the FA Cup.

U's fans step up their efforts for a new stadium in the town ahead of a U's home fixture in 2004.

Layer Road begins to get busy as fans arrive for a home matchday.

The Main Stand looks on.

Steve Brown from Southend but he had gone there instead. He never settled up there, came back to Layer Road and could not stop scoring for the club upon his arrival.

Steve then scored the winner in that game and I had to write my report to file for the game. In my report, I alluded that he scored the goal after being released by Richard Money, and when I filed my report Richard was over my shoulder and he had a go at me after I had finished. He said that Steve's transfer came about because he had repeatedly knocked on his office door and kept asking for a move back down south. 'Why don't you tell people that?', Richard exclaimed. He apparently had not had a chance to reveal that before then.

Neil Kelly of BBC Essex

A panoramic view down the back of the Main Stand at Layer Road.

The Barside make their message clear as the campaign for a
new stadium gathers speed in 2004.

My favourite memory is from when we played Coventry
and won 3–1 in the FA Cup. I thought it was going to be
the usual 'they're a bigger team, we'll lose' scenario but
we fought and carried on fighting all through the match
and won.

The hat-trick from Rowan Vine made the result even
more spectacular because they were three good, very
good, goals. And the celebration after each goal and the
final whistle was good as well, you got squashed in the
Family Enclosure but it was just another thing to love
about the ground. RIP Layer Road.

Laura Aylott

Rowan Vine takes the acclaim after scoring a hat-trick to dump
Coventry out of the FA Cup in 2003.

Not even getting married, starting a family and moving to St Albans could keep me away from watching the U's.

My son Tim, who now accompanies me to many games, was even mascot for Steve Wignall's first game in charge at home
to Barnet in January 1995. My wife Valerie and daughter Caroline both made it to the match for the first time, making it a
true family day out.

Dave Amoss

Chapter 13

An incredible promotion season, and a party that started in the West Country and continued on the Town Hall balcony

The moment that made me realise the effect Layer Road had had on me was when Colchester were going for promotion and played Hartlepool on a Tuesday night, needing the three points. Hartlepool were battling for relegation, and during my commentary, in a pulsating game, they hit the woodwork a number of times. Late on, a player who had been on loan at Hartlepool, Neil Danns, popped up with two late goals to pick up a crucial win for the U's. I have to say, hand on heart, I would not have had the result any other way.

Neil Kelly of BBC Essex (formerly of Hartlepool)

I am a Reading fan who has been introduced to the delights of the U's by my penfriend, who is true blue Col U. Needless to say this has been an unbelievable season of double delight for both of us. We went to the Hartlepool and Rotherham home games and I would be pleased to do a hundred words on either of these games for you. After the Rotherham game we drove back to Reading to take in the Reading versus QPR game and the presentation of the Championship trophy the very next day.

I was pleased to chat and shake hands with my old hero Parky at the end of the Hartlepool game. He is such a level headed and open chap – I do not believe how we let him go so easily, but I suppose our loss was your gain on that one.

Hartlepool (H)

The U's heroes celebrate their elevation to the Championship with a tour around town on 8 May 2006.

A strange one
And one on which so much depends
Twice rearranged
Now on a miserable Tuesday night
Some fixture-maker's humour
Matching Tuesday night at Hanger Park
U's coming off one win in ten
Desperately seeking to resurrect the challenge
Needing points to stay up
Pools show in dismal black
Of all referees
It had to be Trevor Kettle
Woodwork hit in many painful moments
Nightmare defeat potentially looming
Keep on plugging and plugging away
A shaft of light
Hanger's Williams sent off
More frantic plugging
Time running out
Salvation!
Invisible all night
Dannsy wakes to put two away
One last twist
Davison spills over his line
Mr Kettle waves play on
And that's it
2–0 to the U's
The strangest and best 3 points so far

Ted Matthewson

When my son Joseph was aged four we decided to start getting into football. We got a complimentary ticket for the U's versus Yeovil Town game in October 2005 when Joseph joined the Eddie the Eagle club. We stood in the Family Enclosure and loved every minute, and being at that game was amazing for both of us. We were instantly hooked. Not only that, we won the game too!

We went on to watch more games, including beating Ipswich at home in an exciting game that was also Joseph's first late-night kick-off. Another win. Joseph seemed to be a lucky mascot every time we went.

We also went to Stamford Bridge and sung our hearts out from the moment we got into the ground until we left, overwhelmed by our experience. We also went into the High Street to watch the triumphant boys move up. What a season to join, magical. We have been going ever since.

On Joseph's sixth birthday he was a mascot at the ground and he was bowled over. Such a U's fan. He wants to play for Col U when he is older above any other club. Joseph trains weekly and learns football skills at Layer Road.

I am an East End girl originally but have lived in Colchester for the last 20 years and I am now a U's supporter. We will miss the old ground, but we are destined for greater things. Come on you U's.

Alison Zammit and Joseph Holmes

I remember chatting amicably to a 'Blue' who had sneaked into the Main Stand for the 0–3 humiliation against Southend in 2006.

I also remember Parky screaming at the Main Stand for daring to criticise the U's' time-wasting tactics…

Nick St George

Nine minutes of magic; the U's take the lead against Chelsea in the first half of the FA Cup match.

Neil Danns tracks Frank Lampard in the U's' FA Cup clash with Chelsea in February 2006.

When my grandchildren were old enough to go to Layer Road I became a regular again, and what a season to go back! Top two in League One, Chelsea in the Fifth Round of the FA Cup and not yet season ticket holder. I queued up from 4am in the pouring rain to get tickets; it was definitely worth it! The crowd at the Shed End were just amazing; Stamford Bridge had never seen the like. We lost 3–1 after leading 1–0. It was a truly astonishing day!

Can anything else inspire lifelong memories like football can? Getting the new stadium is not just a matter of life or death, it is much, much more than that to thousands of people throughout Colchester and all of the surrounding area. We will all miss Layer Road, but only for sentimental reasons!

Tony Vaughan

After 40 years on the terraces I joined the vice-presidents and saw another side of Layer Road that had been a complete mystery until then, the Main Stand, the vice-presidents' and directors' boxes. The conversations were still the same, though. Everybody always knows what the team and tactics should be and where the manager went wrong!

Continued progress followed, and Parky, with his wife and three kids often present in the directors' box, took us to dreamland. We were in the Championship! What a great place to finish our years at Layer Road!

It did not matter where you stood or sat at Layer Road, everyone was passionate about Colchester United. We all have our memories and are grateful for them. Thanks for those fantastic memories, they will not be forgotten!

For the club to be where it is today is a great achievement and I would like to take this opportunity to thank some people for what they have given to the club. Firstly Peter Heard for rescuing us and steering us to the Championship. Secondly John Schultz, who has been a great unsung ambassador for the club, and thirdly Marie Partner who did a great job, always with a cheery personality, since before our Conference days. Finally to all the diehard supporters who appreciate just how special our years at Layer Road have been.

Mike Gadbury

The last home game in the promotion season of 2005–06 was memorable, of course, not least because Wayne Brown scored with a flighted free-kick. You could tell the lads were running on nearly empty, but they still had the determination to hang on for the three points.

Dave Appleby, Nottingham

So to some unbelievable seasons. Terrace Three has been my home for the most exciting times at the old ground. Great nights under the lights, WBA and Coventry City dispatched in dramatic Cup ties, the promotion dash culminating on that warm Saturday afternoon with the defeat of Rotherham to leave our fate in our own hands.

John Grimwade

I have a confession to make. During the 2005–06 season my family and I purchased three season tickets for the Family Enclosure, and by the time we got to the last few games of this monumental season we were taking at least 10 additional people into the ground with us.

 Let me try to explain. I am a third generation supporter, with my grandparents having attended way back when the stadium opened. My kids, Billy and Lucie, were there with me when it all came to a close so we have experienced the whole lifespan of Layer Road within our family history. The additional people we sneaked in through the turnstiles were in fact the family ghosts and spirits, who I am sure all attended those last fixtures. In fact, how could the U's fail against Rotherham on the last home game; the official attendance for that day was 5,741 but I believe it should have been recorded at 57,410 at least.

 How could we fail with every U's supporter that ever existed roaring the team to victory?

 The game was a blur as many were that season but I can still see Yeatesy swallow diving towards the corner flag in celebration of the second goal, an act which was to cut his season prematurely short with a shoulder injury!

 So to Yeovil; Billy and I managed to secure tickets and joined the convoy south. I have three brief memories of that day: Gerken's awesome near-post save, champagne in the car park and a 4ft tall alien regaled in a Col U shirt standing proud through a car's sunroof as it disappeared back Essex bound!

Captain Karl Duguid is overcome with emotion as the U's are promoted to the Championship.

Young fans celebrate promotion at Yeovil in May 2006.

As I write this, of course, more memories come flooding back from over the years. Bouncing on the boards behind the Layer Road goal, Reg Stratton versus WBA, my all-time favourite Brian Hall, the *Post Horn Gallop*, Friday night fixtures, the Conference years, over the wall versus Barrow and the upward climb since then.

 Thank you Granddad for that first visit in 1961, thank you Gran for the knitted hat and scarf and thank you Layer Road for everything. In years to come when the new houses are built on the hallowed ground I am sure if residents stand in their gardens on a damp Friday evening in Winter they will catch the strong fragrance of liniment on the breeze and hear the distance echo, 'Up the U's, up the U's, Up the U's…'

Paul Dickinson

When I arrived at work on the Monday after the glorious day at Yeovil, my boss's PA could not wait to ask me 'What was the matter with you? Everyone else in the photograph is smiling, but you look so serious'. She explained that she was talking about a photo of the crowd behind the goal in that morning's *East Anglian Daily Times*.

It was a day or two before I worked it out. Everyone else had been enjoying the moment as the players went crazy down at the front of the terrace, but my eyes were on Karl Duguid, 'Mr Colchester United', who was cutting a solitary figure far away to our left, silently shedding a few tears of pure emotion.

Jim French

U's fans make Stamford Bridge a sea of colour during the FA Cup tie against Chelsea.

My mum thought it would be a good idea to get me interested in football when I was young. Then aged four, I got a complimentary ticket when I joined the Eddie the Eagle Club. Armed with our first ticket, Mum and I went to our first game. It was Saturday 29 October 2005, Col U vs Yeovil Town.

We were in the Family Stand and got our place down the front. There were lots of other kids shouting out and Eddie the Eagle came round and gave me a high five. I was so happy about that. The game was a three o'clock kick-off. Mum and me loved that game and were instantly hooked. We won the game 3–2 and I think mum had a tear in her eye.

We went on to watch more games including the night of the derby when we beat Ipswich at home. It was an exciting game as it was also my first late-night kick-off. Mum said I must be the U's' lucky mascot as every time I went we won.

On Sunday 19 February 2006 I saw Chelsea versus Colchester United. With our balloons in hand we sung our hearts out from the moment we got into Stamford Bridge until we left, totally overwhelmed by our experience. We were so proud of our performance.

On Monday 8 May 2006 in the High Street my mum and I watched as the triumphant boys paraded up the High Street. What a season to join, magical. We have been going ever since.

Since then Mum and me have continued to go to games. I have also been a mascot for the U's. That was a great moment for me and I especially enjoyed touring the changing rooms and seeing all the shirts of my favourite players hanging up before the game.

I learn football skills at Layer Road every week. I will miss going there but as mum says, the U's are destined for greater things. Come on the U's.

Joseph Holmes, aged 7

Fans throng the High Street as they wait to greet their promotion heroes.

U's players celebrate in the dressing rooms at Yeovil Town in May 2006.

I parked well away from the town centre on the night of the open-top bus parade celebrating promotion to Championship. Walking along Crouch Street, I bumped into Neil Partner, the chief executive's husband.

Ever since the afternoon at Yeovil I had felt a degree of fear and trepidation about the U's facing Championship opponents every week. It is exactly the same feeling that I had 35 years earlier on learning that we would be facing Leeds United. I had to ask Neil the question that was troubling me: 'Do you think we can hold our own in the Championship?'

Neil's reply was that he had been talking to a good friend who knew all about Colchester and was working for a Championship club, and he was told that that if we organised ourselves properly defensively then we would comfortably hold our own. I did not know it then, but those words of wisdom were searingly accurate and would tell the story of our two-year stay in the Championship.

After the euphoric open-top bus parade, I spent an hour or so in the Wig and Pen before walking back down the High Street, just to savour the moment with the crowds long since gone. As I walked past Marks and Spencer, Phil Parkinson and Stuart Ayles ran across the street towards me, in search of a taxi having just left the town hall.

I gave a message of congratulations to Stuart from a mutual friend in the non-League. Something about Phil and Stuart's demeanour made me wonder whether they had just completed their last public duty as employees of Colchester United. I tried to dismiss the thought.

Jim French

Manager and captain celebrate the U's promotion on the Town Hall balcony.

Neil Danns celebrates putting the U's in front against Nottingham Forest in January 2006.

I have been watching the U's since 1974, going along with my dad during the 1970s and 1980s until I moved away from Essex. Ahhh, jumpers for goalposts, Johnny Froggatt, Steve Dowman's afro, Colin Garwood in the 95th minute – do you know what I mean?

Anyway, back to 2006. Although I was still making it back to sunny Colchester on a fairly regular basis to watch the mighty U's, obviously interest went up during 2005–06 as it turns out we were pretty much unbeatable. A couple of memories of that season stay with me in particular...

The first memory is U's versus Nottingham Forest, 2 January 2006. My main memory of this match is that...I did not see it. Having come back to Colchester to visit the family, I thought I would take in a U's game as usual. So me and my brother-in-law took the short walk to the ground at about 2.55pm (Mum still lives very close to Layer Road – I could see the floodlights from my bedroom window when growing up) and strolled confidently up to the turnstile only to find...the back of a queue around 300 yards from the turnstile.

It did not look good. My brother-in-law (not from round here...) obviously did not believe that the game was 'sold out'. I could honestly say that it has never happened in over 30 years of going to Layer Road. There was only one thing for it, we headed to the Drury Arms.

We made it to the bar at 3.05pm, just as they were closing. We pointed out that they were in for a bit of a bonus – the game was a sell-out and a load of disappointed fans would be heading their way for a couple of beers. Record profits are surely on the cards?

The reaction from behind bar was not as we expected – we were asked to take our beers and sit quietly in the corner while they battened down the hatches and pretended no one was in. Now, I have been in a few lock-ins in my time...but never at 3pm in the afternoon!

Events got more surreal when Sky Sports was replaced on the TV with another channel showing live Premiership football. On a Saturday afternoon? Surely some mistake? It turned out to be a foreign channel. Now, I do not even fully understand all the subtleties in the commentaries of your John Motsons or Jonathan Pearces, but Middlesbrough versus Newcastle in Arabic is something else entirely. But, back to the U's. Updates were still available on Sky Sports in the other bar and things were going OK as it looked like a dull 0–0. Things got even better when news arrived that Dannsy has put the U's in front. A dull 1–0 victory was the perfect result – three points for the U's but we did not miss anything too exciting. We headed safely back to coverage of Shearer of Arabia in the knowledge that all was well. Especially as we were arriving at the end of our fifth pint!

Suddenly the pub filled up with U's fans, all of whom had that post-match glow that only the satisfaction of victory can bring. We bumped into a couple of friends who sympathised that we missed the match. Though sympathy did not last long as they regaled with tales of injury-time derring-do and the legend of Garcia. It meant little to us though, as apparently 'you had to be there'. B***ards!

My second fond memory concerns the U's versus Port Vale game on 21 January 2006...aka 'The Legend of Garcia – Part 2'. Firstly an admission. I was never a fan of Garcia. It does shame me somewhat to say it, however, as obviously support for all players in the blue-and-white stripes is unconditional, and we cheer them all on, through thick and thin. But we all know that there are some players who we are quicker to criticise than others. Let us just say we do not quite like the cut of their jib, even though we do not quite know why.

I remember Ian Allinson being such a player, until one game in the early 1980s when he failed once more to get past the opposing full-back and got a mouthful of abuse. As he chased back, he turned to us all and replied with a nice, clear 'B*ll*cks, you w*nkers'. Talk about Oscar Wilde. Though I liked him far more after that – at least he cared.

Anyway, back to January 2006 and the legend of Garcia. Having booked early (to avoid disappointment), I found myself back on the terraces with my dad – just like the old days, only now it was me taking him to the football, rather than the other way around. We relived memories of promotion from Division Four in the late 1970s as we compared the merits of Dowman versus Brown, Leslie versus Danns and Froggatt versus Iwelumo…and Allinson versus Garcia.

Garcia was rubbish against Port Vale for most of the game. He got the ball…and promptly gave it away each time. 'Garcia, you're useless', someone shouted. Oops, it was me. Again. My dad just laughed (in the 1970s I would have got a clip round the ear) and nodded wisely.

What happened next? Well, obviously he goes and scores, doesn't he (Garcia, not my dad). And even though Vale equalised, Garcia went and scored another to seal the victory. I turned to Dad and tried to make myself heard above the roar of the crowd, 'that Garcia, he's useless!' And that was the last time I uttered those words, until the first home game against Barnsley in the Championship, when he made a mistake to give away their winning goal – but that is another story!

Warren Shaw

One U's fan celebrates as the U's go up at Yeovil Town.

Chapter 14 – 2006 to 2008

PUNCHING ABOVE OUR WEIGHT IN THE CHAMPIONSHIP

It is easy to focus on the first and last games, but the Championship season was extraordinary. There were so many amazing games, including the Colchester versus Ipswich game because it was really special for all involved. Especially fans who had been supporting the U's for years and have had neighbours driving up to Ipswich to watch higher division football. At last they were here and we beat them fair and square with Doogie scoring. It was a storybook game.

Another special game was the Sunderland fixture. They came here with Roy Keane having fashioned a side with a fair bit of quality and an excellent work rate. To many national observers, that self belief and ethic had set them apart from the rest. I was looking forward to seeing them at Layer Road because they were a side that played with those attributes. Colchester got in front, and even when Sunderland equalised the U's took a second breath and started taking the game to them again.

Roy Keane was not the best loser but he had no complaints that his side had been beaten by the better team on the day.

That season at Layer Road it did not matter about the state of the ground or the size of the crowd, or the fact that the U's had been in the lower divisions. Time and time again teams came down here and the U's took them apart. Watching the players at close quarters, you knew they were going to do it every time they stepped onto the field.

Despite the fact that the opposition knew what to expect, they simply could not handle the way Colchester played.

Neil Kelly of BBC Essex

Sunderland play at Layer Road, knowing a win will be enough to get them promoted. But the U's defeat Sunderland 3-1 in April 2007.

Early in our first Championship season, Derby, Sheffield Wednesday and the League leaders Cardiff were intimidated by Layer Road's 'cowshed' atmosphere while being totally overwhelmed on the pitch. By the end of 2006, other big name clubs were taking no chances.

The teams are greeted onto the pitch as Wolves come to town in December 2006.

The Barside back the U's in this home game. The chimney pot belongs to the houses behind...

In the urinals behind the Main Stand I once found myself adjacent to and soon in conversation with a smiling and evidently very relieved Wolves manager Mick McCarthy. Hygiene and etiquette perhaps determined that we did not shake hands, but the conversation was sufficiently friendly to elicit that Mick regretted his insurance policy of bringing down his entire squad.

The intake of pre-match fluids, the lengthy journey, the resultant massive queue at the players' facilities and the urgency of his need had evidently flushed him into the public domain. I think he muttered something like 'even my en-suite is bigger than this', while some wag commented 'by the way, we deliberately leave these taps running so your showers go cold'. Wolves lost the game, and I often wonder how much that had to do with mention of the muddy pitch and our plumbing within Mick's team talk.

Phil Wolski

As a true U's fan, I cannot truly explain the joy of the last three years, years summed up in one glorious moment as Dougie scored THAT GOAL against the team from up the road on Sky at the Layer Road End in front of those fans. The Barside that night, where I stand, was unbelievable and I can still remember how up everyone was for that match.

Ralph Wickenden of Dartmoor

Wolves fans look on as the U's defend a corner in the 2006-07 season.

The 2006–07 season speaks for itself. I remember Greg Halford's wonder strike against Sheffield Wednesday in that campaign that should have got every red blooded supporter going. The memories I carry from that time will still be fresh in the minds of current supporters. For me the 'they shall not pass' defending of Wayne Brown deserves a special mention.

Colin Willsher

A packed Family Enclosure and Barside as the U's play Wolves at Layer Road.

Although there have been many memorable games – the 3–2 win over Leeds and three Wembley appearances spring to mind – and individually there have been numerous players of whom I speak highly, I have no hesitation in saying that the 2006–07 side was the best to wear the U's colours with so much pride, skill, passion and commitment.

In February 2007, on the occasion of my 50th anniversary of watching my first game, I had the honour of sponsoring the match against Burnley, which we drew 0–0. I was very touched by the generous applause which greeted me before the match when I went onto the pitch. It was a very nice moment.

In March the following year I took my two young grandsons (Joseph aged six and Owen aged three) to watch their first game at Layer Road, so that in years to come they will be able to tell people that they watched the U's at 'the old ground'. Unfortunately, Wolves beat us by the only goal of the game.

As the town's MP I was very active in the campaign for the new ground. Prior to planning consent being won the club involved me on a regular basis. Perhaps the most important role I played was pursuing matters at Parliamentary level because of the delays in providing the infrastructure in North Colchester which had caused such a long wait for the Community Stadium. This in turn led to a crucial meeting at the House of Commons with a transport minister, which led to agreement for a future junction from the A12 into the site and the go-ahead for the stadium to be built in advance of the junction being provided.

I shall miss the old place. I have already persuaded the borough council, in the 'planning brief' it has prepared for the eventual residential development of the site, that it is important to retain a 'football' connection – for example, that the Estate Road should go through the Layer Road goal with brick posts on the precise site of the uprights and for the centre circle to be retained as a grassed roundabout.

Hopefully whatever is built on the site will reflect the past, and there is also a plaque commemorating the 100 years of football at Layer Road (from when it was first used as an army football pitch and then by Colchester Town before the professional Colchester United FC was formed in 1937).

Layer Road has been part of football talk not only in Colchester but throughout the world of football, at home and overseas. It will be missed. RIP.

Bob Russell, MP for Colchester

A lower-division club on form at home to a team struggling in the division above, a tight yet imposing ground, a partisan home crowd, one club stable and the other on the verge of meltdown – all the ingredients were there for a Cup shocker. And, from a Derby County perspective, shocker was the only suitable word to describe the events of Saturday 28 January 2006.

My first visit to Layer Road was eagerly awaited as it is always interesting to sample new surroundings, and it is one that will live long in the memory, though not necessarily for all the right reasons.

Arriving at the ground, we were greeted by the most helpful staff you could imagine and shown around the various places we needed to go.

'The dressing rooms are a bit tight,' commented one local. 'That's putting it mildly,' I thought as he opened the door.

As the players arrived you could see who was up for it and who was not. Sadly, most of the Rams on show that day were in the latter category, and the look on the face of Silva – a Brazilian striker more familiar with the big grounds in Portugal – as he surveyed the area, was one to behold.

Grounds like Layer Road are the type that I like. The stands are close to the pitch, the fans are all around you, and the away section is made up largely of a modest terrace, evoking memories of stadia some 15 years ago.

The press box, I think it is fair to say, was intimate, swelled by countless national journalists sniffing a Cup upset and a great story to fill their pages. They were not disappointed as Colchester turned up whereas Derby did not.

Indeed, such were the Rams' failings on the day, they were forced to throw on 38-year-old assistant manager Dean Holdsworth before half-time due to an injury to their only other senior striker. Holdsworth had been playing non-League football only a few months previously.

Colchester fully deserved their success with a performance of quality football at a tempo that was too hot for Derby to handle. Their three goals, scored in a 15-minute period either side of half-time, killed the game and sent the vast majority of the near-6,000 crowd into delirium.

Derby, for their part, could only muster a late penalty, though the game was already up and they were crashing out — and the same sentiments could also apply to their manager.

Richard Garcia is felled as the U's grab a third against Derby in August 2006.

Phil Brown had only taken charge the previous summer but things had not gone too well, and this defeat in Essex would ultimately be his last game in the hotseat. His final act was rather undignified. Verbally abused by an angry Derby fan during a live post-match interview with a local radio station, he was out of a job two days later.

So does that all cloud one's judgement when asked for memories of the venue? Not in the slightest. The staff at the ground, as mentioned earlier, could not have been more helpful and friendly, and they sorted anything that needed sorting with the minimum of fuss.

Layer Road itself was packed with character, it was packed with identity, and while Colchester's new home may be more aesthetically pleasing it will have to go some to have the impact of its predecessor.

Gareth Davis, web editor, Derby County Football Club

The first arrivals on a matchday walk down the back of the main stand.

The pull of the Barside drew me in as I got older, and I have spent most Saturday afternoons in recent years with friends who I met on those concrete terraces, singing at the top of our lungs and participating in joyous, uncontrollable bundles down the steps when we scored. What I have always loved about the Barside support is its ability on a good day to force managers to substitute shell-shocked opposition players due to targeted and sustained mockery. Chris Armstrong and Darren Huckerby were very memorable 'victims'.

Of course, standing next to the away end gives a great view of the visiting supporters, looking bemused at the hotchpotch stands and straining on tiptoes to get a view of the game. While they might sing their sarcastic tributes to our little home, I have always suspected that they secretly loved coming to a 'real' football ground.

Layer Road is a monument to a period of football that is, sadly, disappearing. Yes, the facilities were often atrocious, the view obscured and the rusty Barside roof leaky. But the place had a magic. Stadiums four or five times the size never generate the buzz of a big U's home game under floodlights in front of a ferocious support. Surrounded by streets and back gardens, it felt like a part of the town, quietly slotted in among the maze of local roads and houses.

Ben Wright

I never envisaged that we would spend two seasons in tier two of the Football League and finish the top side in East Anglia. I took my camera to the 'last game' at Layer Road about 20 years ago when we thought we were off to share with Wivenhoe, but now it has actually happened.

Paul Hurst

In the first-ever season in the second tier of English football we won 5–1 against Hull, beat all those big teams humbled at the Layerdrome and, of course, beat the team from Suffolk, with a tear in the eye and a lump in the throat.

Perhaps it is a fitting time to leave the 'ground that time forgot', create a new fortress in a 21st century stadium and make a new history. Layer Road, thanks for the memories.

John Grimwade

U's fans make their journey up Butt Road towards the ground.

The floodlights are on for one last time for the game against Hull City.

Eleven home wins on the trot in our first Championship season put us all in dreamland, and what an atmosphere we had for those games. I sat in the Clock End for some of those games with my wife and neither of us will ever forget the experience.

But my first and one of my last games at Layer Road were both with my dad, in 1–0 defeats against Wolves. The first was as a 10-year-old in 1980 for the Steve Leslie testimonial game, and my last Layer Road visit – again with my dad – was for the 1–0 defeat in our second season in the Championship.

David Clark

It was a birthday present from my wife to travel the 250 miles from where I now live in Devon to watch my last game at Layer Road against Coventry City and take a look behind the scenes at the dressing rooms and entrance into the Directors' Bar. Apart from the result (1–5) it was a superb day.

Tony Bryant of Cullompton

In 2007 if Sunderland had won at Layer Road they would have been promoted, but we delayed their success for another week by winning 3–1. After the game as I walked along Layer Road behind the Layer Road End for away supporters a Sunderland supporter inside the ground was leaning over the fence, talking to one of his mates who was still outside.

The conversation went thus (in a broad Wearside accent):

Sunderland fan outside said 'Ha'way lad wassit like inside mon?'

To which the Sunderland fan inside replied, 'Well pet, it's not like the Bernabeu!'

Bill Frame

The two seasons in the Championship were fantastic. The atmosphere in the ground was unbelievable in 2006–07. I stood on Terrace Three for 20 years and over the final few years at Layer Road the atmosphere got better and better. There was a buzz around the ground regardless of what was going on on the pitch.

Ian Craig

Good news in November 2006 as fans in the Town Hall hear that the new stadium has gained approval.

The Town Hall meeting in November 2006 sealed the fate of Layer Road, but I felt barely a twinge of regret as the councillors cast the votes that condemned our old home. How could it be otherwise? I was in the row immediately behind Peter Heard and saw the tear in his eye as he sat down after speaking. I was near enough to Marie Partner to feel her unbearable tension as her work came to fruition in front of her eyes. And I was near enough to the gentleman in his 80s who spoke passionately about the need to get away from Layer Road to grab him by the shoulder and thank him.

Jim French

Over the years, exchanges between players and spectators have continued, and on 1 March 2008 I witnessed yet another expression of opinions.

On the final whistle, someone at the Clock End shouted out an observation to the Wolves 'keeper Wayne Hennessy – and it was not very flattering – and I have it on camera. The expression on his face said it all.

Norman Spencer

With bigger crowds, extra facilities had to be drafted in behind the Clock End.

My last visit to Layer Road was in October 2007 and it was as if the gods had decreed that a special evening would be put on especially for my benefit. Four great goals and a victory over QPR brought an end to my love affair with what was a very special place.

Gordon Evans, Perthshire

For me the 2007 game against Sunderland was one of the very best I have ever seen at Layer Road. Fond memories. But now there is the problem of 'Where to sit at Cuckoo Farm?'

Terry Lawrence

My taste of Layer Road life was a brief one. But the two or so years I spent in its cosy press box were nothing if not eventful.

As the *Gazette's* U's reporter, I was lucky to be able to watch Colchester United play at the charismatic, intimate ground during arguably what was the most successful period in their eventful history.

Like a beating heartbeat in the town, Layer Road was a pulsating place to be during the U's' first-ever season in the second tier of English football.

The campaign had not started particularly well, though. Defeats in Colchester's opening two home games left some supporters fearing the worst. But a thrilling triumph over Derby County got the U's on track – and provided a taste of the thrills and spills that were to come in the eight months that followed.

The U's fans make Layer Road a sea of colour at the end of the first season in the Championship.

A run of 11 successive home wins left Colchester fans in ecstasy and had the old ground rocking. Goals rained in at regular intervals; the U's seemed impenetrable on their own territory. Their home, so often mocked by visiting fans perhaps more used to more salubrious surroundings, had become a fortress, as visiting teams invariably discovered to their cost.

'Welcome to Layer Road,' screamed the Barside with regularity.

It was a joy and a privilege to report on Colchester during that time.

Although there were some exciting away trips during that memorable season, it was their incredible home form that will stick in my mind.

It hardly seemed to matter that part of my view of the pitch was obscured by the police room, which was situated immediately next to the press box, or that fighting your way to pitchside for post-match interviews was rather like tackling an assault course, such was the throng of supporters weaving its way out of the ground upon the final whistle. These were key elements that made the venue what it was; they enhanced its character and offered a rare throwback to a bygone era when football supporting was a wholly different experience.

The season that followed that first Championship year was not nearly as successful on the pitch. It was almost as if the old ground knew that its lifespan was drawing to its natural end. Eventually, the beating heartbeat ceased and tears were shed. But the memories will remain forever.

Jon Waldron

Chapter 15 – April 2008

A FINAL FAREWELL TO LAYER ROAD

Standing at the back of the old Main Stand I was always transported back several decades. I only had to just half-close my eyes and it could just as easily be my first game in 1968. I still miss those green-painted 'proper' floodlight pylons.

I got down for the Stoke City game courtesy of a ticket from John Tweed – a terrace mate since the early 70s. It was very poignant as we made a gentle walk from the town centre down Butt Road, stopping at that point where you get your first glimpse of the floodlights – just too much emotion.

I thought the Preston game would be my last but I had to be at the Stoke game. If I had not made it then it would have been apt that the 2–1 win over Preston was the same score as my first match against Swindon in 1968.

If that is to be my Layer Road epitaph then I will happily leave with that memory and a very big tear in my eye.

Keith Jenkins, aka 'Yorkshire Kipper'

U's fans make an effort to bring the Layer Road days to a close in style.

Layer Road, God rest her soul
Game after game, goal after goal

We move along to pastures knew
With memories of white and blue

This dear old home is soon no more
So what does Cuckoo Farm hold in store?

Thousands of fans packed inside
Let's hope it's not a rocky ride

A modern framework for us to play
This opportunity has made our day

So to the pitch, the stage awaits
Create a fear that others hate

A different place, but still the same
Football moves on, it's a funny game

But everyone who loves the U`s
Knows too well, there will be news

Of good and bad, and tears will shed
The noise we make, could wake the dead

So onto Cuckoo Farm, soon we go
The chants and songs will ebb and flow

Our new home, a great new place
But don't forget a special place

Layer Road, you served us well
When others came we made it hell

Rest in Peace, special one
We all know you're number one

Mark Sapsford

A final message for the U's fans as the Stoke game comes to a close.

The last game; the dressing rooms will be used no more for matches.

The Barside is vacated as the ground falls silent for the final time.

Layer Road is the place where I fell in love with a football team. It is where I watched my kids grow up. It is where I have hoovered up dead bees, cleaned toilets, painted railings, swept terraces, weeded the pitch edges, poured innumerable pints, had countless laughs and first met some very dear friends. I have even walked round the pitch all night with the same friends, taking part in the Night Vision Relay to raise cash for St Helena Hospice, with the pitch edges glowing with lanterns that had written on them the names of loved ones who would never take their place on the terraces again.

I have watched amazing football and I have watched dross. I have seen awesome players just starting out (Lua Lua), older ones coming back to remind us of what they could do (McGavin) and players I had dreamed of pulling on the blue and white (Cureton, despite

The family Enclosure is full of colour prior to kick-off.

everything). I have been to the point of ecstasy and despair (sometimes on the same day) in nearly every part of the ground.

Layer Road was the place where I found one of the few Football League teams that still felt like a real club, where everyone was a part of what went on, even on the pitch. Where if you had an idea you could just contact someone from the club and they would not only listen, they would go for it. Where we were not just customers, or just a crowd, we were musketeers – all for one and one for all.

On 26 April 2008 we said goodbye. Relegation did not bother me too much, but leaving the place that I have loved so much I consider it an extension of my home broke my heart.

Just recently I have been sitting around wondering just what it *is* with me and Colchester United. After all, I am an immigrant to the area, who over the years has easily ignored the charms of teams as diverse as West Ham and Caersws.

Was it the team? Well, as there is only one player from my first-ever game in March 1998 still playing, that is unlikely.

Was it the way that the club was run? To an extent, yes. I had never before been to any football club where the overwhelming ethos was that of a true club, where everyone who walked through the turnstile was a member and part of the team.

I loved the way that you could turn up with an idea and find that people at the club were not only prepared to listen, they were prepared to take your idea and use it. I loved the way that the players were not kept at arms length from the fans, they would turn up at all sorts of club gatherings and were also prepared to sign autographs for the children hanging over the wall armed with their pens and programmes.

But most of all, I have come to the conclusion, it was all because of Layer Road.

I know Layer Road looks like a hovel, but it was *our* hovel. Fans of other teams could mock it and deride us standing on our crumbling terraces, but look at what we had. A perfect playing surface. A compact ground where you could be so close to the action if you wanted, that it sometimes felt as if you were on the pitch yourself. A place where relatively few fans could create such a noise that they would be recorded as officially the loudest fans in the Football League.

A place where players who had graced the pitches of Old Trafford and Anfield could find themselves surrounded by young kids breathing down their necks as they stepped back for a throw-in.

I loved being on the Family Terrace in blazing sunshine, using my magazine to shield my eyes from the lowering sun, or on the Clock End seats peering out through winter rain. I loved the sense of theatre at floodlit matches, the gleaming pitch under the lights, almost impossibly green, players looming large on their stage in the frosty air.

Layer Road is where my children grew up. I have loved every minute, from the first days of Lottie barely able to reach over the wall at the front of the family terrace to pummel the advertising hoardings when we

A view from the family Enclosure as the two teams prepare for kick-off.

Terrace Three prepares to greet the teams onto the pitch.

scored, through Milli falling asleep *on the terraces,* to recent games when they gather with their friends on the terraces while their poor old parents take to the seats.

Some years back when I was working part-time I spent most of the summer holidays helping to prepare the ground for the new season. The girls came with me, cleaning, sweeping, mopping and painting. The ground felt like it belonged to all of us after that.

My first game came towards the end of the 1998 promotion season, and I had gone just to avoid ironing and to shut the family up. Thirteen goals in two games, and suddenly I was seriously interested. When I joined in the pitch invasion after the Barnet Play-off semi-final and stood on the pitch under the floodlights teaching my tiny kids football songs, I knew that there would be no going back, not ever.

Lea Finch

Wow, what a day 26 April 2008 was! Of course it was the last-ever home game played at Layer Road, and saying farewell to the old place was always going to be emotional for me. At 41 years of age, I have been a Colchester fan ever since my dad took me to my first-ever game at aged five.

The opposition and even the score escape me now, but I do so clearly remember sitting in B block and the atmosphere was like like nothing else I had ever encountered – I was hooked.

Now, 36 years later, there I was standing in the Family Enclosure, complete with a full face painted head of blue-and-white stripes, with my own son Elliott, aged 7. He is now a dedicated Col U fan of three years standing, and my eldest son Ross, aged 15, is also a fan. There truly is something about Colchester United that gets under your skin and into your very being.

For this occasion, though, Elliott, Ross and myself were not alone. My girlfriend Ruth and several of her friends as well as my mum had come for the occasion. Strange, I thought, as none of them – particularly Ruth – were interested in football.

Anyway, there I was, standing in the place that truly felt like home to me, looking all around the ground and reliving so many very special memories. Looking at where I sat with my dad, now departed, that first time, and where I stood when we suffered the anguish of going out of the League, onto where I stood that momentous day against Barrow when we entered the League again.

Oh so many memories, all of them special, all of them engrained in my mind for evermore.

My partner Ruth and I have been with each other for 13 years now, and I love her dearly; although she vies with Colchester United for who is the love of my life, a battle in which I think she believes she is the constant runner-up!

On the day I was getting fed up as I kept asking to look at the commemorative matchday magazine the club had brilliantly put together for the special last match. Every time I asked for the programme one of her friends asked a silly question about the club or ground that they did not really want to know the answer of!

The final whistle went, but to be honest for once the result was not important to me. Anyway at last I got hold of the matchday magazine and was just skimming through the pages with the intention of having a proper read when I got home. It was now just before the Player of the Year presentations and I was on page 57 of my quick read, when I heard, almost subconsciously, the PA system declare that there was a special announcement, asking Rob if he will marry Ruth.

I looked up at Ruth, thinking how strange, two people with the same name as us…

She took the magazine off me and opened it up to page 71, and there in black and white was her proposal to me! I instantly accept and burst into tears – the emotion of the day getting to me, you see!

Wow, as a diehard Colchester fan that to me was the ultimate proposal, my club's ground and on the last ever day there to boot.

Ruth then went on to tell me that it was just as well I accepted as the wedding was booked for just under four weeks' time, she had chosen my best man and invited about 140 guests as well – now I knew why my mum and her friends were there!

We were married on 23 May, and in keeping with the unusual we had a BT van as our wedding car as that was how I met her, by mending her phone.

Layer Road really was a theatre of dreams for me over the years, and I have so many memories. And now, thanks to Ruth, I had one more very special memory to store on top.

I am looking forward immensely to our new home at Weston Homes Community Stadium, but one run down small corner of Layer Road Colchester will be ingrained in my heart forever.

Rob Cherry

Scott Vernon and Kevin Lisbie kick-off the final ever game at Layer Road.

26 April 2008. There was no way I was going to miss the last ever game at Layer Road. However, I also recognised that there was no way I was going to get a ticket given that the priority was rightly given to season tickets holders, regular attendees, etc. So I scraped together the pennies and bought a hospitality package. I booked a hotel for a couple of nights and told Mrs Col U that I was taking her away for a fabulous holiday (never let her tell you I don't show her a good time). She would still rather poke needles in her eyes than watch football so I went off to the game while she went off for some retail therapy.

The hospitality package included a seat in the stand. I had spent 50 years standing on Terrace Four and I was not changing then so the marketing people arranged a switch for me. I got to the ground at 12.15pm and spent a pleasant couple of hours eating lunch, drinking a few pints and inspecting the memorabilia in the board room (this was done before the directors arrived so that I did not risk unceremonious ejection).

I then watched the game from Terrace Four. It was probably one of the poorest games I had seen at Layer Road. Back to the bar for another couple of pints and then it was time to spend 30 minutes walking around the pitch remembering old times. I talked with a number of supporters, young and old, until it was 6.15pm and Mrs Col U had come to pick me up because she wanted her dinner.

And that was it. Layer Road has been part of my life for 50 years and that is why I love it, and that is also why I have taken the time to explain why I love it.

David Hicks

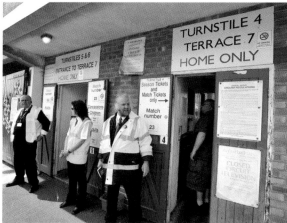

Stewards prepare to greet the fans for one last time.

Karl Duguid's lengthy association with the club comes to a close as he is substituted late on.

Terrace Three's message of condolence as the Stoke game unfolds.

Terrace Three gets behind the team for one last time at Layer Road.

This U's fan takes in the view of Layer Road for one last time.

One fan's message as Layer Road's life comes to an end.

Leaving Layer Road

By Maddie Cuff – St Michaels Primary School

Tears drip as supporters cry.
Voices lower,
They sing no more.
Drooping heads match setting sun,
Darkness falls and colours vanish.
Players feel lonely and sick,
Never again to taste victory at Layer Road.
Winter is bleak…

Match Days at Layer Road

By Jordan Lawson – St Michaels School

The smell of fresh cut grass makes me anticipate
Match days at Layer Road.
Hot dogs, burgers and onions remind me of
Match days at Layer Road.
Sweaty trainers, smelly socks   memories of
Match days at Layer Road.
Mascots always there encouraging the players during
Match days at Layer Road.
The ball dives through the air on
Match days at Layer Road.
The players always talk before the game on
Match days at Layer Road.
Fans cheering when a goal is scored on
Match days at Layer Road.
The commentator says his speech before kick off at
Match days at Layer Road.

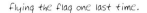
flying the flag one last time.

Chapter 16

LOOKING INTO THE FUTURE

I will miss the standing terraces; plastic seats are comfortable but they are not conducive to a good atmosphere. I will miss the billiard table perfection of the green playing surface glistening under the floodlights (although hopefully Cuckoo Farm will be just as good). I was going to say that I will miss the sense of anticipation waiting for the *Post Horn Gallop* to be played as the players run out onto the pitch, but hopefully this tradition will be continued.

I went to as many games at Layer Road as I could in our final year at the ground. After all these years it will feel strange walking down Layer Road and not being able to see the floodlights in the distance.

I hope that the new stadium will remain the home of a genuine football club and will extend a warm welcome to genuine football fans, both U's supporters and our visitors. To this end, I hope that we will employ well-trained, intelligent stewards, not the strutting bullies in florescent jackets who seem to delight in creating a tense atmosphere at so many other grounds.

Talking to fans of so-called bigger clubs during the two seasons in the Championship, it was apparent that many envy us because we Colchester fans still have a real football club to support, whereas their clubs have become soulless plastic corporations that treat them not as fans but as 'customers' to be ruthlessly exploited.

Read the comments on BBC 606 and you will see that opposition fans enjoy coming to Layer Road, not for the facilities (that is for sure!) but to get a taste of a traditional football atmosphere. It will be sad if we are relegated at the end of this season but it will not be the end of the world. Success and failure are fleeting shadows; the most important thing is to ensure that our beloved club keeps its character, its integrity and its soul.

The U's: not just for better or worse, not just for richer or poorer, but forever.

An empty Family Enclosure after a U's home game.

Dave Appleby, Nottingham

The steps leading up to the side of Terrace Four and the Clock End.

The walk down the back of the Main Stand towards Terrace Four.

One fan's message as Layer Road's life comes to an end.

Leaving Layer Road

By Maddie Cuff – St Michaels Primary School

Tears drip as supporters cry.
Voices lower,
They sing no more.
Drooping heads match setting sun,
Darkness falls and colours vanish.
Players feel lonely and sick,
Never again to taste victory at Layer Road.
Winter is bleak…

Match Days at Layer Road

By Jordan Lawson – St Michaels School

The smell of fresh cut grass makes me anticipate
Match days at Layer Road.
Hot dogs, burgers and onions remind me of
Match days at Layer Road.
Sweaty trainers, smelly socks – memories of
Match days at Layer Road.
Mascots always there encouraging the players during
Match days at Layer Road.
The ball dives through the air on
Match days at Layer Road.
The players always talk before the game on
Match days at Layer Road.
Fans cheering when a goal is scored on
Match days at Layer Road.
The commentator says his speech before kick off at
Match days at Layer Road.

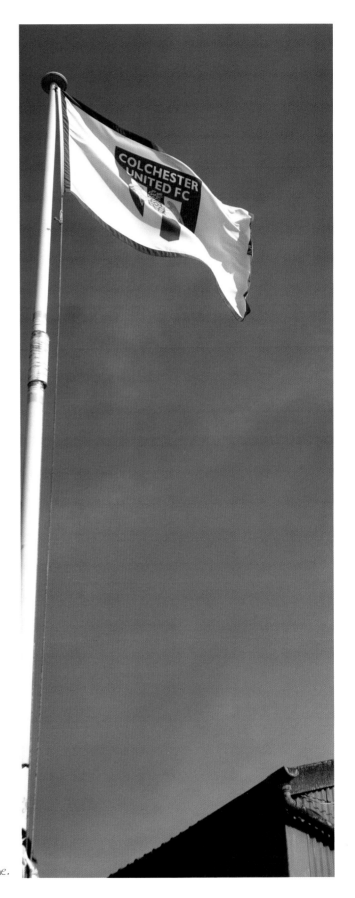

Flying the flag one last time.

The whole day of the Stoke game was so busy for so many people, but the closing of Layer Road did not really hit me until the final five minutes of the game. I was commentating the final period as the U's burst forward and pelted the Stoke defence with shots galore in a desperate attempt to score but the defence held firm.

I somehow kept my voice together for the end and my emotional speech that was aired on radio and via our roadshow out into Layer Road itself, I could not hold back the tears though.

Dave Buckingham

Somebody mentioned that they were at the very first and very last floodlit games at Layer Road. Well I was at the very first League game at Layer Road, but unfortunately, being so far away, I was not able to be at the last League game at Layer Road.

Malcolm Murray of Niagara Falls, Ontario, Canada

My worst moment was not being relegated to the Conference at Cambridge United but the last game at Layer Road. Overall, though, we have not had many bad memories along the way, but of course we have had bad games and rough results.

I will miss the camaraderie of Layer Road. We knew where everyone was standing week in week out; people became creatures of habits. I made a lot of friends going to Layer Road and there were always a lot of comedians in the stands waiting to make a funny comment.

Charlie Brown

And always, top of my wish list was a tiny striker called Jamie Cureton, of awesome ability but who always seemed to end up on the losing side…and I even saw him in a Colchester United shirt, albeit for one magical loan spell and one unbelievable season where we became everyone's favourite team.

And in between, I got cold, and wet, and bored, and watched some fearful dross and some terrible players. But there was always the atmosphere of our tight little ground, and the feeling that at any time something wonderful might just happen.

One day I became the barmaid for the CUSA Corner Bar, and suddenly another area of the ground became much loved as time that had been spent with our children who were off doing other things became time spent with new-found friends. The place was like the old TV series *Cheers* – everyone knew your name, and you were only a stranger once.

I do not have a Colcestrian history. My grandfather never stood on the terraces with me. I was not there for the Watney Cup, or relegation to the Conference, or even the Auto-Windscreens Shield Final – these were all before my time. Yet in such a short time I have come to love that place as much as I love my own home.

It's five to five and the final whistle is about to blow on Layer Road.

The media looks on as the game unfolds.

The fans head for the Barside for one last time.

I know that it is foolish but it brings tears to my eyes to know that I will soon never be able to stand and gaze across at the Family Stand and see my pigtailed daughters in my mind's eye, filled with excitement as they battered the adverts, full of excited chatter about their favourite players (David Gregory and Sam Stockley for one and always, always Doogie for the other).

I will not be able to sit in my seat near the clock, clambering over people apologising for my late arrival and early departure as I attend to my bar duties. I will not be able to meet with friends after the game for a companionable discussion about the game (even if being trapped behind a bar means you have to suffer all sorts of weird and wonderful interpretations).

And then there was always that last game of the season bacchanalia, where everyone slowly subsided into a drunken stupor, celebrating the successes and failures of each season with a kickabout on the hallowed turf of dubious and drunken ability – sometimes even with a player putting in crosses for them.

Should my own children have children of their own, I will never be able to take them to the places where their mother stood, or show them how to sweep a terrace or clean out a turnstile.

I know that we are getting a wonderful new stadium. I know that we will have 'proper' facilities, and clean loos, and that the club will have resources so that it can make money. And I know that I always took part in campaigns to get it. But I know that in doing so, I have lost the one thing that made me a true Colchester United fan.

In 2008 we suffered the first relegation that I have known. It hurt, but on the other hand I saw it as a future excuse for another open-topped bus parade. But on 26 April 2008 a part of my heart was broken.

Lea Finch

Chapter 16

LOOKING INTO THE FUTURE

I will miss the standing terraces; plastic seats are comfortable but they are not conducive to a good atmosphere. I will miss the billiard table perfection of the green playing surface glistening under the floodlights (although hopefully Cuckoo Farm will be just as good). I was going to say that I will miss the sense of anticipation waiting for the *Post Horn Gallop* to be played as the players run out onto the pitch, but hopefully this tradition will be continued.

I went to as many games at Layer Road as I could in our final year at the ground. After all these years it will feel strange walking down Layer Road and not being able to see the floodlights in the distance.

I hope that the new stadium will remain the home of a genuine football club and will extend a warm welcome to genuine football fans, both U's supporters and our visitors. To this end, I hope that we will employ well-trained, intelligent stewards, not the strutting bullies in florescent jackets who seem to delight in creating a tense atmosphere at so many other grounds.

Talking to fans of so-called bigger clubs during the two seasons in the Championship, it was apparent that many envy us because we Colchester fans still have a real football club to support, whereas their clubs have become soulless plastic corporations that treat them not as fans but as 'customers' to be ruthlessly exploited.

Read the comments on BBC 606 and you will see that opposition fans enjoy coming to Layer Road, not for the facilities (that is for

An empty Family Enclosure after a U's home game.

sure!) but to get a taste of a traditional football atmosphere. It will be sad if we are relegated at the end of this season but it will not be the end of the world. Success and failure are fleeting shadows; the most important thing is to ensure that our beloved club keeps its character, its integrity and its soul.

The U's: not just for better or worse, not just for richer or poorer, but forever.

Dave Appleby, Nottingham

The steps leading up to the side of Terrace Four and the Clock End.

The walk down the back of the Main Stand towards Terrace Four.

Nothing will replace the atmosphere of Layer Road. The memories will last for my remaining years. The build-up prior to the game was something special. Likewise the crowds pouring out of the ground after the game and clogging Layer Road as a sea of people walked towards The Drury Arms and the town centre. Layer Road when the U's are home was a unique experience. I will miss it.

Other games I can recall are the record 9–1 wins against Bradford City (when Bobby Hunt and Martyn King each scored four goals) and the more recent FA Cup victory by the same score against Leamington (but the visitors' goal was the best one of the match!), the 8–2 thrashing of Stockport County, drawing 2–2 against the mighty Arsenal in the FA Cup and cheated with a 1–1 draw against West Bromwich Albion in the year they went on to win the Cup. Not to mention the thrilling Cup ties against the likes of Manchester United, Newcastle United and Aston Villa. But there have been dire games as well, like losing 0–5 at home to Luton Town.

However, for me, there is more to supporting my home-town team than simply cheering them on, which I do from the terraces where I have been a season ticket holder for many years.

Bob Russell, MP for Colchester

It will not be the same without the Layer Road atmosphere. I only hope Cuckoo Farm takes us on to new levels – while retaining some of the best of the old club ethos from Layer Road.

Andrew Mann, Didcot

Anyone passing by Layer Road in 2008 would have little indication that a football ground lay beyond its modest façade, apart from the floodlight pylons. But inside was a remarkable sporting venue: intimate, friendly and full of character. Even visiting radio commentators recently remarked how much they liked this traditional style of football ground.

Norman Spencer

Eric Lee, my granddad, had been visiting the U's for the past 50 years by the time the ground closed. He is an avid fan and has watched numerous generations come and go. He has stood on the terraces for this period of time and has followed the team come rain or shine and, up until recently, he would walk to Layer Road from his home on Mersea Road. Something that, as a 76-year-old, is quite a feat.

The walk to the Weston Homes is possibly a bit too far; although he will often meet me and my cousin for a drink in The Bricklayers Arms and he walks this on occasion.

About 10 years ago the club advertised for staff to clean Layer Road in exchange each week for a free match ticket. My granddad jumped at the chance as it gave him something active to do and also allowed him to delve further into his beloved club.

A wider view of Terrace Three.

A view down the rear of the Main Stand towards Layer Road.

A low view across the pitch towards Terrace Three from the Barside.

A view down the back of the main stand.

The Layer Road turnstiles.

He has told us numerous stories about his encounters with players who were training on the pitch and how he would engage in long chats about what they were doing right and how they could improve their game! On some occasions he would even demand a lift home from some of the players; something I think they felt they could not deny him.

As a former employee for what used to be British Rail, Eric would travel the length and breadth of the country following the U's, as well as jumping on the coaches to follow them. Recently he was able to go to see the U's at Leeds, which was a special moment for him as Leeds is his town of birth. But he was happy that the U's showed mercy and got their deserved 2–1 victory.

A special moment for him was when my cousin Lee hired Layer Road in the summer of last year for a game between his friends and his Sunday League side.

He also had the opportunity to hit home a penalty at the Layer Road End. My grandad has seen generations come and go at Layer Road and has been a true, loyal fan of the club.

Clinton Davies

The transient nature of our lives means that we often mark out the vital landmarks in our lives by places we have been at key times. For me, outside of my home, Layer Road became the most important of places – somewhere to forget the real world and escape. So when people used to say 'Everyone old enough remembers exactly where they were that day in the 1960s when Kennedy was shot or when man first landed on the moon' I have to reply that I actually do not, but I do remember exactly where I stood in November 1962 for my first U's game. United 4 Brighton 1, and Martyn King got a hat-trick. It was an introduction into a world where all the emotions, the elation and the despair could be experienced within a couple of short hours, but by the time you got home reality will usually have made you remember it was just a game…but, thankfully, not always.

Having followed the U's man and boy, home and away, I have witnessed them leading at Chelsea and losing at Cheltenham, felt inspiration at Elland Road and incredulity at Edgar Street, but it was always comforting to return to Layer Road where significant experiences and life's real education took place.

So hence my journey of nearly 50 years is mapped out by my inability to find a sense of ownership of any one part of the ground, perhaps reflected by my passage from childhood through to my present state of near senility. The map reflects these endless shifts…

1. 1962, my first game with my brother Chris.
2. 1963, the first time I saw grown men fight. The important world issue under debate was whether John Fowler was a dirty player or not.
3. 1965, I learned the nature of how society dealt with mental illness as this was where the Turner Village inmates were always crowded together.
4. 1965, I first inflicted pain on another human being – the over enthusiastic use of my rattle was to blame.
5. My first smell of linament which was blown out from the changing rooms on to passing fans.
6. 1965, my first feeling of real disgust when I experienced those Clock End toilets.
7. 1967, my cousin Paul and I seriously thought we could influence the outcome of a football match by throwing a piece of fudge on the pitch. We could not.
8. My first TV appearance. This is where I would run on to the pitch at the end of a game being televised by *Match of the Week* so I could watch myself the next afternoon. True fame.

The tunnel area at Layer Road, looking towards the home dressing room.

9.   1970, my first feeling of guilt as I cheered after Chic Brodie, the Brentford 'keeper, got injured by that dog chasing the ball after being let loose on the pitch. He never played League Football again.

10. 1971, I stood for the greatest day of my life (marriages and births excluded). U's 3 Leeds 2. And I watched in amazement and amusement as I first saw grown (Yorkshire) men cry.

11. The stand where pre-decimal currency lasted more than a decade after it had gone out of circulation. *The Colchester Express* was still 3d.

12. 1972, my formative fumbling years with my attempt to chat up Janis and Julia failing as their infatuation with the physiques of Steve Leslie and Steve Foley grew.

13. I experienced the loudest voice I had ever heard before or since, a legend called Les who would shout at the 'Shakey Old 'keeper' and keep cracking the joke about him being called Cinderella because he always misses the ball…endlessly. And it was always funny.

14. 1979, I watched the cocky Man U supporters try to invade the pitch at the end of their lucky FA Cup win only to find the U's had sorted out security that day by buying 200 white coats and giving them to 200 squaddies who marched in formation across the pitch. The invaders ran very fast in the opposite direction!

15. and 16. The only place that has two memories both highly significant…Burnley in 1990 and Barrow in 1992. No more needs to be said.

So, from those early days of paying 1 shilling to get in and barely being able to see over the wall through to the days of being able to walk the length of the ground at half-time so you could always be behind the U's goal, and then four decades later driving halfway across the country with my son to watch our final game – Layer Road has always held a real sense of place.

Let us not get carried away…you may be relieved to know that I have now changed my will and am no longer going to have my ashes scattered across the turf! But Layer Road's memories will undoubtedly stay with me forever.

Tony Wright, Bristol

Trying to think back over favourite memories of the ground is complicated. I can, of course, name my favourite games, such as Ipswich at home in 2006–07 or the win over West Bromwich Albion in the League Cup. My favourite goals are easy to recall – Mike Masters' first against Barrow or Greg Halford's strike against Gillingham.

Entering the ground to sit in Block D of the main stand.

But cherry picking these popular moments in our history only tells half the story. Why is it that I have clearer and fonder recollections of eating fruit toffo's in the Main Stand as a child? Patting our goalkeeper Mark Walton on the back by the tunnel after we thrashed Exeter City? The smell of bonfire smoke wafting over from a nearby resident's garden? The midweek game against Slough played on a quagmire of a pitch?

These are personal memories that supporters who have been standing at Layer Road for longer than I have might not even remember. But they will all have their own recollections of particular moments at the ground that are bigger than the promotions, the goals and the results.

Ben Wright

And so the time came to depart Layer Road, unfortunately more with a whimper than a bang (despite the fireworks) in view of our hopeless League position. It was a time to consider cherished memories but also a time to look forward. We now have a structure in place to carry the club forward and hopefully the chairman's ambition of a consolidated position in the Championship will be achieved.

A view through the rear of the Clock End towards the main stand.

In Paul Lambert and his backroom staff we must have potentially one of the most motivated setups in the lower Leagues and with careful selection of players we should be able to give the other teams a run for their money. We need some measure of success. The loss of local support to our friends down the A12 is nothing short of criminal. Let us be successful and then we might get some Suffolkites coming to see games here!

Colin Willsher

I had no reason to drive past Layer Road the other day, no reason at all. In fact it took me out of my way but I just felt I needed another look — maybe the last, who knows. It was a pretty sorry sight. Letters were missing from the front of the building and weeds were growing up the front of the stands and around the entrances. That said, to be honest it did not look that much different from when I first rolled up there with my dad 25 years ago!

It was a freezing cold Friday night and I had been on at Dad for a while about going to see a game at Colchester, and he finally relented. There were just over 1,700 people there, the U's lost an awful game 2–1 to Darlington and we traipsed back to the wilds of Norfolk. I thought that would be the end of it until Dad piped up: 'When's the next home game?'

A view of the back of the main stand, looking its age.

And that was it, we were hooked. We tried out every area of the ground, even the rickety wooden terracing at the Layer Road End (it was split half and half in those days between home and away fans and we used to swap ends at half-time). Finally, after serving the apprenticeship in the family terrace we graduated to the Barside.

The tea and coffee were awful, the ground was far from full (far from half full, if we are being honest), and we got showered with rust when the ball hit the roof. You could smell the 'Deep Heat' if you walked past the dressing rooms behind the Main Stand and you always came out stinking of cigarette smoke as all those around you puffed away on seemingly endless fags.

Yet there was something which kept drawing us back. As fans we can probably all mark out stages of our lives and marry them up with Layer Road. I took my girlfriend (now wife) to a game on our third date (yes, and she STILL married me) and we watched Lua Lua and Aspinall argue over who was going to take a penalty.

The ghosts of fans of the past mixing with supporters of the present?

There was the night of the Sheffield United FA Cup replay when it was all a bit misty, a night game against Darlington when the fog meant you could not see both goals but the referee allowed the game to go ahead as long as the Darlo fans could sit in the Main Stand.

There was the night the U's beat Exeter 4–0 to stay in the League and home fans were applauded out of the ground by the visiting supporters. The night Scott Barrett bought Wycombe fans a cup of tea each during at Bob Lord Trophy tie, and there was the 5–0 demolition of Barrow to get back into the League. The countless Cup ties and more recently the promotion to the Championship and that great first season.

I have been lucky enough to earn a living reporting and commentating on the U's and there was still the buzz of driving up to the ground, seeing the floodlights and spending 15 minutes looking for somewhere to park. You know, you used to be able to park on the Garrison!

Then there was the walk along the Main Stand roof to get to the commentary box perched precariously atop the Main Stand, breaking possibly every health and safety regulation. The hole in the side of the box got progressively bigger each season and there always the odd visit from a squirrel.

The games were all played out in shabby, decrepit, tumbledown surroundings. But it was our ground and away teams and fans did not like it, but who cared, we did. And we will miss it.

It will disappear sooner or later but maybe I will take one more drive past, out of my way, and maybe Dad will come with me and we can thank the old girl for all the memories and for all the rust we had to shake off ourselves as we made our back down Layer Road.

Glenn Speller of BBC Essex

Supporters of other clubs have told me that it takes 10 years for a new stadium to feel like 'home'. Part of me suspects that – while the move is necessary and timely – nowhere else will *ever* really feel like home.

The thought of driving home in years to come and not seeing a football ground on Layer Road is immensely sad, but I hope that what made the place special was not just the wooden stands, the cramped seating and the uneven terracing, but the 'us against the world' spirit that it engendered among our supporters and players. The feeling that those who saw our ground as nothing but an outdated relic could never really understand our club and what Layer Road means to us.

If we can take a little of that Layer Road spirit with us when the ground is no more, then I hope that, given time, our new stadium can provide just as many memories.

Up the U's.

Ben Wright

I suppose I first became aware of Layer Road when watching the highlights of that never-to-be-forgotten FA Cup tie against Leeds in 1971. I remember all the chairs and benches that the manager, Dick Graham, had ordered placed around the pitch to make the playing area seem even more claustrophobic that usual.

But it was only when I first visited the ground in person that I realised what Layer Road was really like.

I can recall visits in the 1980s, before I had become a commentator, to see the likes of Mike Walker and Mickey Cook in action – usually on a Friday night. I remember being amazed that a football ground, and all the other facilities and offices that go with it, could be squeezed onto such a small site.

More recently, my vantage point has been an aerial one from the television gantry that could easily double as an air traffic control tower. You got a great view from up there, across beyond the elegant buildings and gardens of 'The Cannons' and into the far distance. You also got a really good impression of just how higgledy-piggledy the stadium was. Since the demise of Oxford's Manor Ground, it probably has more different stands and terrace areas than any other ground.

Yet despite the limited capacity, the atmosphere never suffered. I especially enjoyed being at the games against Stoke and Sunderland during the first season in the Championship, when 6,000 people managed to sound like many times more.

I will be sorry to see Layer Road pass into history. Too many grounds these days lack character and are merely copies of one another. You could never say that Layer Road was anything other than unique.

Jon Champion, commentator of ITV on football from Division Two to the Champions League

I have supported the U's for 20 years, and even though my son Philip was only five I wanted him to experience the pleasure that Layer Road had given me. He was very excited and wanted to tell his friends at school that he had been to his daddy's club. So I bought him a scarf and he wore his CUFC leisure shirt and loved the entertainment even if the game itself was not very good.

So I created my own bit and history and this is something that Philip can tell his grandchildren. I plan to take him to the new stadium and hope that he is bitten by the bug.

I am proud to support this great club and be part of the Colchester United family. They are true supporters who will back the team no matter what.

CUFC, the best community club in Britain.

Up the U's.

David Welham and Philip Welham, aged five

The media watch out over Layer Road as the sun sets.

I remember most of the players and all of the managers, but I also remember the fans that have stood in our little area of the ground. There has been Witham, Tiptree, Braintree, all now sadly passed onto the stadium in the sky. It is funny how we seldom got to know names but instead took more notice of where they came from. There were the moaners, the comedians and the familiar faces, one of which appeared at my local church and I could not place him because he was not in his right place, so to speak.

There have also been those that have become friends in the truest sense of the word.

I am going to miss them all and I am going to miss our home ground. No doubt I will see some familiar faces occasionally, but who knows who I will be sitting next to!

Perhaps the new ground will eventually find a place in my heart, but it is likely to take at least another 60 years before it can begin to compete with my memories of Layer Road.

John Foskew

A view along the Family Enclosure; the red paint showed the area where smaller fans were allowed to stand.

Probably the biggest change when we move from Layer Road will be that I can see all of the pitch! Over the years I have missed at least two broken legs, six players sent off and dozens of free-kicks and long-range goals.

Two years ago I decided to move a yard to my right, but a post still blocked the action and still things went on behind it. Seeing a corner or throw in being taken in the South West Corner will be a first when we move to the new stadium.

I will never forget when we were asked to stay behind after an evening game to walk in line across the pitch to press down any divots before a frost that night as we were playing Manchester United the next match. Just over halfway across I was feeling tired and remember missing a few, and this just happened to be around the place where the ball bobbled up, hit Jimmy Greenhoff's knee and went into the net.

Later, Mike Walker our 'keeper said he had it covered until it hit the bobble – the goal came in the last few minutes and we lost 1–0 and missed the chance of a replay at Old Trafford. Did I cost the club the replay money that could have stopped us going into the Conference? Could we have gone into the Second Division 20 years earlier?

I have not missed the outside toilets at the back of the Main Stand, however. The rhubarb next door has never been as good since they closed I hear!

I will always remember Lua Lua putting defenders on their backsides. In a friendly against Norwich he went past two defenders, turned around and then dribbled back past the same defenders a second time.

Chris Coe

It was Wayne Hennessey's look of wry amusement which personified an appreciation of the fairness of the Layer Road crowd, even in the modern high pressure monetarist game of today.

Layer Road really has been unique in terms of personal connection between supporters, the players and the club itself. When only memories and ghosts of the past remain many will lament its passing.

Norman Spencer

I was an outsider when I first arrived in the 1980s, but I have since commentated on many hundreds of games over the years, covering 350-plus for BBC Essex during that time. Layer Road has become my home and I am very familiar with it. It was a great place to do commentary, and although the average crowds were low there was always a terrific atmosphere which you cannot quite recreate in the bigger grounds.

In those grounds, when goals go in it is deafening, but the intimacy at Layer Road and the sense of access you got during your time at the ground meant that it was a fantastic place to watch football. It was a great place and one with so many fantastic stories.

Neil Kelly of BBC Essex

The best players I have seen down the years would have to be Peter Wright, Mark Kinsella and Greg Halford. The best moment was watching Colchester United at Wembley and seeing the open-topped bus leave Layer Road when we were promoted to the Championship.

I think four words sum up Layer Road. They are not mine, but instead come from an incident at the evening game against Hull City during our first season in the Championship. The two seats beside me were empty up to the half-time interval. Then two guys turned up, having travelled round the M25 through the Dartford Tunnel and A12 to get to the match.

At the end of the game, they turned to me and said the four words, 'That was real football'.

David Cheeseman

BBC Essex's Neil Kelly prepares for work in the commentary box.

When I first came I was in awe of Hal Mason and the reputation that preceded him. I was a junior reporter and the likes of Hal and Bernie Webber always impressed me. Hal always used to bring sweets and Bernie liked them – but one day Hal had a packet of laxatives and no one told Bernie that and so he took one or two, and, not surprisingly, he struggled in the second half of the game!

They are the ones that should be revered – they are the trailblazers who covered the club initially in the papers and people like Carl Marston, Francis Ponder and myself who have done a long stretch since the 1990s, step in their shadows.

You had to earn the respect of these people, and when it is a small group of people it is particularly tough. You have to build up the relationships and travel with these people. There has been longevity in many of the journalists and they have enjoyed working here, and that says a lot about the vibe of the ground and the family club feel that United possesses. It has been a great pleasure to work here because in an age of huge salaries for top players, this place has remained immune to it and retained its living proof of the old world of football.

Neil Kelly of BBC Essex

Sights, sounds and smells always summed up Layer Road. Back in the days of standing up at the Clock End on Friday night matches, the people who lived in the houses behind the goal would pick that night to have a bonfire and the smoke would waft over the ground, and we did often wonder if they were burning the balls in a protest!

After the final whistle of the Leeds United match in 1971, something I will remember forever is going onto the pitch with so many others celebrating. It was one of those special sights that you see, but of course the roles were reversed in the Bedlington game.

I had been a bit of a schoolboy Manchester United fan and used to try and go and watch them in London. My family was living in Straight Road at the time and I had a Manchester United coffee mug. When we lost to them in the Cup I was so disappointed I threw it against the wall. I had to throw it two or three times to break it though!

My favourite characters over the years have been many of the managers – Dick Graham, Bobby Roberts, Steve Wignall and Big Roy. Clubs had gone out of the League and had not come back, so it was important to have someone like Roy in charge. Managers these days isolate themselves from the fans and Roy was more of a man of the people.

Mickey Cook was always one of my favourite players because I used to go and watch him in the youth team, and it was great to see him come through the ranks. If he wanted to he could have made it to a bigger club and had more success in that period of time. He would always speak to you in the street and was a real gentleman.

There are also characters among the fans: Michael 'Charlie' Brown is a Layer Road character if ever there was one. I made friends with him on the terraces, and there are a lot of friends that I have these days who I met at the football.

John Tweed

The first games that I attended were in the 1970s and even then I can remember paying attention to the music that was being played, and I remember walking in and every game I used to arrive at the same time and they would be playing Peters & Lee's *Welcome Home* and then, at the end of the match, they would play the Three Degrees' *When Will I See You Again*.

It stuck in my mind and here I am playing the music today.

In more recent times, that game against Bristol Rovers has stuck in my mind. I was working that day and can remember announcing the scorers, and whoever scored I said that it was not over yet and there was more to come. Sure enough Lomana came on and scored the winning goal.

Colchester played Norwich in a friendly and they had about eight subs and decided to put them on at the same time. They all stood up, I read out their names but they did not match up with the teamsheet, and all of the Norwich fans started laughing. I forgot the mike was on and said 'Oh b*ll*cks!' and the crowd all laughed even more. 'OK,' I said, 'a load of canaries coming on and a load of canaries going off!'

I have been doing the tannoy for about 10 years now and it has been really good fun. One way that I have kept up with play is to listen to a commentary, as I often get disturbed either by the phone or a melee of players making it difficult to tell who scored.

Neil Kelly obviously did commentary for the internet and BBC Essex, so, to listen to that commentary and ensure my facts were right, I used to get a feed from a baby alarm, with one in his commentary box and the receiver right next to me!

More recently, with the smoking ban, I was able to make some off-the-cuff remarks about no smoking inside the Layer Road stadium which led to a certain amount of infamy.

The press picked up on them and they ended up in *The East Anglian Daily Times,* and some of the nationals picked up on it too.

It is hard not get caught up in the emotions of it all. Sometimes I have had to take the mike away as I am a supporter first as well as an announcer. I have supported the U's since 1972, and I picked up on the fact the club was there from the Leeds game and I think that still happens today when the club have a big match.

The announcers' seats at Layer Road were right in among the directors' seating and we have often had some famous faces in there, including Teddy Sheringham of course last season. Delia Smith and famous ex-players have made appearances, and Martin Jol was also there last season as well.

Going on the pitch was nerve wracking at first and even now when I do it, for the first time of the day, I have to take a deep breath. The crowd are very good and I enjoy doing it though.

When I have been out and about or when I am on the phone in the office, people have said that they recognise my voice. It can be quite strange, but it is still good fun.

At the new stadium, I think we have got to modernise what we do a bit but having a better sound system will make a big difference. There is some responsibility to try and recreate the atmosphere and make sure the crowd are kept entertained. People get there an hour before kick-off sometimes and you have to get them ready for the game.

One time I was in the bar and Roy McDonough was the manager, and I was working as a DJ in the clubs that the squad used to go to. I said to him that I supported the club for years and always wanted to play. There was a friendly coming up at the end of the season against an Arsenal XI and he said that I could a sub in that match. He came off before the end and I ran around like a headless chicken but at least I can say I played on the pitch!

Tannoy announcer Peter Sleigh hits the headlines.

Colchester played at Wembley versus Torquay in the Play-off Final in my first season. They asked whether I could come help warm the crowd up. Torquay had Helen Chamberlain and the U's had me! That was quite nerve-wracking, though not many people can say that they have done a gig at Wembley!

Peter Sleigh

Now I have paid my last visit to Layer Road and I could not help but notice the nice cars the players arrived in (they used to come in on the same bus as me in the 1960s), but one thing had not changed. That is the friendliness and good natured humour of the supporters who belong to a great community football club.

At the new ground the torch will be passed to a new generation of supporters. The club must nurture and embrace them, some of whom will never have been to Layer Road. We must make them aware of the great legacy to which they are about to be entrusted but at the same time be ready for the new challenges ahead which will make the new stadium a famous venue in its own right.

Layer Road has now entered the sporting history books and there are those who say sentimentality over a football ground is out of place in the modern world. This may be the case, but it will not alter my view of things. Goodbye Layer Road and thank you for everything. Thank you for giving me an interest in sport and in people. The lessons I learnt in companionship and adversity helped me in times of trouble and will stay with me always.

Norman Spencer

As I stood there for the last few games it was the sights, the sounds, the smells, the humour and the tears that will be the abiding memories of Layer Road. Players who gave 125 per cent for the shirt; and even the opponents and players such as Frank Worthington or Ian Wright that I have enjoyed seeing us beat.

If the new ground can continue to deliver a similar atmosphere then it will be a fitting new future for the greatest team in the world and more fantastic memories will be created.

Ralph Wickenden of Dartmoor

A view across Terrace Three from the front of the stand.

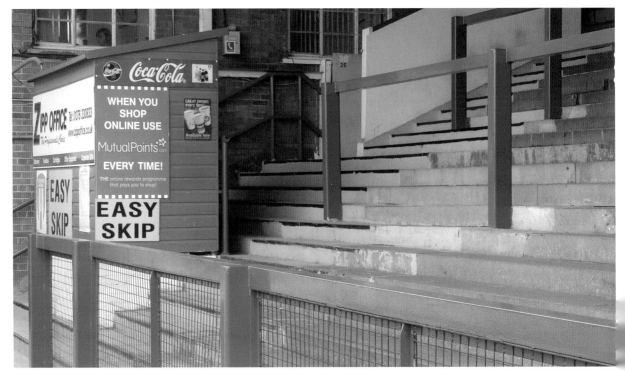

I rarely go to games now, but in 2008 as a birthday treat my daughter and son-in-law arranged for my brother and I to go to the Hull City game and attend a celebration dinner. The club made a great fuss of me, but unfortunately the game was called off shortly before kick-off because the pitch was waterlogged.

It was re-scheduled for a Tuesday evening and I went then and they again gave us a lovely meal and we went onto the pitch to be introduced to the crowd. John Schultz took me under his wing and took me into the boardroom where there was a photograph with my father on.

I was very sad when it became obvious that Layer Road would cease to be our home and yet when I went to the Hull City game I realised how dilapidated the ground had become. I used to object when visiting clubs said what a dreadful ground it was but I said to my daughter that I could now see what they meant.

Mrs Jean Bell

Layer Road was the first football ground I ever set foot in and in photos and memories it will stay alive as we move to a wonderful new stadium and a new chapter in the club's life. We must never forget Layer Road and its magic which has made Col U the well run, friendly and wonderful club that it is.

Layer Road has brought so many people together, friendships between fans and staff to name just one example.

They think it's all over…ah no not a chance!

Dave Buckingham

The greatest things about Layer Road were the friendships that were formed over the years, and the whole wonderful atmosphere of the club. It was just a lovely place.

Judith Musgrove

The hospitality suite at Layer Road – holding just 40-odd places compared to the 700 available now.

Like most people of a certain generation I remember the bar on the Barside, mostly because when you walked in it was almost impossible to see the bar itself because the room was so smoky. It was like Victorian fog. But I stood on all parts of the terraces over the years.

I started on the Barside, where I used to stand behind various members of the band Modern English, watching the game, while admiring their unfeasibly long and trendy overcoats. Then I moved to Terrace Three, where I suspect most of Perry Groves' family used to be. There certainly seemed to be a lot of squealing, every time he scurried into view.

Then I did the 'change ends at half-time' routine for a while, before ending up back on the Barside. And I then had a four-year spell at the end on Terrace Four.

And I remember the big games. But weirdly it is the daft ones or depressing ones which really stick in my mind. For example, losing 1–0 at home to a hopeless Mansfield on a Friday night when Big Roy missed a sitter (which I chided him for very loudly and got, in response, a well-known hand gesture which he aimed back at me).

The view that greeted fans leaving the Layer Road hospitality lounges.

And for a while I used to go to some reserve games, so I was there in the early 1980s when we beat Haverhill Rovers 8–0. I think there were only about 30 people in the ground, including the girl who used to go round the pitch at half-time selling rosettes and programmes out of a sort of choc ice tray. That always struck me as quite an unenviable job to be honest.

Bournemouth, called off at half-time because we were wining 3-0, but the pitch was too wet – anyone remember that? And my own personal nemesis, Luton Town who beat us 5–0 when I first sponsored the match ball: a game only cheered by the first sight of Greg Halford throwing the ball so far you suspected he was actually the bloke from the *Fantastic Four* with elasticised arms in disguise.

Steve Lamacq

The last few fairytale seasons were nothing short of outstanding. To reach the Championship and be moving to the new ground has been like living in a dream world. After 50 years of coming to Layer Road, it is sad to leave such a special place, but life goes on and moving to Cuckoo Farm could very well lead to bigger and better days.

Dave Amoss

I have got a confession to make. Well no, it is not a confession, it is a proud boast. You remember that petition for Cuckoo Farm that eventually collected about 30,000 signatures? I never signed it. Yes, I know the club needed to move to provide an acceptable quality of backroom facilities for the players and the day-to-day running of the club (given that it was not possible to acquire the land around Layer Road to redevelop there) but that move was really for the club – not for most of the fans. Watching football anywhere else than from the terraces at Layer Road is not the same, and I have seen U's play at most of the Football League grounds and probably even more non-League ones. A packed Layer Road under floodlights. . .now that is real football.

A view down the back of the main stand towards Layer Road.

My 10-year-old daughter does not agree by the way. She far prefers Cuckoo Farm with her cushion under her bum, her rug over her legs when it is cold and a flask of hot chocolate on tap. She was a late starter though – she has only been a regular since early 2008. Not the best time to start as school playground banter is much easier when you hook up to a winning team, but once she found out what a win felt like

Entering the Clock End, with seating either side.

Main Stand seating.

A view along the Clock End stand, erected in 1995.

(against Preston) she was hooked, and when she experienced the emotion from T3 and realised the songs you could sing as we stuffed Ipswich again I knew it would cost me a second Cuckoo Farm season ticket.

My mum tells me I was under two when my dad first took me to Layer Road, so that would have been 1956–57. Apparently if he wanted to go he had to take me. It adds up because that was the season second-tier football nearly came to Layer Road – we blew it in the last four games – so you can understand my dad being desperate to be there and my mum objecting to being stuck at home with two very young children. About 40 years later I asked him if he knew what my first game had been, but he could not remember.

I went to various first team and reserve games from then on but my earliest memories are from around 1961–62, and having done so much historical research of the U's and the ground I have to be careful to be sure that my early memories are indeed first hand and have not been acquired along the way. That research, though, does let me put them in date order and informs me that two of my memories are from the same game. Brian Abrey heading into the Layer Road End goal, and Martyn King and one of the Brady brothers walking off after being sent off. That was 28 October 1961 versus Millwall. I can also remember the home defeat to Wrexham – it was dark, we were losing and a lot of the crowd had left, so late in the game we moved from our usual place on the bench seats at the front of the Main Stand to the back of the stand. When I asked if we could leave as well I have no idea whether it was my dad or someone close by who replied by saying that you do not leave just because your team is losing, you stay and support them. Another memory is from the 9–1 game versus Bradford City on 31 December 1961, in which I remember a penalty being taken at the Clock End. Match reports have subsequently confirmed that Bobby Hunt converted a penalty at that end.

My family connection to the club goes right back to Stan Drury, one of my great-grandfather's younger brothers although by age only a couple of years older than my granddad. Stan joined Town aged 19 a year after they had moved to Layer Road, and over the next 10 years he played about 170 times and scored over 80 goals, including four hat-tricks. Those 10 years include the all but five-year gap from the end of April 1914 to the only game the club played in 1918–19, Easter Monday 21 April 1919. He was one of very few to regularly play both sides of the World War One. This I found out over the last couple of years, after what started as a search for information regarding the opening of Layer Road (prompted by a thread on the U's message board) turned into a major research project on the history of Colchester Town. Stan was always referred to within the family as 'Stan the footballer' but I did not realise how prominent a player he had been until my research began, and I only wish I had found out three or four years earlier when I could have asked my dad about him.

My granddad spent most of his working life with the corporation, initially as a driver, later in the admin, and he used to drive the football specials to Layer Road and stay on to watch the game. He and my dad spanned the club's change from Town to United. I do not think Dad saw the U's first game on the Thursday evening versus Bath, he would have been 11 years old and it was probably a schoolday, but he was certainly there on Saturday 4 September 1937 for the 3–3 draw against Ipswich. I have the programme he bought on the day, although it has lost the team photo insert.

My father spent the war in the Far East with the Royal Navy – something he would never speak about – but was demobbed in time for the main part of the 1947–48 Cup run and is one of the Mason's employees wearing the funny little hats in the crowd photo from the Bradford game on the

Watching from Terrace Three at Layer Road.

front page of that week's *Essex County Telegraph*. Purely by coincidence I found myself watching the closing few minutes of the last game versus Peterborough Reserves from the end of Terrace Four right next to the surviving piece of the old terracing that was once part of the Spion Kop (or Masons Corner, because that was where the Mason factory employees congregated). Although I have got a copy of the newspaper I do not know what happened to the copy of the original photo that my dad had. I could pick him out on that but I will not pretend I can do the same on the newspaper copy, which unfortunately is damaged by a fold.

As I said earlier, I started on the bench seats at the front of the Main Stand but from 1965–66 it was time to save money and stand on what later became the family terrace. By now we had moved to Shrub End – my sixth different home and fourth different school before I was 10 years old – and certainly during the 1966–67 season if not from the start I was going up with lads from the estate and moved to the Layer Road End in the days when Twiddle, cigar in hand, led the Zigger Zagger chant.

The Layer Road End was home until I went into exile up North in 1973 although the (cheaper) counter attraction of spending Saturday afternoons in the local coffee bars meant I was hardly a regular for the last couple of years. I came back to Colchester at Christmas 1977 and was an erratic attendee until Autumn 1979's charge to the top of the old Division Three brought me back for good. From the 4–0 home win over Wimbledon on 23 October 1979 I did not miss another home league game, a home FA Cup tie or a home League Cup tie, ever. I did skip a few friendlies though especially the Summers during which I played cricket. RIP Colchester Grasshoppers.

So, which matches stand out?

Leeds – packed so tight into the Layer Road End behind the goal on the Terrace One side (part of a big group of Gilberd 5th years) that I could not get my fags out of the top pockets of my denim. Coming off the Shrub End Estate I had had my first ciggie when I was nine but I packed up in my early 20s.

Macclesfield – the FA Trophy semi-final first leg. Squid's goal which made it two in a couple of minutes midway through the first half – 2–0 up and I knew I was going to Wembley for the first time. I was a seasoned away traveller by then – on my way to my fifth ever present season and I had been to way over 100 grounds (listed in the programme column I wrote for the next game) but I had always refused to go to Wembley until it was with the U's. (I have still never been to Wembley unless the U's are there and I do not reckon that will change now).

Barrow – Mike Masters' thunderbolt. We had got our league place back. It is sometimes difficult to appreciate that many present-day U's supporters are too young to remember the 1980s and the Conference. Season after season just missing out on promotion while the club survived on a shoestring; then the seriously underperforming side of 1988–89 that latterly rallied the crowd and town with the successful fight against relegation, but should never have been that deep in trouble in the first place, and finally the poor 1989–90 squad that unfortunately got what it deserved. It happens that I was distracted from football for much of 1989–90 because I was on the 14 or so month course leading to the exam that would get me a significant promotion. I actually sat my exam on 24 April 1990, rushing back from London for the penultimate home game against Doncaster – which we won 2–0 to prolong the mathematical hope for a few last days.

Barnet in the second leg of the Division Three Play-offs in 1998 was a rocking Layer Road night but I think the greatest for me was a recent one, 29 September 2006. Karl Duguid on nine minutes. Colchester United 1 Ipswich Town 0. I had waited nearly 50 years for that.

As I get older I think I have to acknowledge that I am tribalist. Maybe it is genetic but I have this fundamental instinct that tells you stay loyal to your own even if they are not always completely to your taste. I have done the family history research thing and I know who all my 62 direct ancestors are for the five generations before me, from my parents back to my great-great-great grandparents. One of my great-great-great-grandfathers, William Price, was a tinman who came over to the Stour valley from Broseley in Shropshire by 1830. His wife was born in Stoke By Clare and their daughter, who is one of my great-great-grandmothers, was born in Sudbury. They had settled in Colchester by the early 1840s though, in the high class yards off Magdalen Street, and apart from another great-great-great-grandmother from Halesworth in Suffolk, but whose family had moved to Colchester by the time she was 18, every other one of the 62 was born in North Essex – none further west than Toppesfield, none further east than Wivenhoe and none further south than Great Wigborough.

Back in the early 1980s I did one of those 'this is me' forms in a football context and in the dislikes column I put people who support a 'big' club instead of their local team. That was before the days of Sky Sports or Setanta, and I can understand the mentality that wants to attach itself to the perennially successful Manchester Uniteds and Liverpools and Arsenals and the arriviste Chelsea, particularly with the incessant indoctrination of much of the media that they are all that really counts. But I cannot get my head round how anyone with integrity can give their football allegiance to their town's greatest rivals. To me it says something about them as a person, and it is not complementary. And believe me, the town of Ipswich are our historical rivals, not Southend or High Wycombe. We did not start playing Southend, for example, until 1950 (and Ipswich did not start playing Norwich until 1946). Those modern rivalries were a substitute when events conspired to put a hiatus to the real deal. The Colchester versus Ipswich rivalry has history that goes back 130 years, and you do not hear of Ipswich refusing to play a League game with Norwich, or Southend refusing to play a League game with Colchester, because of what the locals might do to them. Nor do you hear of them giving them a tin shack to change in in retaliation for being made to find and pay for their own changing-rooms for the reverse fixture earlier in the season! But those are pre-Layer Road tales. Maybe you will get a chance to read about them one day.

For me the greatest U's player I have seen at Layer Road is easy – the 'unique treasure' Lomana Tresor Lua Lua. Tony Adcock possibly heads the rest.

In terms of memorable seasons, the 1991–92 season became something special because of the way we did it, Big Roy and his pub team mentality was the right man at the right time, but the middle two-thirds of 2006–07 has to take the prize. If the season had ended at 23 games, 'little' Colchester United, everyone's pre-season banker for relegation, would have been in the Play-offs for promotion to the Premier League. Personally I thought the announcement early in 2008 that the Premier League would not allow us to play at Layer Road under any circumstances was the psychological killer blow and after then it did not really matter.

Kevin Drury.

I think my father would have been very sad in many ways to see the U's leave Layer Road. It obviously held many poignant memories for him, so much hard work and heartache had gone into the years when professional football was played there. However, being the forward-thinking man that he was, I believe he would have realised only too well that a larger ground would be needed, capable of accommodating larger crowds if the U's are to go forward in the football world, and he would readily have given his blessing to the project.

I too was very sad to go through those gates for the last time. I know it was a small ground but in many ways that was its beauty. It was so compact and had an atmosphere all of its own. I realised how much work would be needed to bring Layer Road up to the standard required and I am sure the right move has been made in creating the new stadium. Given time, I believe the U's will settle in their new home and will go from strength to strength. I send them every good wish for the future and will keep a watchful eye on their progress.

Mrs Jean Bell.

Chapter 17
TIME MOVES ON...

Three months after the final whistle was blown against Stoke City, Colchester United were beginning their new era at the Weston Homes Community Stadium.

But while nearly 6,000 fans watched the U's take on Spanish side Athletic Bilbao at the U's' fantastic new home, the sands of time were beginning to take their effect on Layer Road.

In only a few months since the curtain fell on the historic home of the U's, the ground was already starting to show signs of being forgotten. Scrap metal merchants had taken away the metalwork surrounding the pitch and it left behind a ground stripped back to its roots, in more ways than one. And while the aftermath painted a pretty sorry picture, there were glimpses of the past being brought back to life, as the sweeping terraces of the 1940s came alive at the Clock End for one final time.

These final photos show the stadium as it appeared at the time of this book going to print in the Spring of 2009 and, with the global economy in a state of flux and housing developments put on hold across the country, uncertainty remained over the future plans for the old ground...

Layer Road lies abandoned as the U's host Bristol Rovers at the new stadium, in October 2008.

A view out over the pitch from the Corner Bar window.

The bookies' hut at the rear of the Barside.

The Corner Bar lies abandoned.

The abandoned Corner Bar building.

fans leave their messages on the walls of the Corner Bar.

The empty physio's room.

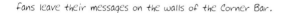

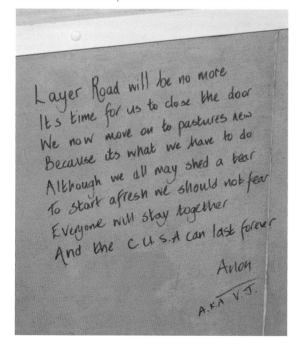

Layer Road will be no more
It's time for us to close the door
We now move on to pastures new
Because its what we have to do
Although we all may shed a tear
To start afresh we should not fear
Everyone will stay together
And the C.U.S.A can last forever

Avton

A.K.A V.J.

The Layer Road pitch now resembles a meadow as nature takes hold.

Seats from the Clock End ready to be transported to Newcastle Blue Star.

The dugouts are gone and are now housed at Stanway Rovers' ground.

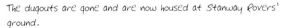

A view of Block D after season ticket holders came to collect their seats.

The Clock End, stripped of seats.

The sun shines down over an abandoned Family Enclosure.

The Barside is stripped of its barriers for scrap metal.

All metalwork is gone from Terrace Four, again revealing that familiar sweep of terracing.

Nature begins to take over an abandoned Layer Road.

The Barside roof, felled as the scrap metal merchants grab their wares.

Two fans survey Layer Road long after the U's departure.

The message from the fans is clear.

The Barside and family Enclosure are fully exposed.